D1553048

FIFTH WARD to FOURTH QUARTER

SWAIM-PAUP SPORTS SERIES

Sponsored by James C. '74 & Debra Parchman Swaim and

T. Edgar '74 & Nancy Paup

FIFTH WARD to

FOURTH QUARTER

Football's Impact on an NFL Player's Body and Soul

Delvin Williams

Forewords by
BRUCE TAYLOR and DARRYL S. INABA

TEXAS A&M UNIVERSITY PRESS

COLLEGE STATION

This paper meets the requirements of ANSI/NISO Z39.48–1992
(Permanence of Paper).
Binding materials have been chosen for durability.
Manufactured in the United States of America

Library of Congress Cataloging-in-Publication Data

NAMES: Williams, Delvin, 1951– author.
TITLE: Fifth Ward to fourth quarter : football's impact on an NFL player's body
    and soul / Delvin Williams ; forewords by Bruce Taylor and Darryl S. Inaba.
OTHER TITLES: Swaim-Paup sports series.
DESCRIPTION: First edition. | College Station : Texas A&M University Press,
    [2023] | Series: Swaim-Paup sports series | Includes index.
IDENTIFIERS: LCCN 2022016275 | ISBN 9781648430718 (cloth) | ISBN
    9781648430725 (ebook)
SUBJECTS: LCSH: Williams, Delvin, 1951– | Football players—Texas—Houston—
    Biography. | African American football players—Texas—Houston—Biography.
    | Football—United States—Psychological aspects. | Football players—
    Retirement—Psychological aspects. | Football injuries—Psychological aspects.
    | LCGFT: Autobiographies.
CLASSIFICATION: LCC GV939.W488 A3 2023 | DDC 796.33092 [B]—
    dc23/eng/20220509
LC RECORD available at https://lccn.loc.gov/2022016275

CONTENTS

A gallery of photos follows page 162.

FOREWORD

BRUCE TAYLOR,
SAN FRANCISCO 49ERS,
1970–1977

I was privileged to play with and against some of the greatest players in NFL history as a member of the San Francisco 49ers throughout much of the 1970s. As a defensive back, I had to be fast enough to a cover lightning-quick wide receiver downfield on one play and strong enough to come up and tackle a powerful running back on the next.

One thought went through my mind more times than I can remember: *I sure am glad I am playing with Delvin Williams instead of against him.* As I watch football today, I marvel at the size, power, and speed of running backs such as Derrick Henry, Christian McCaffrey, and Todd Gurley. But I would put Delvin right alongside any of the great backs in football, past or present. He was that good.

I joined the 49ers in 1970 and saw plenty of hotshot rookies come and go. But when Delvin stepped onto the field in training camp in 1974, I knew he was going to be special. Every good running back has speed, but Delvin also was *quick,* which is something else entirely. As soon as our line opened even the smallest hole in which to run, Delvin shot through and was in the defensive backfield before they knew it. And if he broke free with his world-class speed, it was a foot race to the end zone, one that Delvin usually won.

Delvin put up some amazing statistics with the 49ers and later the Miami Dolphins, but no statistic can measure a man's heart. Delvin and I quickly became good friends, and you won't meet a more good-natured person. He was down-to-earth, dependable, and respectful to everyone, including the players' wives. I know my wife, Terry, loved Delvin.

Delvin is smart and well-rounded, and we loved to talk about everything under the sun. He occasionally mentioned his upbringing, from the tough streets of Houston to learning disabilities to substance abuse. But with Delvin, a difficult past was never an excuse. It simply was the fuel to exceed everyone's expectations, including his own.

We all were shocked when the team traded Delvin to the Dolphins and brought in O. J. Simpson. The Juice was a hometown hero in San Francisco and had the name recognition, but having played with or against both, I can tell you that Delvin was a far superior player at that point in their careers.

The story doesn't end there. Those of us who played in the NFL realize that our years outside the game far exceed the ones in it. Delvin and I have remained in touch despite the years and miles, and I am proud of the hard work he has done for children and the rights of former players.

Reading this book will make you smile, cry, and perhaps grow angry at injustice. Above all, it will inspire you to be more like Delvin and never, ever give up. I was proud to call Delvin Williams my teammate, and I am even prouder to call him my friend.

FOREWORD

DARRYL S. INABA,
CEO AND PRESIDENT OF HAIGHT-ASHBURY FREE CLINICS,
1995–2005

Fancying myself one of the "Niner Faithful," I had the privilege of watching Delvin Williams weave and power his way through tough NFL defenses to win the rushing title in the NFC West in 1976. Following his football career after his trade to Miami, I was also able to appreciate his efforts in winning the NFC West rushing title in 1976. Yet it was a much greater privilege for me as a prevention/education professional to personally witness Delvin Williams inspire youths to heathier and more fulfilling lifestyles through his work with Pros for Kids upon retiring from the gridiron. As Delvin notes in this book, the career of a professional football player is both brutal and very short on and off the playing field. A star performer like Delvin goes overnight from 70,000+ avid fans (like me) cheering for him on the field to wondering what next to do with his life. Del shared with me that he had greatly missed his cheering fans and wondered what if anything could ever replace that now that his pro football career was over. Then, working with him at a Pros for Kids event to help youth avoid substance abuse, Delvin said that watching the faces of youth coming into new understandings, motivation, and hope for the future had replaced the feelings he had sorely missed playing before thousands of adoring fans in the NFL.

In *Fifth Ward to Fourth Quarter*, Delvin Williams provides a very candid and intimate narrative about the inner goals and ambitions that enabled him to weave his way through a tough life of abandonment, poverty, neglect, exploitation, betrayal, and deceit. Suffering through brutal physical and emotional injury, facing challenges from dyslexia and severe sleep apnea, he realized his goals of achieving Pro Bowl status as a professional football player and also being the first of his family to earn a university degree. Del then went on to a career in youth and community services with Pros for Kids, positively impacting the lives of hundreds of youth and their families. It was these efforts after football that won him the recognition and support of First Lady Nancy Reagan and President Ronald Reagan and even put Del on the A-list for state dinners in the White House. Best of all, this also gave me the opportunity to personally meet and then work with him in his efforts to prevent youth substance abuse.

Fifth Ward to Fourth Quarter exposes the great illusion projected by the National Football League to both its players and its fans: that the NFL is a great and caring family organization where family members are well cared for beyond just the few years that they can contribute on the field. Pro football players are expected to play through injury and pain with reasonable expectation that they will be well cared for in the future. This expectation is assumed, and so, since never committed to contract, it is a rude reality that awaits players when they retire from the game. It is also a great disappointment to fans to learn that once players are deemed no longer able to contribute on the field, they are abandoned by the teams they sacrificed so much for.

The way Delvin Williams faced the many challenge during his retirement was the same way he faced fearsome defenses throughout his days as a running bac, weaving and powering his way through it to the best of his abilities. Despite all the challenges thrown at him, Del's appreciation of football—the sport, not the institution—transcends the trauma. Football and his love for the game provided him the opportunity to realize his life goals and gave him the ultimate opportunity to be of service to youth struggling to find their way in life. It is wonderful to read this honest and unassuming narration of his life journey.

ACKNOWLEDGMENTS

It's an old cliché in football, but a running back would be nothing without his teammates blocking and opening holes for him. Writing this book was possible only with the support of dozens of "teammates," from my childhood in Houston to my retirement in California:

my inspiration, Marilyn Patton;

my biggest fan, former First Lady Nancy Reagan—I have nothing but love and respect for her; Ken Barun; David Rabin;

my family: my father, Delvin Williams Sr.; my mother, Dorothy Jean Williams; my maternal grandparents Robert and Pearlie Young; my paternal grandparents Jesse and Priscilla Williams; sisters Delva Diane and Saundra Michelle; brothers Donald Wayne, James Anthony, Tommy, and Ricky; daughter Dositheia Ross; grandchildren Je'Marcus and Anjeniqua; four great-grandchildren; and cousins Cecil and Darlene Mayfield, whom I thank especially for the gift of music appreciation; Uncle Sonny; aunts Maddie and Sandy;

my contributors: Brian Fobie, Mike Oriard, Alan Goforth, Dr. Fred Leavitt, Dr. David Smith, and Dr. Darryl Inaba of the Haight-Ashbury Free Clinic;

my surrogate father, Thomas Hendricks;

my high school instructors in Houston George and Mattye Carson, Mrs. Goins, Mrs. Hill, Mr. Leon "Mad Man" Parker; Kashmere High School coaches Billie Matthews, Thomas Hendricks, Walter McGowan, Julius Simon, Kirby Jones, Major Abrams, and Weldon Drew; teammates Willie Ferguson, Leon Strauss,

Donald Charles, Russell Charles, Jesse Lamb, Larry Gray, "Backfield Willie," "Shack" Skillern and Shelton Zenon; Tony "Little Dick" Stevens; Tim Gray; LJ Jenkins; Sammy Johnson; Michael Smith; upperclassmen Clarence "Bubba Dick" Dickerson and Larry "Big Lou" Edwards; and Mona Lisa, Annette, and Maxie B. Jones;

my college roommates: Don Goode, Emmett Edwards, Randy Robinson aka "Edward Carson;" James Bowman, and Carlos Matthews;

John Novotny, assistant athletic director at Kansas;

the late coach Don Fambrough;

fellow alumni Bob Billings and Skipper Williams;

all those who let me use their cars to go to work my freshman year;

and, for focused support, Michael Oriard and Todd Trigsted; editor and true believer Marie Morgan; editor Michael Hurd; Glenn and Lisa Borromeo, Joey, Maria, Bobby, and Letty; Marianne Sibaila; Elvira Ehrlich; Jeff Koppelmaa; Sharon de Monet; Rick and Lynn de Monet; Adam, Alex, and the rest of the de Monet family; Mary, Charles, and Jim Hunt and the Hunt family, Larry, and Nicole Thomas; Harry, Ruth, and Dylan Leroy; Jim and Patty; Elizabeth "Teenager" O'Boyle; Marilyn Pera; Jeanne Corrigan; the Hamiltons—Kenneth Hamilton Sr., Bertha, son Kenny and wife Geraldine: Neal Colzie, Mr. James aka "Pop" and Mrs. Colzie, and the Colzie family; Shawn Welch; the Levine family; Gary, Melanie, and kids Loni and Justin, Lora, Carol, Joanie, Sid and Lillian; Barry "Cowboy" Savitt; and Nancy "Sista" Olson, Bill and Joie Tipmore; Gary Fronrath's Chevrolet;

my friends and associates at Pros for Kids: Orle Jackson, Byron Kunisawa, Terry Adelman, Jon Sagen, Dick Keys, Art Agnos, Anna Eshoo, Jay Gellert, Jackie Spier, Colette Winlock, Carol Burgoa, Manny and Liz and all the kids who came through the program, and program supporters Dave and Judy O'Neal, Fred and Dolly Marcussen, Steve Schaiman, Tim Anderson, Jack Tatum, and Sherman "Shoes" White; Leo and Kristen Johnson; Pam McCubbin and her kids, Danny and Robin Ortner; the Northern California Olympians: Ann Cribb, Jim Hines, Diana Nyad, Jim Nabor, Mary T. Maher, Julie Inkster, Rosie Casals, Vida

Blue, Ricky Henderson, Brett Saberhagen, Ken Barun, Marty Cohen, David Rabin, the Gatlin Brothers, Doug Henning, Rich Little, Ben Vereen, George Brett, Joe Montana, Keena Turner, and Bubba Paris;

Enneagram: "The One" David Daniels, "Spiritual Force" Helen Palmer, Beatrice Chestnut, Pete O'Hanrahan, and the rest of the Enneagram family;

Don and Anne Solem, John Kauffman, Barbara French, Eileen "Easy Money" Collins, and Kate Cutting;

my spiritual sister, close personal friend, and organizer: Mary Kay Fry—I was stuck in mud and you pulled me out (God bless you!);

William "Coach" Wyman and editor, fact checker, and project teammate Bo Crane (Bo, thanks for your valuable contribution of seeing things with a different perspective)

Eli and Alice Zelkha (I feel Eli's presence, and he's tickled pink; I wish he were here to celebrate the accomplishment);

the Nessan family;

Pete Gent and *North Dallas Forty*;

all of the ones who came before and those who no longer are with us, may they rest in peace;

and finally my wife, Kim Yen Chau Williams: thank you for the sacrifice you've made to bring peace and comfort to my life; love you.

The list of those to whom I owe gratitude is long, and it is almost inevitable that I have forgotten someone. If so, I hope you still know that I couldn't have done it without you.

FIFTH WARD to FOURTH QUARTER

INTRODUCTION

Our path through life is rarely a straight line. Mine has had more ups and down, twists and turns, than I can remember.

However, one thing at which I have always excelled is running with a football. This skill carried me from the tough streets of Houston to a four-year degree at the University of Kansas and ultimately an All-Pro career with the San Francisco 49ers and Miami Dolphins.

Just like every other man who has played in the NFL, what I could contribute on the field determined my self-esteem and sense of identity. But what happens when the day comes when they tell you that you no longer are good enough?

That day came for me in September 1981, when the Green Bay Packers released me just two weeks after I signed with them as a free agent. The news came only a month after the Miami Dolphins released me, and I was trying to keep my career alive. The questions flooded my mind:

When did the game I fell in love with as a kid change into Football, Inc.?
What is a retired football player supposed to do?
Where do I find my identity as a man now?
Where do I fit in?

People other than my friends and family knew me only as No. 24— if they knew even that—and what I used to do soon would fade from memory as new players took over the sports headlines. I had to convince the outside world that I could do something else. Although I had excelled in my career for fifteen years during school and the pros, it was the only thing I had done and the only thing I knew.

As a player, I ultimately realized that the glorified life was just an illusion. In truth, few understand the price an individual must pay to be called a football player. Over and over, the game tests your will, your desire to compete, your emotions, and the limits of your body and mind. The rewards can be the highest emotional experience of your life, but pro football can also take you to the depths of depression, despair, and unparalleled physical pain. The game I played as a man was different than the game I saw on TV as a kid.

My football career resulted in a head-on collision between the starry-eyed kid and the industry of football. In addition to the ongoing physical pain, concussions, and often injuries requiring surgery, professional football is a trigger for depression and substance abuse and can lead to addiction. Although I don't speak for other players, I can say with confidence that I'm not alone.

Memories can make childhood seem more innocent and pure than it was. The truth of the matter is that, in many ways, football was never just a game for me. The innocence of my early years was broken long before I picked up a football, and I was looking for something to fill the void within me. Football to me was like an ever-changing kaleidoscope, from pure joy to a ticket to a college education to a coldhearted business that beat me down, physically and emotionally.

I had spent nearly three decades trying to be what other people—whether parents, teachers, or coaches—wanted me to be. Now I was on my own to find my place in the world and, more importantly, my identity as a man.

The more I pondered these questions, the more my thoughts returned to my childhood in the Fifth Ward of Houston.

1

A *football game is divided into four quarters,* and life is much the same. Looking back, I realize that for me, those four quarters are my childhood, college football, professional football, and finally retirement, which for athletes comes at an age when many people are just getting established in their careers. And, just as in football, decisions made in the first quarter can have a profound influence on the eventual outcome.

My story begins when I was born on April 17, 1951, in Houston, Texas. It would be impossible to understand Delvin Williams the athlete without first understanding Delvin Williams the man. Like everyone else, I was shaped by the places, people, and experiences of my childhood. Although I may have experienced higher highs and lower lows than some people, we all share the same dream—to be significant, matter to someone else, and be a part of something bigger than ourselves.

Houston always has been a city where great fortunes are made and lost, from the Wild West days through the boom-and-bust cycle of the oil industry and the heady days of the Space Age. It always has attracted more than its share of dreamers, doers, and hustlers.

By the time I was born in the 1950s, Houston was a city on the rise. As millions of Americans began moving south and west, the population of cities such as Houston exploded. Between 1951 and 1967, when I entered high school, the city's population doubled. However, although Texas was growing richer and more populated, many politicians worked night and day to keep the state's black population from enjoying its share of the state's newfound wealth. I was four years old when the US Supreme Court issued its anti-segregation decree in *Brown v. Board of Education,* but state officials fought tooth and nail to prevent Houston schools from integrating for most of my youth.

The question of integration had special importance to the folks of Fifth Ward. Founded in the immediate aftermath of the Civil War by former slaves, Fifth Ward has always been the center of black life in Houston. Some people may not think of Texas as southern, but when you're a black kid who grows up watching white people refer to even the most respected members of the black community by their first names, while blacks defer and refer to them as "Mr. So-and-So," you understand that the racial dynamic is as southern as it gets. No white people lived in our neighborhoods, and unless we went downtown or had a run-in with the police or fire department, we could go days without seeing a white face.

Between Interstate 10 East and Clinton Drive was a neighborhood called "The Bottom." Most major cities have an area of this type where blacks traditionally settled. My maternal grandparents, Robert and Pearlie Young, and their children put down roots in The Bottom. My grandparents had six kids—one boy, Edgar (or Uncle Buddy, as we called him), and five girls—Lilly Mae, Mary Ella, Phoebe, Dessie and my mother, Dorothy Jean, the baby.

It gets really hot and humid in the South, and you know what it's like if you have lived there. Houston is defined as much by its climate as by its geography. In summer, you can count on it consistently getting to ninety to one hundred degrees, with 90 percent humidity. The heat is intense and stays that way for days or sometimes weeks. However, winters are cold, and it isn't unusual for the temperature to drop to single digits.

At Home in the Fifth Ward

When I was born, we lived on Baer Street in a shotgun house. Shotgun houses are long and narrow, with two or three rooms. When you walk in the front door, you can see through the house and out the back door. The old saying was that you could fire a shotgun through the house without hitting anything. The houses sat on bricks, about two feet off the ground. You would be hard-pressed to find houses in the neighborhood with a cement foundation. Some areas resembled a town right out of a western movie, on dusty streets with wood-siding houses that often were unpainted.

If a car drove down the streets in The Bottom, you had to cover your face because of the dust. People screamed at speeders to slow down, because the dust was everywhere. When it rained, the streets were one big puddle of mud. If your car got stuck in the mud, you were going to need help to get out. If you tried to push a car from behind, it was a good bet you'd get mud all over your clothes. Eventually, they upgraded the streets from dirt to seashell chips. That helped with the dust, but we no longer could take off our shoes and go barefoot as we were used to doing.

In the summer, we played in the street—more accurately, the dirt road—until dark. We had to go to bed early on Saturday night to make sure we got up in time for church. It also gave the women time to start preparing Sunday dinner. I can't recall being read to or even if there were books in the house that we could read, except for the Bible.

Greater Mount Olive Baptist Church, where I was baptized, was the cornerstone of the community. Church was an all-day affair, and from my earliest memories as a four-year-old, like anyone my age, I didn't like going. We started with Sunday school around 8:00 a.m., with a short break before the main service began.

Our family often moved to different parts of the neighborhood, and I imagine it was because we were poor. The need to earn enough money for the essentials—rent, clothes, and food—was ever-present. I remember overhearing my mother asking for more time to get the money to pay the rent. Everybody pitched in to help one another. We were happy children but troubled about monetary stuff that we didn't understand. As I would learn time and again throughout life: we didn't know what we didn't know.

I didn't know how difficult it was for our parents to make ends meet. In hindsight, as a child, I sensed the need to know what I could count on, what could I predict, whom I could trust, how I could use the limited amount of resources I had, and who could best get me the resources.

In 1956, when I was five, my grandparents separated. My grandfather, Papa, was a proud individual and a stern disciplinarian. He was the consummate patriarch, and all six of his kids revered him. When they separated, all of the girls got together and decided where Papa should live. The eldest

> *We didn't know what we didn't know.*

son, Uncle Buddy, already had left for the army. In the end, the daughters decided Papa should live with Aunt Dessie, who had moved to the northeast side of Fifth Ward to a house on the corner of Kirk and Stamp Streets.

My grandmother was no pushover. Her daughters got their sense of entitlement from her. She spoke her mind, and you took heed of her opinions. She also moved to Kirk Street, one house away. Mr. Garrett's store was across the street from my grandmother's house. We used to get those moon cookies there. Papa loved them.

My brother Wayne continued to live with my mother, and my youngest brother, James, lived with Aunt Mary. My parents were divorced, and I don't remember them ever being together. I had never lived in a two-parent household. That generation kept secrets about family issues, and trying to put the pieces together now is too late, because the sources are not with us anymore. Before I started kindergarten, I spent the nights at my grandmother's house and days with Papa. Living one house away made it easier.

Papa moved in with Aunt Dessie and her two children, Cecil and Brenda Ann Mayfield. Cecil was a musician in high school. During TV commercials, he would beat on the chair arms as though they were drums, and Aunt Dessie would yell at him to stop, because he had worn them out. I felt closer as a family during those times than at any other point in my life.

Mama was sixteen and living with Papa and Grandma in Fifth Ward when I was born. She was the youngest child, left alone in the household, most likely spoiled as well as dominated by her older sisters, perhaps wanting to grow up like them and be independent before she was ready. Although it wasn't preferable, it was not unheard of to be a parent at sixteen. My grandparents took care of me while my mother continued to do what sixteen-year-olds do, which in her case meant having another baby before she turned eighteen. That was in 1952, when times were difficult for blacks, especially for an uneducated teenage mother with two children.

I come from a large, extended family that spans several generations living together. Dorothy Jean Williams, my mother, had four children— three boys and one girl, who was born much later. Delvin Williams Sr., my father, also was the father of my younger brother, Donald Wayne, known simply as Wayne. From a second marriage, he fathered three kids—Delva Diane, Tommy, and Ricky Williams. Willie Jones is the father of my half-siblings, James Anthony Williams and Michelle Williams. Because my mother was married only to Delvin Williams, she gave both of them her last name.

Wayne, who is a year younger than me, lived with my mother. My youngest brother, James, lived with my mother's sister, Aunt Mary. I found out about my sister Delva from a letter she sent me. It caught me off guard when I was nine or ten years old. The emotional space was crowded and disjointed—I was just getting used to James! How do you deal with that information at that age? However, D.D. is a good sister, and we are very close. We stay in contact, and, like most sisters, she makes sure we do.

Wayne and I didn't care for Willie Jones, but what could we do? We preferred for our own father to be in our lives. Although we didn't like Willie, we respected him, because we had to. He never tried to discipline Wayne and me, and I don't think he could have. He would have had to fight us first. There was always a strain between us. I believe that's why I always picked on James when we were little. I don't think my mother would have gotten married again, given the circumstances and what she had experienced with my father. It was clear she was bitter about that, because she got upset any time I would mention him. She would say, "I don't know why you want to talk about him."

Meet the Williams Family

My father was the seventh of Jesse and Priscilla Williams's nineteen children. I knew who my father was, having been with him when I was young, but I didn't know him well at all. When we were kids, he wasn't around. My mother would say to me, with some disdain and a half smile, "You look just like your daddy!" I often thought, "Maybe you're the reason he's not here," but I never said it aloud. Even as a kid, I knew that saying that would hurt her. She wasn't happy with him, and I never had an opportunity to find out what had happened between the two of them. My cousin Morris said my father left her because he didn't want to pay child support, but I like to think there was more to it than that.

After Wayne turned two, Mom had James with Willie Jones. I figure something happened between them after Wayne was born or maybe before, but my parents are not here, and I don't expect to ever know the truth.

The Williams family was from Industrial City in Austin County, Texas. I met my paternal grandparents when Grandma Priscilla was in St. Joseph's Hospital in Fifth Ward and my father took me with him to see her. My grandfather, Jesse, was visiting there as well. That was the first and only time I would see them. My grandmother did not live much longer.

My father was five foot nine and about 160 pounds. He was serious, straightforward, sensitive, and private, with a strong personal constitution. If provoked, he could be violent, particularly when protecting people he was close to or defending himself. To this day, I believe he had deep emotional pain.

In high school, I met only two of his eighteen siblings, Luciene Williams, known as Uncle Sonny, and Aunt Mattie. Pat is Aunt Mattie's only child, and over the years we've developed a close relationship. I stay in contact with the three of them.

Seven of my father's siblings are still alive. Aunt Sandy is the oldest, and Uncle Sonny is the last of the boys. However, I was as close to Aunt Mattie and Uncle Sonny as I am to any of my mother's family (there aren't many left). Uncle Sonny is the last boy alive in the Williams family, and I get to see my father's side of the family through his eyes. The Williams family were sharecroppers and lived on a plantation. They raised all of their own food, from hogs to corn. Grandpa Jesse was fluent in German, because his mother was German and Native American. Although it was never talked about, Grandma Priscilla was said to be half-white. They worked the land, and, at some point or another, all of their kids picked cotton.

When he first came to Houston, Uncle Sonny lived with my father. He and Aunt Mattie were the only Williams family members who had met my mother. I talked to him about the Williams family history.

He began by saying, "Your daddy would probably tell you if he were here, and the family won't talk about the things I'm telling you, such as how we grew up, what we experienced, and where I come from. I know a white man who whipped a black man and hit his wife. The white man would do all that. In fact, I've seen that in my lifetime. Lots of people think I'm too young to say I've been close to slavery. That's right—they talk about that show, *Roots*. But I've seen so much pain. *Roots* ain't nothing for what I've seen. They're just playing for TV there.

Many people don't think about seeing the things that I've seen, so when I got to the place I didn't understand, I also couldn't then understand my daddy. That's when I walked away from home at sixteen years old. I've been gone ever since."

Wayne has spent more time with our father, Delvin, than I have, and he got to know him better than I did. Given what little I know about how little my parents interacted, I can try to guess why they were not together. Was it really a child-support issue? If so, why two kids? Could it have been my grandfather, Papa, not allowing his underage daughter to marry? Was it my father not believing he could support my mother? Was it for lack of love or money?

I'm not speaking for Wayne, but today I can say I believe that it may have been in our best interest that they did not stay together. I don't carry the burden of "what ifs." It doesn't matter if they had stayed together. What I know is that they didn't yet saw to it that I had a home and was loved. When we were kids, it was my parents' job to raise, protect, and nurture us. When we become adults, it's on us. Given what was handed to them, they did the best they could. I forgave my parents years ago for whatever as a child I felt I was entitled to and did not receive. I loved my mother and father, and nothing will ever change that.

My grandparents, especially my grandfather at this stage, had a profound impact on me—more than my parents would have. I didn't realize it until later in life, and I love them dearly for the impact they had. The male influence of my grandfather's presence was important, because my father wasn't there. That is what I believe contributed to my pursuit of defining myself as a man by hanging out with older guys and seeking their approval.

My grandfather, Papa, shared his name with Robert Young, the lead actor in the TV show *Father Knows Best*. We watched the show quite often, and I remember everybody smiling when they rolled the credits and put his name on the screen. Somebody would always say, "There it is, Papa, Robert Young." Of course, Papa never minded the part about knowing best.

Papa would do different types of odd jobs, although mowing white folks' lawns is what I remember most. One day when I was seven, he took me with him on a job in Tanglewood, an affluent neighborhood and one of Houston's most desirable places to live. It seemed to take us forever to get there. Tanglewood was beautiful, with tall green trees and spacious, manicured lawns, and it was quiet. When they developed it years ago, they planted two oak trees on every lot. When the lawn mowers stopped, it was quiet and peaceful. You could hear the birds chirping.

I was running around while he was working and cutting the yard. I noticed there were several tricycles in an area where the children kept their toys. My first reaction was, "Wow, look at that." I was struck, because they had new toys and bicycles. I was curious and wondered why I didn't have what they had. I got on one of the tricycles and started riding it up and down the driveway. The next thing I knew, my grandfather was upset and yelled to get off of that tricycle. At the time, I didn't know why he was so upset, but it was clear that he was. I know now he could have lost his job. The owner wasn't angry, however, and said to let me ride the tricycle.

In my mind, Papa was a towering figure, but he was brought low with every encounter with a white face, because custom and convention required him to defer and show respect to even the lowliest white man by sheer virtue of the color of his skin. Small children notice these things and internalize them.

On some level, I knew there was a difference between the two cultures, black and white, which was obvious by daily mannerisms. Cousin Cecil would get upset with Papa for saying "Yes, ma'am" and "No, sir" to white adults who never responded in kind, which seemed even worse when they were younger than he was.

Losing Papa

I was about eight years old when Papa died. I remember peeping in his bedroom and seeing him resting in bed. I was sad, because he wasn't up and active, and I knew something was wrong. Aunt Dessie wouldn't let

> *The weight of racism cracks the foundation of a child's mind and hollows out one's self-esteem.*

me go in, but this day he saw me and gestured for me to come to him. I climbed into bed and laid next to him. He had a bunch of coins in his hand and gave them to me. After about five minutes, Aunt Dessie made me leave so he could rest. I didn't want to leave, but I knew he was sick. The short time I spent with him couldn't measure the impact it had on me. In those final minutes lying next to him, just from his presence alone I felt loved and safe.

Everyone in the family said that he really loved me. I know he loved all of his grandkids, but he was more important to me than I knew at the time. He would take me places with him and over to his friends. "This is my grandson," he would say, smiling. My mother once said to me, "Papa was crazy about you." Losing my grandfather was hard for me. He was the head of the family, a patriarch and my role model of a man. He commanded the respect of his children and the people around him, solely because of his presence.

We all cried while riding in the family car on our way to his funeral. For a long time, I had the feeling of being left alone. I thought maybe he was coming back. My parents were separated, and Papa was bigger than life. I was the first child of his baby girl, and a boy. He was a giant of a man to me, and I've never felt closer to any other male figure in my life. I was lost, and his death left a huge void in my life.

Grandma was the matriarch, and members of the family would come by to see her. She was receiving my grandfather's social security and had a steady income, although it wasn't that much. She would help her daughters, especially Aunt Mary, and others with the little money she received. There were times I went to school without lunch money. Mr. Hubbard, Aunt Mary's husband, as we called him, was always in the house, and we didn't see him much. They had one son, James Hubbard Jr., who went to the navy. I have a vague memory of him coming and going, but I remember him coming home only once or twice.

Whenever someone came over and asked how she was feeling. Grandma would always say, "I'm just as sick as a woman needs to be." She then would ask for a cigarette, or, if they didn't smoke, she'd ask for a couple of dollars, and we'd all laugh. I don't recall her going to see a doctor, and you never knew if she was sick.

The family would congregate at Aunt Dessie's house during the Thanksgiving and Christmas holidays. Everyone brought something.

My life's journey came into focus when Papa died; it set in motion a lifelong pursuit to fill the hole that could never be filled and replace the loss.

At times there would be two of everything—turkeys, hams, and most of all dessert. She would get up early in the morning and start cooking her sweet potato pies and cakes. The children would fight for the mixing bowl she used for the desserts. We would take our fingers and clean the batter out of the mixing bowls.

She had a chicken coop in her backyard. We'd get fresh eggs in the mornings. During the holidays, there would be a couple of hens on the menu. I saw my grandmother wring the neck of two chickens at the same time. The headless chickens jumped around squirting blood until they died. My cousin Robert and I had to pick the feathers and gut them. I didn't like the job when it was my turn. Those were the happy times, and it didn't matter that we were poor. Back then the community was family. I felt closer as a family during those times than at any other point in my life.

After my grandfather died, Aunt Lillie talked my Grandma Pearlie into moving from the Kirk Street in Fifth Ward North to Kashmere Gardens to be closer to her. Although my grandmother picked up where my grandfather left off, the void was still there. However, she instilled in me the belief that faith gives rise to hope. Belief in something better and the room to grow instilled and nurtured life's fundamentals for me. Pearlie Young was a petite woman with black hair and brown eyes. She smoked, would have a swig of whisky, and occasionally dipped snuff and sold bootleg liquor. She was the second of three children between Aunt Millie and Uncle Louie.

Aunt Millie lived in Baytown, Texas, and from time to time would come to visit Grandma and Uncle Louie. He lived in a back room at Aunt Lillie's house and worked for her husband cutting white folks' yards. (They call it landscaping today.) Uncle Louie looked to be about six foot three, with a thick brown mustache and light complexion. He kept to himself for the most part. He would sit on the back porch at Aunt Lilly's house, smoking his pipe and whittling a piece of wood. He was one of the nicest and gentlest men I have ever known. However, Uncle Louie, and his girlfriend, Willie Mae, were alcoholics. They drank together and would get into arguments, and sometimes they were violent.

Uncle Louie was a tormented man and must have experienced something tragic in his life. He was like Dr. Jekyll and Mr. Hyde. At the end of the week he would by himself drink a bottle of Gypsy Rose wine. He would sit in the back room, drink it, and start talking to himself. It would get worse when he would start walking through the house blinking his eyes and cursing, or if he was having a conversation with someone. Willie Mae would drink just as much as he would. They would get into violent fights and do terrible things to one another.

Whether the men's behavior we saw was due to what we would now call mental disorders or learned in order to cope, patterns were handed down over the years. What else was there to make them feel like men when their only outlets were alcohol, drugs, or taking it out on their wife? How can you fix years and years of going to bed not knowing there's a different way of looking at things? How can you know that if no one has shown you a difference? Their behavior in part was a residual by-product of years of systemic segregation.

The repressing of anyone's emotions for long periods of time can manifest as rage. How do you relieve emotional pain and the burden it has created and still be a man? It perpetuates itself and is passed down from generation to generation. It will continue until someone pays the price to break the chain in a more responsible way, such as having constructive dialogue. It requires trust, which was in short supply, but I was filled with hope.

I am convinced that education is essential to break the chains of poverty, ignorance, and prejudice. However, the educational system of segregated Houston in the 1950s was ill-equipped to meet the needs of a child desperately wanting to escape the tyranny of low expectations and discover his identity and ultimately his destiny.

When I tell people my life story, they often are impressed that I was able to go from grinding poverty to earning a comfortable living playing what I perhaps naively thought was a game. What was far more rewarding to me, however, was overcoming an inauspicious start to my education to become the first member of my family to graduate from college.

When I was in elementary school, I was talkative and hyperactive. I had a hard time focusing on things that I needed to get done. Paying attention was a problem for me, and furthermore I was a distraction to the other students. I was trying to make my classmates laugh, but it always seemed to be at the wrong time. This is why I would end up standing in the hallway next to our classroom door. It's called a timeout today. There were other times my teacher had to send me to the office.

Reading was difficult for me, and I had a hard time concentrating. When I had to read, I used my finger to follow the words. Somehow my eyes would end up on another sentence. Every time that happened, I would have to start over again. My mind was going faster than I could get the words out, so it was a success if I finished reading the sentence without starting over. In reality, though, it wasn't, because I didn't understand what I was reading.

The other students laughed at me, and it took me a while to figure out why. It was because I couldn't read. However, some of them were in my group who couldn't do much better. I would get angry when they snickered at me. I could beat them up, so I would push them when the teacher wasn't looking. If they told on me, I would get three licks in the palm of my hands with a ruler. Even during punishment, I tried to do something to make them laugh. That was frustrating.

By the fourth grade, I was somewhat inattentive and aloof. Wayne was a better student, getting A's and B's on his report card, plus being listed on the honor roll, along with music appreciation certificates and other awards. One semester, I got so many D's that I thought the teacher was giving them to me because my name started with a D. I was glad the school year was coming to an end, but I was not looking forward to getting my grades. I got all F's, which meant I failed fourth grade. I was upset and angry but most of all frustrated. I wanted to do well in school, but I was not able to demonstrate it in the classroom. Wanting to be a part of something, I felt like an outcast because I had to go to summer school and had to then repeat fourth grade at Dogan Elementary starting the next fall. It wasn't until years later that I learned I have dyslexia, along with ADHD.

The black community was expanding to the northeastern part of Houston. The school district had started construction on a new elementary school named J. C. McDade, where I started fifth grade after repeating fourth grade at Dogan Elementary. The newly built school was closer to my new home. I didn't mind being away from Dogan. Any school was better than having nothing to do. There were no gyms around, nor playgrounds, neighborhood parks, swimming pools, organized sports, or anything else geared to youth activity. When we played basketball, we'd attach a bicycle wheel rim to some plywood and nail it to a telephone pole. Because we used tennis balls for basketballs, we couldn't miss.

Kashmere Gardens Life

The intersection of Wayne and Rand Streets was the epicenter of our Kashmere Gardens neighborhood. Hing's Grocery Store was on the northeast corner, and the front door faced the intersection. A church across the street from Hing's on the northwest side was a tent for quite a while. My cousin Bonnie, Aunt Lillie's oldest daughter who lived next door, opened a burger and soda joint on the southwest side. Avery Scarborough owned the Sinclair service station on the southeast corner. Facing Rand Street and next to the service station were three shotgun houses.

Most of my immediate family on my mother's side lived within fifty yards of one another, and it was an interesting time when we were living there. Although I was not with my mother, she didn't live far away. At this time, she was living next door. I lived in the middle house with my grandmother and Wayne on the left, and James lived with my Aunt Mary on the right. Aunt Lillie lived on Wayne's street right next door to Hing's grocery store. The Hirsch Road bus ran through the neighborhood and stopped on the corner of Wayne and Rand.

There was a lot of activity on the corner. Hing's had good business, and customers were coming and going all the time. The service station, church, and Bonnie's hamburger and soda business all were active. Gas was about twenty-five cents a gallon for ethyl, and if they had a gas war it would drop down to fifteen cents. You could get a package of cigarettes for twenty-five cents, a soda for ten cents, and my favorite dinner snack of cinnamon rolls and lunch meat for twenty-five cents.

Our lives are shaped as much by the mundane, day-to-day activities as by the big moments. We learned from the experiences that we witnessed or picked up things that were talked about and did them to one another. Disagreement and conflict resolution were handled violently or repressed. Smoking cigarettes, sniffing gas, and drinking are ways that we learned how to deal with the problems of stress, depression and boredom. We were taught to keep things in and not to air the family's dirty laundry, such as alcoholism or abuse. Almost all personal needs were handled within the invisible boundaries created by our color.

We lived in a gray standard shotgun house on Rand Street. It sat on bricks and was higher than most. The front porch was all wood and half-screened. There were a couple of chairs, including a metal lawn chair that rocked. After heavy rains, city trucks drove through the neighborhood spraying pesticides. They said mosquitoes carried a disease called encephalitis. To keep from breathing the chemicals, we would put a scarf or something over our noses.

We sat out there in the summertime fighting mosquitoes. My grandmother was smoking cigarettes, and I was trying to catch fireflies. When entering, you had three steps up to the front screen door to the porch. Once inside, you turn right to enter the front door and go into the front room. Looking straight ahead, you'd see a window with a couch underneath it. You could find Grandma sitting there looking out the window and absorbing the neighborhood activity. A coffee table sat in front of the couch, with a big family edition of the King James Bible sitting on it. To the best of my recollection, it was the only thing in the house to read. Most houses in our neighborhood had one.

Our family was splintered, and so was my mother's love. Wayne lived with Mama, James stayed with my Aunt Mary, and I was with my grandmother. We all were struggling for our mother's love, but the biggest impact was the absence of our father. Among the three of us, Wayne probably struggled the most, because he spent a lot of time by himself, but to me he was getting our mother's love, and I wasn't.

A Fresh Start

Adulthood and its challenges could wait. For now, I welcomed the opportunity for a fresh start at a new school. My sixth-grade teacher's name was Thomas Richard Manning. At that time, he may have been the only male teacher in the school. He was the first positive role model since the death of my grandfather, although I never let him know it. In fact, I didn't realize it until I started thinking about positive male figures in my life.

Like most kids, recess was my favorite part of school. I now was getting interested in organized sports, especially football. I was a better athlete than most of the kids, and they always wanted me to be on their team. Although most of the students were better in the classroom, recess was a time where I could excel, and I always tried to do my best. Sometimes we played team sports, but most of the time it was group participation, which I did not like, because we had to play with the girls. Not that I did not want to play with the girls, but I would not get a chance to excel if girls participated.

Mr. Manning had just graduated from college, and I think it was his first teaching job. He dressed well, and I thought he was cool. All of the girls at school liked him, and some of the teachers had a crush on him as well. I was talking to him one day and asked where he lived. He never really told me, but he was a Kashmere fan, so I assumed Kashmere Gardens or Fifth Ward. Sometimes at recess, he would play football with us. I saw him once at one of Kashmere's football games and called him Thomas instead of Mr. Manning. He didn't appreciate it. I think one day during school I called him Thomas under my breath, and he heard me.

What is called child abuse today was called discipline when l was in school. Corporal punishment was sanctioned by the schools and the parents as well. Most students would rather be disciplined at school than by their parents. I don't remember getting many whippings at home, although I know I got some. However, I did get three licks with Mr. Manning's board. I was angry with him for doing it, even though I instigated it. However, with Mr. Manning as it would be in other situations, I wanted to know what my boundaries were, so I pushed him and he responded in the way I subconsciously knew he would. My grandfather would have been all over me for behaving that way, and I knew it. I needed to be clear about recognizing my boundaries.

Behind McDade but part of the school was an open field we used at recess. A chain fence divided Kashmere Junior and Senior High School from McDade. During football season, some days I would see the Kashmere football team practicing when we were at recess. If it was in April, I could see spring practice. When they scrimmaged, I could hear the collisions, pads popping, and coaches yelling. At the time, the guys were big and intimidating to me. I thought maybe I should change my mind about playing organized football.

What I remember thinking about those players was that they were special. My thoughts took me back to failing the fourth grade and feeling like an outcast. But it was starting to come together in the sixth grade. My father was not in my life, and I had two uncles who were alcoholics. My friends were going to Gatesville Juvenile Correctional Center, getting killed, or overdosing, and I was on the edge. Thanks to my grandmother, I did not go over to the other side. I have told many of my friends I knew in the sixth grade that I wanted something different. The great professional football players I had watched, my sixth-grade teacher, and

> *I didn't know what it would be or how it would show up in my life, but I wanted a change.*

the Kashmere football players had become, in my subconscious mind, positive role models.

As a kid, you don't realize what's happening. We're able to recognize on a surface level what we want, but we don't understand our motivations for it. Neither did our mother. It was "do what I say and not what I do," and you were disciplined accordingly if you didn't. There was no child-development guide or how-to-love-your-kids program around. We want what we want, and sometimes we don't get it, and because of our learning curve we want to know why.

Every kid in my neighborhood—just like every kid in every city with a pro football team—liked to play pick-up games where we emulated our favorite players. Guys in the neighborhood would come to watch us play. I also was called "Sonny," and I remember one intense game when I played quarterback and called a rollout, right fake, double-reverse pass. I was supposed to hit my cousin Robert on a post pattern, but I had no intentions of passing the ball. I faked the pass, pulled the ball down and started to run.

The defender had a good angle on me, but I was faster. I made him think I was going to try to outrun him for the touchdown, but as he got close to me, I made a cut, went behind him and scored a touchdown. When I put the move on him for the score, I heard my friend Artis emphatically say, "Damn, Sonny is good!" Those were words I never heard in the classroom and rarely heard at home. I knew it was something I could do well, and I felt drawn to the game. For the first time in my life, I had done something well.

Just as importantly, people *told me* that I had done something well. I had just ascended to the rank of neighborhood football star. In that moment, I was forever drawn to the game. I had found my sense of self. This is a defining moment for any kid, but especially so for an African American who repeatedly had been told what his place was in life.

Growing Sense of Manhood

Between the ages of eight and thirteen, I had experiences that left me traumatized but motivated. However, given how things worked out, it definitely was more the latter. I was developing a sense of manhood since Papa's death, and I was unaware of the void left from the death of my grandfather. I was learning how to be a man and felt like I wanted to be on my own. Much later, I realized how many football players had shared not only that dream but also my pursuit of a place where they could fit in. Many tried to find that place on the streets.

One summer night, I walked in on the middle of a conversation. Robert Rogers, one of the leaders in a Kashmere Gardens gang, was talking about retribution and respect. Apparently, someone had gotten beaten up by a rival group, and I missed that part. It felt like I was learning part of a doctrine I had not been privy to before, an aristocratic code of sorts. He said, "You can't be afraid of getting your ass whipped, and if a fight is inevitable and you're outnumbered, make sure you get the hero first." He was referring to the lead instigator, because at the very least you'll get respect.

Although he said more, that part of the message stayed with me. It transcends "street cred" for me, and I applied the concept to several areas of my life, including football. I wasn't afraid to take on the best player, especially if I was in a new neighborhood. I would carry that into my professional life. I had to gain their respect.

I have evolved and adjusted my philosophy since those days, but Robert was referring to the ultimate respect, that shown to those who display willingness to die.

In the South and particularly in the black communities, people passed through, needing a room for a night or two. Families also rented rooms in their homes. My grandmother did that. Sometimes she would have a roomer for a night or two. I didn't like it, but there wasn't anything I could do. Sometimes, especially at night, they used the back door to the bedroom when they came home. My grandmother had rented a room to a man who

> *A platform built on respect was key to how I would define myself.*

seemed to be quiet, shy, and respectful. He would come and go, minding his own business.

About two o'clock one morning, my grandmother and I woke up to a loud banging on the front door. From our bed, grandma asked who was there, and a voice said it was police. She peeped through the window curtains, and several cars were in front of the house. When she asked what the problem was, they said a girl had been raped and said she was brought to this house. As my grandmother got out of bed, she protested that nothing had gone on in the house and that she had been home all evening.

They asked if a man was living here, and she said there was. When she opened the door, three police officers entered. Asking us to step aside, they opened the bedroom door. When they turned the light on, we saw blood all over the bed and on the floor. I couldn't believe it. A trail of blood led to the kitchen into the bathroom and out of the back door. They ask us to step out of the house while they searched it.

By this time, my mother and Aunt Mary were awake and outside with us while the officers searched inside, outside, and underneath for what seemed to be a long time. By this time, there were police everywhere. They were getting ready to call off the search, when one of the officers shined his flashlight under the house again. He saw something moving. It was the man! The other officers pulled out their guns, and he yelled, "Come out from there, nigger!" I watched Grandma's roomer as he crawled out from behind one of the brick stacks supporting the house. It was cold, he was in bloody pants, shirtless and barefoot, and could hardly move. As soon as they could reach him, one of the police officers grabbed his arm, handcuffed him, and dragged him out and through the yard into the paddy wagon.

Everybody was in shock that something like that happened in our house—and even worse that we had been unaware of it. It was a long night for all of us, and I didn't have to go to school the next day. In the weeks to come, my grandmother and aunt had to go to court and testify. We weren't told about what happened in court, because it wasn't good. The accused had family in the area who would come to our house cursing and yelling at my aunt and grandmother. After that, I was afraid to be in that room with the lights out. On several occasions, my grandmother asked if I wanted to have my own room, to which I would always say no.

Sense of Belonging

When I started junior high school in the fall of 1964, I saw football players, and they were always together. Nobody messed with them, and the coaches and players were like a family. I said to myself, "I don't know what all of that is, but I want it." Later I realized it was a level of group consciousness, this sense of safety and the tribal needs of support and love. The coaches were like father figures. It was what I had been looking for but didn't know it. The whole school was behind us. I thought of this later. I knew it was something that made me feel good, but it later became clear why I was drawn to this. Football was bigger than simply a game. Now it meant more.

I grew up in a community that had the images of the powerful, imposing black athletes broadcast into our homes every week. Six days a week, we saw nothing but representations of white America. In Jim Crow Texas, we were made to see and understand that only white people ever accomplished things, earned respect, or showed off their full potential. But on Sundays, we could see black men such as Jim Brown of the Cleveland Browns dominating and expressing themselves as powerful, capable, respected leaders and celebrities. I wanted to be a part of that. Television illuminated football and something that seemed otherwise hidden and impossible in American life: a way for a black man to matter. Not only could I find validation, one day I might even get paid for it.

I wanted to be a halfback like Lenny Moore of the Baltimore Colts, the prototype elusive professional running back at that time, who led the league with sixteen rushing touchdowns in 1964. We used a beer or soda can as the football, always being careful not to fall on it and get jabbed. I had an announcer in my head whenever I ran the ball and broke free: "It's Moore to the thirty, to the twenty, and what a great move to the ten! He's going to go all the way for a touchdown!" And the crowd would roar.

Most star runners in the NFL were black, but the quarterbacks were white. At the time, it was just the way it was. A lot of times I played by myself. You can't hand off to yourself, but you can throw. I would be Johnny Unitas, the Colts' quarterback, throwing to his favorite receiver, Raymond Berry. I would drop back in the pocket and imitate an announcer: "Unitas manages to get away from one, he dodges another would-be tackler! Oh, he's hit from the blind side for a loss."

CHAPTER 2

Inevitably, I would be in an almost insurmountable situation: "It's now fourth and 20. What will they do now? Here is the snap. Unitas drops back . . . he's looking, he's looking . . . and he spots Berry! He throws!" Simultaneously, I would throw the beer can in the air high enough to run underneath it. "What a catch! One of Berry's patented sideline receptions." After the first down, I would repeat desperate heaves and acrobatic catches until I scored.

One afternoon, I had just finished our traditional Sunday meal, and the preseason 1965 College All-Star Game was on television. My idols, Jim Brown of the 1964 NFL champion Cleveland Browns and Gale Sayers of the University of Kansas were both playing. That year, 1965, would be Brown's last season and the rookie year for Sayers with the Chicago Bears. They were, in my opinion, the best two running backs who had ever played the game, even to this day. Throughout the game, I was imagining being Brown on one play and Sayers the next.

When the game was over, I met some friends and played a pickup game of football. I pretended to be Sayers and tried to imitate his moves on the field. We played until dark and talked about the All-Star Game on our way home. When we stopped under the streetlight, I said how much of a thrill it was for me to see those two great players together.

Like any other Sunday night, I had school the next day. After I finished some chores, it was time for bed. I remember waking up in the middle of the night from this dream. My heart was beating fast. It was pounding. I didn't know what was wrong. Then it came to me: I had just run for the winning touchdown in a professional football game. It was vivid. The crowd was roaring, and my teammates were congratulating me. I lay there not totally awake, contemplating the thought of playing professional football. It was scary, surreal. Before I drifted to sleep, I consciously thought, "That would be great!"

That dream one day would become a reality with the San Francisco 49ers, Miami Dolphins, and Green Bay Packers, but it began with the Kashmere High School Fighting Rams.

My long journey out of the Fifth Ward and to the NFL began with a vision. Literally.

I remember seeing the local Kashmere High School football team practice, and I wanted to be a part of it. Most of the neighborhood guys had always encouraged me to try out. Even though I had all the normal fears of failure and acceptance, I decided to do it. You always hear guys say they are not afraid of this or that, but I disagree. Fear is a healthy and natural emotion, and it will manifest in other ways if repressed. In a certain way, football is played to get over the fears. But little did we know it would create the biggest fear of all, which is living without it.

The high school building was behind us. At recess, I used to watch the high school practice. You could hear the coaches yelling at the guys. I said, "I want to play football." It was something I felt I was good at, but it also had that discipline and unity I didn't know about at the time. I was willing to pay the price of discipline to be a part of it.

I tried out for the team before school started. All of the coaches were there, including Tom Hendricks and Mr. Simon, whom I had seen from afar but never up close. The coaches at Kashmere, especially the football coaches, were a different breed. It was like they were the school enforcers. They were intimidating because they had to be.

Mr. Hendricks was the junior varsity football coach, as well as receivers and defensive ends coach for the varsity team and head track coach. He also taught history. Mr. Simon was the main enforcer, and the coaches would get into fistfights with some of the students and non-students. Some of them would attack Mr. Smart, who was the junior high football and basketball coach, simply because he was smaller. However, if the enforcers caught one of them, that person would be in trouble.

They were preparing for summer practice, and this would be the time for signing up new players. The line stretched out of the coach's office, down the steps, and around the corner. I had looked forward to this moment, and now it was happening. The reality of the occasion was more intense than running for a winning touchdown in my dream. I saw dejection on the face of some guys as they left the coach's office. They were bigger than me, and I had thought for sure they were going to make the team, but some didn't.

> *Football was an introduction to manhood.*

When it got to be my turn, I was nervous. I walked in the door, and Mr. Abram said in a deep voice, "What do you want to do, son?"

I said, "I want to try out for the football team."

He said, "Okay."

Although I had never been in that situation before, I knew going in that I had to strip down to my underwear. When I pulled my pants off, they laughed. I had on some boxer short that were too big for me. My grandmother would buy them large, because her thinking was I would grow into them. However, when I stepped on the scale, I weighed ninety-seven pounds, and the coach told me I was too small to play. He suggested that I try next year.

I was disappointed and hurt, because I wanted to play football, and I didn't think size should have been a factor. I knew I could play, but now I thought I was a failure. How would I face the fellows? What would I tell them? Would it expose my façade of being tough?

Although I did not make the team that year, something was starting to change. The circumstance with the overlarge underwear was a metaphor. It is a quintessential example of what can happen when you don't have someone to guide you through the uncharted waters of adolescence.

A New Phase

There have been several important phases in my life, and starting junior high school would be the beginning of one of them. I was starting to meet new people, and they were my age and height, unlike my neighborhood friends. In fact, I could go through most of the day and not see anyone from our neighborhood. It dawned on me that I wouldn't see them, because most had dropped out of school. I realized that all the street cred I had from the neighborhood didn't matter. I was on my own.

All the things I had learned from the streets in our neighborhood led to a heightened social awareness that would come into play. It would manifest as common sense and instinct. Observation of potential danger proved to be a valuable lesson in survival. As a seventh grader, I was comfortable around all the high school kids, although I maintained my distance, and a healthy dose of skepticism always helped.

It's easy now to look back at my early years and focus on the negatives, such as poverty, a broken family, lack of positive role models, and pervasive racism. I choose to look at the positives. I could have easily embraced victimhood and ended up a dropout, in prison, or worse. In fact, I was one of the lucky ones. I didn't know it then, but, given my behavior, I did not want to be a victim. I would get angry when I was told I couldn't physically do or participate in something. Getting emotional about things of that nature and pushing back or not accepting something was my way of being persistent.

The absence of my father and the loss of my grandfather left me confused and in search of my identity as a man. For better or worse, I was about to fill that void in the 100-yard-by-160-foot dimensions of a football field.

I recognize that others who take the gridiron in the NFL have not had my exact experiences, but I believe that most of us come to the game damaged and in need of something. Although I am several generations removed from the current crop of NFL superstars, most players in the league come from backgrounds that look far more like mine than the idealized *Father Knows Best* 1950s TV world of mythical America.

Only 20 percent of players grew up in two-parent homes, and, if anything, the NFL today looks more like where I came from than it did when I played. More than two-thirds of players are black, and most of these are from the South. Men enter America's football factory pipeline—high school, college, and NFL—and carry with them all of the dysfunction and brokenness of the neighborhoods, cities, and cultures from which they came. They arrive hungry for acceptance and for a vision of manhood to which they can cling.

Because the core emotional and psychic needs focus on such things as acceptance, tribe, masculinity, strength, meaning, and purpose, they accept or ignore the myriad ways that football further breaks them. The exchange is one in which the football factory offers a temporary emotional reward in return for the sweat, labor, blood, and vitality of the players.

Because of Grandma's poor health, before ninth grade I went to live with my mother and brother Wayne, who had moved around to various apartment houses and now were in Kelly Courts apartments in the south part of the Fifth Ward, close to The Bottom. Moving into the projects meant living in a slightly more urban environment but still with open lots and mostly one-story homes and wider streets. Kelly Courts Park, on the corner of Green and Grove Streets, was the central location where everybody congregated. Afterschool programs and activities such as Ping-Pong, basketball, baseball, and football could be found there.

When I think back on life in Kelly Courts, I didn't realize much of what was going on around me at the time, which probably was for the best. The environmental intensity alone created an enormous amount of stress at every level. We were emotionally vulnerable kids who were put in adult situations more than we should have been or wanted to be, and we were expected to survive. There was no alternative, and whether you survived largely depended on how well you disguised your fragility with your ego.

Choices and Consequences

Inside, however, fear was driving me, although having a healthy dose of skepticism is a good thing. We were trying to dodge the landmines of the neighborhood. It was easy to succumb to the traps of drugs, stealing, and violent fights where you could wind up in the hospital or cemetery. Another life lesson was emerging: everything depends on the choices you make.

The focus was on surviving, and we were not even aware of the concept of self-actualizing. It wasn't until I started playing football that any possibility of going to college became more than just a foreign thought. At the time, the only college graduate I knew was Koonie, who had a PhD but also was a heroin addict. Although there were some fathers in homes, single mothers were in charge. Johnny Peacock, Richard Ross, Johnny Hines, Ron and Don Pearson, and my best friend, Willie "Chucksey" Ferguson, all lived without fathers in the home. Our mothers were all heads of the household and ruled with an iron fist.

I was now in junior high and would have to take courses such as Spanish, history, English, and algebra. English, because all the reading and writing I would have to do, and any kind of math, because of the sequences of numbers to remember, both would be challenging. Math was my least-favorite subject. Moreover, the thought of reading Shakespeare was enough to make me want to cut English every day. Even though my grades were not getting any better, school was becoming an interesting place to be, and I was starting to like it.

Kashmere was a predominantly black junior and senior high school, with four thousand students enrolled. There would be more freedom in terms of moving around the campus, because I would have six classes instead of one. My academic confidence was shaky at best, if I had any at all, and I still remembered having failing fourth grade. I wasn't a dunce, but I would struggle throughout school. Given my challenges and background, I was always a candidate to drop out of school.

I was not raised in a home environment that pushed education. My grandparents were functionally illiterate. Education was only talked about, because survival was the main objective. Therefore, reading and writing were not something that would come naturally to me, nor was there anyone at home to teach me There were no books, magazines, or anything that would have given me a hint about how important reading was to education. I entered the seventh grade with lots of things on my mind, the least of which was school. Although school was a major concern, foremost was the uncertainty of my immediate future.

After attending Kashmere Middle School for seventh and eighth grade, I was transferred to E. O. Smith Junior High for ninth grade, because I was living at Kelly Courts with my mother. After not making the football team in middle school, I didn't try out at the new school. Although 95 percent of the students at E. O. Smith went on to Phyllis Wheatley High School, Leon Strauss, Michael Smith, Johnny Ray Peacock, Willie "Chucksey" Ferguson, and I attended Kashmere High. We got the E. O. Smith principal's permission to leave after our fifth-period class for Kashmere's spring football practice. After two failed attempts to make a team, I finally received my first uniform. I felt good about being a part of the team, but if it were not for Chucksey, I probably would not have tried it again.

I had met Chucksey in the summer of 1966, and he would turn out to be my best friend. He talked me into trying out for Kashmere's football team one more time. We had discussed my two previous attempts to make their junior high team in eighth and ninth grade. Chucksey had seen me play as a teammate and opponent at the park in the neighborhood and respected my ability. However, I had never played organized football. I thought about giving up the dream of playing—but, thanks to Chucksey, I did not.

He was the youngest of four children, one girl and three boys. His siblings were Rose "Lil Honey" Ferguson, Charles Hines, and Alex "Boardwalk" Ferguson." "Walk," as we called Alex, had been a standout the year before as the starting center and middle linebacker for Kashmere. He was finishing his senior year and had several scholarship offers. As a football player, he was our first role model. Others were Kenneth "Booty" Foots, Andrew "Slab" Clifton, and T. C. Gray. Walk had a lot of potential and could have gone further but chose a different path. Although he had given the coaches some background information on me, I was nervous and somewhat pessimistic about making the team.

I wanted to be a halfback, but I wanted to be on the team more, so I played where they put me. Right away, they realized I was fast and moved me to the flanker position on offense. I didn't want to play defense, but that was not an option, so I was assigned a cornerback position.

Mr. Hendricks, who also was the head track coach, saw my potential, and right away he recognized the raw speed I had. He'd pull me aside from time to time and give me pointers on running pass routes and receiving. Mr. Hendricks had a reputation around the school as someone you did not want to mess with. He was also one of the enforcers and was a big man, about six foot two and 230 take-no-prisoners pounds. He had a dark complexion and deep voice, and when you heard it, you knew it was him.

He had played football and run track at the University of Michigan and had a short stint in professional football. A no-nonsense type, he would not tolerate a lack of effort and expected nothing less than

100 percent. There was no middle of the road with him. A passionate man and motivator extraordinaire, he was liked, loved, and feared by some but respected by all, especially those of us who played for him. However, all he wanted to know was what you were made of. A player's heart was his measurement.

Running with the First Team

Although this was my first time playing organized football, I was picking up the game faster than I expected. A week into spring practice, I started running plays with the varsity's first team. Benny Mitchell was the starting flanker, and a couple of times they pulled him out and put me in. That was pretty heady stuff for someone who had never played organized football before. But it was embarrassing for a senior, and Benny didn't like it. He made some comments about it being his position, trying to intimidate me. He said, "This is my job."

We were supposed to rotate every other series of plays. Then when it was my turn, and when the coaches were not looking, he would beat me to our spot in the huddle and run some of my plays. In some way, I was being used to push Benny to get better, but it was good for me to be in that group. Mr. Hendricks was taking me under his wings.

I had run a post pattern. Calvin Burleson, the defensive back, read it and came unabated, putting his Riddell helmet right in the ear hole of my helmet. WHAM! As a rookie sophomore, I had probably tipped my hand, but he was a senior and knew the plays. To break a player in or test him, sometimes the offensive coaches would tell the defense what play we were going to run. It wouldn't surprise me to learn that they had set me up.

When someone says they got their bell rung or they were seeing stars, I know exactly what that is like. The field hadn't been watered for a few days, and it was hard. When I hit the ground, my head was ringing. I saw red, blue, and yellow flashes of light. I paid the price for being on the team when I hit the ground after one play. Calvin played with a chip on his shoulder and always brought it to you. I lay there for a minute or two, but I could hear him saying "He's not going to get up, he's not going to get up" and then start laughing.

I believe everybody in the sport has a moment of questioning themselves: "How badly do I want to do this? Is it really what I want to do?"

That was my moment, and it was a point of no return. That experience became my reference point of what it took to play football. There were going to be days like this, and this is what I had to go through if I wanted to play. I got up, and by doing so I let everybody know I could take a hit. Your teammates' affirmation that you're now a part of the team is subtle. Acceptance was not as overt as I hoped it would be—it's a nod of the head when you make a big play, maybe a half-smile from the head coach. Taking a hit and getting up results in the ultimate acceptance. After all, that's what the game is all about—hit or be hit, and sometimes be knocked out cold. When you get hit and hear "Wahoo!" while you hold onto the ball, nothing else needs to be said.

I had a good spring practice and had run some plays with the varsity. This was far beyond my expectations, and I was looking forward to the fall. That summer, someone told Chucksey about a high school sports magazine that mentioned both of our names. We walked into a Ralston drugstore looking for the magazine, although we did not think they would have it. Much to our surprise, they had it, and we bought a copy. It mentioned our names as up-and-coming players to watch for at Kashmere.

Integrating the Leagues

Although sports, like everything else in Houston, had long been segregated, integration between the two primary high school athletics leagues occurred in the fall of 1967. Andrew Patterson was the head football coach at Jack Yates High School. The African American high schools in Texas played in what was officially known as the Texas Interscholastic League of Colored Schools from 1920 until 1964. Coach Patterson came up with the idea of changing the name to Prairie View Interscholastic League (PVIL). At the encouragement of Coach Patterson, the overall Houston Independent School District was the lead supporter to integrate the PVIL along with the University Interscholastic League for statewide high school play.

The PVIL began to merge with the University Interscholastic League during the 1967–68 school year. Coach Patterson would end his career with a 184–61–9 mark and five state championships. He was one of the most successful high school coaches in Texas history. A lot of great football players have come through the PVIL, such as Ernie Ladd, Jerry LeVias, Bubba and Tody Smith, Gene Washington of the Vikings, Gene and Marvin Upshaw, Don Goode, J. V. Cain, Eldridge Dickey, Joe Greene, Kenny Houston, Otis Taylor, Emmett Thomas, Dick "Night Train" Lane, Warren Wells, Eldridge Small, Leo Johnson, Greg Pruitt, Dwight Harrison, Mel and Miller Farr, Joe Washington, Cedric Hardman, Lester Hayes, Cliff Branch, and Robert Miller.

The 1967 opening weekend went off without a hitch, because no black and white teams played each other. The next weekend was different. Yates played Westbury, and other games included Bellaire versus Wheatley, Worthing versus Milby, and Williams versus Lamar, all night games. All the black teams won except Wheatley, but outside of the usual racial epithets, there were no incidents of note.

I was on the junior varsity team my first year as a sophomore, not having made varsity as I had hoped. We played for the J.V. championship but lost the game to Sam Houston, 21–20. That was my first taste of championship defeat, and I didn't like it. It didn't feel good, because I couldn't do anything to change the outcome. It felt like I had lost a fistfight, fair and square, and I couldn't hit back any more. I had to sit with that feeling until the next season.

When I started playing, validation was instant, and I was redefining who I was through football. I didn't like the feeling that came with losing, and I was not conscious of the impact it was having on me. I don't think any of us knew. Making the team and getting to play wasn't enough anymore. There was a connection between competition and self-worth that was tied to winning and losing. That transcended the game, and now it was personal. When I took the uniform off, the game was over, but the feeling of the loss didn't go away. It was as if my manhood and pride had been attacked. I believe it happens to all football players, in times and places not of their choosing. That started a lifelong commitment in me to football and winning.

During the season, our intensity grew to a point that when we won, we wore it as a badge of honor. The competitive edge that we gained was internalized but surfaced as a defense of manhood if we were challenged. With a smile on your face, it was who you were, in all your splendor, at an early age. However, if we lost, the feeling of failure was present. We couldn't wait for the next week. We didn't lose much in high school, so we usually felt good about who we were. Especially during this season, I felt a balance between the emotions of winning and losing. Given my genetic makeup, environment, and desire to succeed, little did I know having a drink after a game, whether winning or losing, planted the seeds of addiction that ran deep into my subconscious.

That same year, 1967, the varsity lost the city championship. However, college scouts were on campus recruiting the seniors and keeping a watchful eye on others. Kenny Adams and John Sanford went to the University of California, Berkeley, and Larry Edwards and Henry Glenn went to Texas A&I, where they would go on to win two small-college national championships.

Just as I had envisioned, being a part of the team gave me an identity. It was clear that the football team was a united group of guys. We supported each other for a common goal, which was to win, game by game. More than anything, the support was what I longed for. Team had now taken the place of family, the one that was so disjointed for me.

Up until then, football was an end in itself. Whether in the sandlot or the stadium, I played solely for the love of the game and the identity it gave me. As I was about to learn, football also could be the means to reach the ends I desired.

After that first season, my paradigm shifted: I began to see football as a means to a better life, not simply as an end.

Before playing football, my goals were simple: I wanted to finish high school and get a job so I could move out of the neighborhood. I thought these were solid goals, but after the season, I started wondering, was that enough? Were these goals something every kid wanted, or was it short-sighted because of my circumstances in life?

What football meant to me was changing again. I could have gone over to the other side and chosen a life of crime and violence, but football started meaning something different for me. It no longer was just this fantasy, but it began to be part of the plan. In the sixth grade, I was inspired and hopeful with visions of getting out of the neighborhood and changing my lot in life. I wanted something different for myself. Not making the junior high team, I didn't get into organized football as early as others did. Then in high school, I began to see football as a way to make it out. I wanted to play professional football.

Coach Billie Matthews

Playing varsity football began a long and complicated relationship with Coach Billie Matthews, who would precede me to the University of Kansas. Coach Matthews had been the head football coach at Kashmere High School from the day it opened in 1957. Midway through my junior season, something happened that changed the course of Billie's and my future in football.

I was a defensive back, wide receiver, and punter. It was fourth down, and I was waiting to punt. When the center snapped the ball, it went over my head and into the endzone. I ran back and picked up the ball, and when I turned around all I could see were the opponents bearing down on me. My instincts took over. I dodged the first wave of would-be tacklers, made a move, and started running. I outran everybody and scored a touchdown.

At first, it didn't seem to be that big of a deal to me. After I got past the first guy, it was just a matter of outrunning the rest of the team. I was happy I didn't get trapped in the endzone. However, from what I've been told, it was my speed that blew everybody away. The next week I was playing fullback. I finished that year with a better-than-average season, considering that I had played half of the year at fullback. I looked forward to the next year.

I was hoping I could get a scholarship, but my grades would be an impediment. The coaches reminded all of us about getting good grades. If we didn't have the grades, we wouldn't be able to get into college. The coaches would give the senior players the letters they received from colleges and universities.

In 1968, my junior year, we were 6–4, and with a break we could have been 8–2. But we ended the season on a high note. There were four or five games that were very important for us to win. We had to get out of our district, and that meant beating Washington and Sam Houston High Schools. Washington had finished 13–1 the year before and lost in the semifinals of the state championship playoffs. In 1969 we would start the season playing the Beaumont, Texas, schools: Charleston Pollard and Hebert. We were returning fifteen lettermen from the season before and felt good about our team. Some thought this team was better than the 1967 Kashmere team.

Unexpected News

During my junior year, as I was still finding my way into football—and by extension, into manhood—my mother announced to the family that she was pregnant. I was stunned when she told me, and I felt somewhat uncomfortable with it, but what was I going to do? I wasn't prepared to discuss my mother's sexual activity with her. On March 28, 1968, Saundra Michelle Williams was born. She was James's sister and a half-sister to Wayne and me. Wayne was in Gatesville State School for Boys, a juvenile detention facility, and I was ending my junior year in high school, and now we had a new baby sister. We wouldn't know until a few years later that she was born autistic. I assume that after the doctors told my mother, she didn't want us to know, but you can't hide autism. And this would not be the last time that family complications would impact my aspirations.

Heading into my senior season, I felt good about my abilities on the field and was feeling better about my classroom work. However, news that came like a bolt out of the blue nearly derailed my dreams of a college scholarship and a professional career.

In May 1969, I had been finishing my junior year of high school. I had just gotten home from work. I had started working before school was out for the summer, doing maintenance work at a machine shop. It had been a better job than my two previous ones. Working on the railroad tossing crossties wasn't fun, especially in the middle of the summer. It would get so hot that we had to wear long-sleeved shirts to keep from getting sunburned.

In those days, the goal was to graduate from high school, because college was out of the question. It became clear to me that if I did not graduate from high school, I would have to resign myself to manual labor. I was convinced this was something that I did not want to do. I saw the importance of graduating from high school, and I wanted to do something better.

One job I had was breaking up cement using an air hammer. The job I had with a machine shop was one that I started before school was out. With two weeks to go in school, I worked from 6:00 p.m. to midnight, making $1.60 an hour. The buses would stop running at about 11:00 p.m. or midnight, so I had to walk about two miles to get home. I would get home at about 1:30 a.m., take a bath, and flop down on the bed and go to sleep. Before I knew it, it was 7:00 a.m. and time to get ready for school and go catch the bus or hitchhike to school.

This went on for about two weeks. When school was out, I then worked from 6:00 p.m. to 6:00 a.m. or longer for seven days a week. One payday, I had my regular 80 hours for two weeks plus 74.5 hours in overtime. I netted $275 on my paycheck and said the government was killing me. But in midsummer I bought my first car, a green, four-door 1957 Chevrolet.

I was home alone one day and had just gotten out of the bathtub when I heard someone at the front door. From the top of the stairs I yelled, "Who is it?" Someone responded, but I couldn't tell who it was. I wrapped a towel around me and started down the stairs, and before I reached the bottom I again asked, "Who is it?"

Then a voice said, "Hanna Mae. Is your mother home?"

By now I was at the front door. I stood on one side of the door and opened it just enough to peek around. I said, "No, she is not here."

She said in a soft voice, "Well, can I talk to you?"

Now I was really wondering why she wanted to talk to me and what was going on. I stepped back from the door, walked toward the stairs, and said, "Okay, come in. I was just getting out of the bathtub. Let me get dressed, and I will be right back."

As I was getting dressed, I was thinking, "Why does she want to talk to me?"

On my way down the stairs, it dawned on me that this could be about her daughter Kathy. Kathy was the sister of Richard Ross, who was a friend of mine. They lived two buildings over from our house. At the time, Kathy was about sixteen years old, and I had just turned eighteen. She would stop by our house and talk with my mother from time to time.

I didn't think much about it at first, because Kathy was not a woman I was interested in. I don't say that to demean her but to put it in perspective. She would pretend she was there to see my mother, but I knew she was there to see me. It got to a point where I did not turn away her advances, and, furthermore, I would encourage her to come by.

One night she stopped by to see my mother and was there only for a few minutes. She stopped downstairs, and we talked for a few minutes. In that conversation, we talked about sex. We also talked about the fear of her getting pregnant. She told me she could not have children. I thought about it for a second, but I didn't think about it any further. However, soon one thing led to another, and we had sex. This would continue for three to four months. During that time, nothing else had been discussed. It had been strictly sex.

As I sat down on the couch, I wondered what Miss Hanna Mae wanted to talk to me about. She said, "Kathy is pregnant, and she said it is yours." I was shocked. All kinds of things were going through my mind. How could this be true since she told me she could not have children?

My response was the typical one, "Are you sure it's mine?"

Miss Hanna Mae said yes and began to cry.

I sat there stunned, not knowing what to say. Miss Hanna Mae continued, "I knew something was wrong, because Kathy didn't have a period for a long time, and she is now six months pregnant."

It was May, I had just turned eighteen in April, and now I was going to be a father. She was saying other things, which were going in one ear and out the other. She stood up and said, "Have Dorothy Jean call me when she gets home."

I said I would do so, and she left. I also thought about the hardship this would bring to their family. I was embarrassed: How would I tell Mama? What would she say? Sooner or later, everybody in the neighborhood would know, and how would I explain it? How would I hold up under the pressure with all the attention I was going to get?

I didn't know how my mother would react, and I was not looking forward to telling her. My relationship with my mother was confusing sometimes. There were times it was as if we were a sister and brother, but there were also times I felt like I was the man of the house. I'm sure Wayne felt the same way. Although we had the freedom to explore our independence, what I really wanted was for her to be my mother. I believe this hurried me into premature adulthood.

When she got home, I told her that Kathy was pregnant and that Miss Hanna Mae wanted to talk to her about the situation. I told my mother that I was having sex by informing her she was going to be a grandmother. Much to my surprise, she started smiling and pointing her finger at me.

It was strange that she accepted it instead of scolding me, as I had expected. In fact, she wasn't surprised. I've thought about that evening over and over, trying to figure out what that was about. I've concluded that my mother may have sanctioned Kathy's pregnancy. My mother was close to several young women, and she had her favorites. She knew the neighboring families, and Kathy lived two units away. I have long tried to reconcile some unanswered questions. If she were alive today, I would ask if she set up me up with Kathy.

It is interesting how a child feeling emotionally abandoned by a parent still holds on to the unconditional love for their parent. You spend most of your life seeking a parent's reciprocation of love, no matter what has happened. You reach an age where you think it doesn't matter anymore, but that isn't so. We can turn off the pursuit of love for a little while as a coping mechanism for emotional safety, but it never stops being important. I've always felt like that, and I can imagine that's how my daughter feels. It becomes an act of love for one's self to forgive your parents. The irony is the feeling on the other end. I created the same situation for her that I was trying to get away from.

No "I" in "Team"?

During summer practice my senior year, Coach Matthews asked me if I would like to go to the Oilers-Bears preseason game at the Astrodome. I was a Gale Sayers fan, and he knew it. In fact, that's why I wore number 40. My first thought was "Wow! A professional football game and to see Gale Sayers . . . yeah!"

However, I thought it was strange that he asked me. He had always been partial to the quarterbacks—particularly Shelton Zenon, the starting quarterback. Billie would not let anyone touch Shelton in practice, and that included the coaches. That in and of itself is not that big of a deal, because most coaches protect their quarterbacks due to their value to the team. But he asked me and not Shelton. It felt kind of clandestine, and it put some pressure on me in accepting the offer. The oneness and purity of the team starts to get convoluted if coaches show preference. In the pure essence of team, I wasn't supposed to be treated special.

I had bought into the concept of "there's no 'I' in 'team.'" The denial of self for the team is something we struggle with, and, unbeknown to the players, it becomes a lifelong pursuit to retain their individualism apart from the team. Professional football does not honor personal growth. A college degree doesn't prepare you for the industrialized game. What I saw was that if you had success on the field, you couldn't enjoy it, because it could influence the team, and so you suppressed pride and even self-esteem.

I thought that personal success after football was over was the reason I was playing. But I also thought that it was a game and that you were supposed to enjoy it. We were taught subliminally and directly to deny ourselves for the good of the team. At the same time there was a continuum of trying to find your individual

> *Most of the time in football, we struggle with trust, and it permeates your personal life.*

self. We sacrificed for the team, not for one player to be treated as special and better than the others. In this case, my getting invited to the Oilers game, I believe my teammates were affected in some way. Maybe a seed of distrust had been planted. This would be the start of how I began to measure coaches: not by what they said but what they did. Subconsciously, trust was violated and replaced with partiality. I eventually would abandon that questioning somewhat, because you must be all in to play football. However, doubts were awakened in me.

We were a team. Why ask me and not the other players—or at least explain it to all of us? Professionals refer to it this questioning as a defense mechanism, but I call it a bullshit detector.

The Kashmere High Rams played in four stadiums: Jefferson, Delmar, Dyer, and Butler, and all games were played at night. Before integration, black schools used Jefferson Stadium. When we were on the J.V. team, Mr. Hendricks used to create a night game mystique and use it as a carrot, teasing us about playing at the big stadiums and under the lights.

He might say something such as, "Hey, baby, if you keep blocking like that, you are not going to be under the lights this week." Everybody wanted to be under the lights and play at night. The stadium fields were in great shape and neatly manicured. The white lines and numbers were clearly defined, and ten yards didn't seem so far. I remember getting tackled and bracing to hit the ground. You could get hurt falling on the ground at school, but this was soft grass. It was special to be under the lights. On our way to the stadium, we had the team bus rocking. The coaches would think something was wrong if we weren't laughing, talking, preaching, and teasing one another.

Before the games, we all were getting dressed or sitting there in a serious frame of mind. After we were dressed, Coach Matthews would read off the names of the players who were starting. He would go over the assignments and talk about the first couple of plays we wanted to run. In the meantime, Coach Hendricks was slowly walking around the locker room with white tape in his hand. He'd look everybody in the eye and stop in front of the starters and tear off two pieces of tape and put it over your heart in shape of a cross. Everybody wanted a cross, and not for religious reasons. The significance of the cross meant you had the heart to play. He talked about having heart and hammered it into our psyche: there was no place for the faint of heart, only for the pure-hearted. If you were chosen to start, you didn't want to let him down. That's what it meant to me.

There was no place for the faint of heart, only for the pure-hearted.

When Coach Matthews finished with his instructions, he asked if we had any questions about any of the information. No one ever had a question. All of us sat there waiting on Coach Matthews to finish. When he was done, he turned to Coach Hendricks and said, "Tom, you have anything you want to say?" and his response would be, "I just want to say this, baby," and then he would say a few words that would get us so fired up.

You never knew what he would talk about. It might be the struggle of our ancestors or the sacrifices our parents had made to give us a better life. Go out there and make that sacrifice mean something, make them proud parents, a win would mean so much to them, you're doing something good with your lives. I don't know another coach who has reached so deep inside of me, to get me to play for something bigger than myself. It was unbelievable!

The year before, Charlton-Pollard had finished with one loss and was rated one of the top teams in the state. In our 1969 game against them, I scored our first touchdown on a two-yard run. Our defense was dominating, and their quarterback, Hardy Malvo, didn't have anywhere to run. One of their punts landed practically on our goal line, and we had to start deep in our own territory. Quarterback Shelton Zenon called "37-off-25," a fullback carry that would become our signature play.

I made a read off the guard's block on the linebacker, turned upfield, saw only grass, and sprinted for a ninety-seven-yard touchdown. Late in the fourth quarter with a big lead and time running down, we ran 37-off-25 again. This time I broke away for an eighty-yard run and was tackled on the two-yard line. Two plays later, I scored the game's final touchdown. As time ran out, the score was 25–0.

My stats were eighteen carries for 294 yards and three touchdowns. I got on the bus, not just tired but drained, waiting for the rest of the players. Nobody spoke very much to me about the game until Chucksey walked up to me and said, "Do you know what you've done? You're going to have college scouts all over you!" Although it was one game, I sensed things were starting to change, something more than just high school football.

Whenever there was a car parked on the street watching our practices, Coach Matthews would have our trainer see who it was. For the Sam Houston game, to make sure we weren't spied on, we practiced at Brock Park, a golf course in a wooded area about six miles northwest of the school. After a fifteen-minute bus ride, there was no one else around, reinforcing that it was a big game.

We were both undefeated and state-ranked. The Sam Houston Tigers had beaten us 24–14 the year before. More than that, the teams still represented their segregated neighborhoods. The Tigers had been playing football since 1896. The stands were packed. It was a tense game from the start. The players started calling us niggers, and we responded with "Fuck you, honky!" When one of their players tried to spit on me and missed, I almost went to the next level but didn't.

Finally, someone pushed Jesse Lamb, and he pushed back. It was on. The officials quickly stopped the fight between Lamb and their player. More fights broke out, and a whiskey bottle flew onto the field. Still in the first half, two players from both sides were thrown out of the game. Joe Tusa, the Houston Independent School District athletic director, came down from the stands and stopped the game to speak with the officials and both coaches the middle of the field. Tusa, a respected former football coach at Reagan High, would later say, "I could see the thing was going to explode. I just laid down the law to both. Clean it up."

It was a tough, close game. After I fumbled, they started to move the ball downfield, which I knew was my fault. But our safety Sammy Johnson intercepted a pass and ran it back close to the goal line. As time ran out, we scored the final touchdown and won 23–14. Both teams left with respect for one another, which was the whole point of integrated play.

On a Roll

We kept winning games, big at times. At 5–0, we were ranked number one in the greater Houston area and number two statewide behind Austin Reagan, which had been undefeated and state champion the preceding two years. *The Houston Chronicle* previewed our Washington High School game in the sports section with an article headlined, "A Guy Named Williams May Decide Eagles-Rams Battle." Booker T. Washington's quarterback, David Williams was having a great year, just as I was. They had two other great players on that team—tight end J. V. Cain and linebacker Don Goode, who both went on to be NFL first-round draft choices. The Eagles had been 13–1 season the year before, when they were city champions, having blanked us 20–0.

After watching the films of the Washington game, our defensive line coach, Mr. Simon, started to indirectly tease Donald Charles, one of our leaders and most experienced lineman, that he couldn't handle Washington's Goode. Coach Simon kept it up all week, and we teased D. C. that he better get his ass ready for the paddle.

The district championship was as stake. Fifteen thousand people attended Delmar Stadium. The defense led by D. C. on the line shut down David Williams and J. V. Cain. The final score was 35–14, and we kept envisioning our goal of winning the bi-district and then the city and state championships.

We ran the table and finished 10–0, the best record in Houston. We beat Jefferson Davis 64–0, Reagan 56–0, San Jacinto 60–0, and Milby 34–8. All those opponents were all-white high schools. Kashmere was number one team in the state on both defense and offense, even with the Reagan and San Jacinto games ending four minutes early because the score was so lopsided. Due to an ankle injury, I missed our last two regular-season games and so lost the city rushing and scoring titles to Robert Miller of Yates.

Yates, which happens to be the high school that George Floyd attended, had close games with the two Beaumont schools as well as a tight 8–0 loss to Washington. Kashmere had not beaten Yates since 1966. Their quarterback, Jeffrey Allen, was the only Houston high school player then who wore white shoes. (Future Houston Oiler star Billy "White Shoes" Johnson was still playing high school ball in Pennsylvania, with shoes dyed white, but we didn't know that at the time.) Our defense was out to stop Allen.

The game was played in their backyard stadium in Third Ward, where our Coach Matthews also lived. The place was packed. Our starting halfback Willie Skillern, aka Shack, did not play, but Russell Charles, our two-way back, intercepted a pass and returned it to the Yates one-yard line, and the next play he scored a touchdown. They punted to us and the ball was on our fifteen-yard line. On the first play, Shelton fumbled, and Yates recovered it, and then we were tied at 6–6. However, by the end of the first quarter, we were leading 20–6. Russell proceeded to score again, once on an eighteen-yard run and once on a pass reception for three touchdowns in the first half.

At halftime, the score was 33–14. I started the game, and, as my ankle held up, I had two touchdowns on thirteen carries for ninety-one yards. The final score was 62–20. Russell, whom we called Moses, had the game of his life, playing all forty-eight minutes, which included special teams. He intercepted two passes and scored three touchdowns. He never came off the field.

Victory—Then Defeat

Our next opponent was Robert E. Lee High School. We had beaten them 26–7 in the fourth game of the season, but they had won another shot. This was going to be for the Houston city championship. The Yates game had been the best we had played. We were three games away from our goal of winning the state championship. Kashmere High was excited! KYOK, a Houston black radio station, broadcast a pep rally from the school courtyard. We went to the Brock Park hideout again to practice. and everything was going smoothly. We were psyched up. Fifteen-thousand-seat Jefferson Stadium was sold out and standing-room-only. People were crowded on the track around the field, black on one side and white on the other.

After taking the opening kickoff from the Lee Generals, we marched down the field and scored. Soon after that, we got the ball back after a Lee punt and scored a second touchdown. At halftime, it was 35–0. I came out early in the fourth quarter, with 253 yards on twenty-nine carries with scores of five and seventy-eight yards. We continued our dominance, beating them 41–15.

Chronicle sportswriter Bill McMurry called me Roadrunner. In an article, the Lee head coach was quoted as saying, "I've seen lots of good backs with speed and lots with power but none with both the speed and power of Williams." I had scored nineteen touchdowns for the year on a team that was averaging forty-two points a game. We were on a roll.

We had already beaten our next opponent, Hebert, 26–7 in the second game of the season. This Friday night game was at Marston Teach Stadium, and it was pouring. Seventy-eight hundred people sat with umbrellas in the wind and fifty-degree temperatures. Fumbling away the ball in the mud and throwing interceptions, we gave up three touchdowns in the first half.

Desperate, we played better in the second half but couldn't score until the fourth quarter, when I punched in from two yards out. I gained 162 yards rushing in the slop and returned a punt forty-seven yards, slipping and sliding, but it was too late. We beat them in every statistical category, but we lost 29–12.

I woke up the next morning as if out of a bad dream. I didn't want to believe it. I still don't. When you know you were better and you let it get away, it's painful.

Everyone felt sick about losing. It had rained all week long and we thought we might play at the Astrodome. How different that would have been. With our records, we thought that all of Houston would want to watch us. Thinking about the dome and fussing over the weather were distractions. Hebert was a good team. Our game early in the season with

---

When you know you were better and you let it get away, it's painful.

---

them had been our closest. Continuing in the postseason, Hebert then lost to undefeated Lee High of San Antonio 21–18 in the semifinals. San Antonio then lost to undefeated and once-tied Wichita Falls in the state championship. Who knows what we could have done? Though I obviously didn't know it at the time: it would be closest I would ever come to being on a championship team.

Instead, the football season was over. It was painful. I was back to being a high school student with class on Monday. I also was an unwed father with a newly born daughter and a need to find a university where I could play football and get my student draft deferment. I was sure a football scholarship awaited me, although I knew I wasn't ready for college academically.

I had a great senior year, rushed for eighteen hundred yards, and made high school All-American. During the recruiting season, I received hundreds of letters from colleges and universities offering me a scholarship. Because I was busy running track during the spring, I had time to visit about five schools. I was committed to running track but more importantly to Mr. Hendricks. Most of the guys on our team stopped running track when they became seniors. Players talk about the team and say that no player is better than the other, that we all should be treated the same, and that there shouldn't be any preference, but advantages are taken.

Although the season didn't end the way I would have liked, I had made a statement on the field. Recruiters from the top college football programs in the nation were lining up to try to convince a kid who had failed fourth grade to commit to their college. I was about to learn that my best interests as a person, student, and athlete were not always their top priority.

Although my high school football career was over, I was not yet done with sports. During football season, I had chipped a bone in my ankle. The injury caused me to miss two games, and I subsequently failed to win the city rushing title. I had then questioned whether I was going to run track in the spring, but the injury hadn't bothered me much over the winter, so I did go out for track. As in football, I was a three-year letterman, running the 100-yard and 220-yard dashes and the 440-yard and 880-yard relays.

We had our first meet in February, which I believe was the San Jacinto Relays. In the preliminaries, I ran a 9.5 in the 100-yard dash. I would have a track meet every weekend. The top sprinter in the city and probably the state was Kenneth Curl out of Houston's Worthing High School. He ran a consistent 9.3 in 100-yard dash but tore a hamstring and was out for the season my senior year. I had been looking forward to competing with him, but with him out I was the top sprinter in the city. Curl went on to Stanford University, became a dentist, and now practices in Houston. Another top sprinter also was out of Worthing, Cliff Branch, who would go on to play fourteen seasons in the NFL as a wide receiver for the Raiders. They were the best sprinters I've ever competed against. Cliff died in 2019, may he rest in peace.

I had a good track season, particularly in the 220, in which I competed at the state regionals. The top two finishers went to the state championship. The final was going to be a close race, because the best 220 sprinters in the area were in the field. I was confident but frustrated, because they stuck me in lane eight. But, as I stepped into the blocks, my confidence was high.

"Runners take your mark, get set. . . ." (and before the starter shot the gun, you could hear a rat walk on cotton). *Bang!* I was out of the blocks with a good start. I ran the curve well and knew that I would be strong down the stretch. As we came down the stretch, we were bunched up. I thought when we crossed the tape that I had won, and it was so close that a tenth of a second separated five of us. I finished third, and my track season was over. That season I had set school and track meet records. But I didn't like track—football was my love, and running track made me a better football player.

I wanted to go to the state meet more for Mr. Hendricks than anything. He worked hard to get me ready for the meet. This was important and would have been a big win for him as well. A coach from San Jacinto Junior College asked me if I wanted to go to his school. There were other things that we talked about, but the main topic was a scholarship.

I said, "Well, I don't know. I'll have to talk to my coach."

When I told Mr. Hendricks what the coach said, he was indignant. He said, "You want a scholarship? You're going to have more scholarship offers than you can imagine! You want to go to Oklahoma?" Sure enough, before the year was out, I got a letter from Oklahoma.

However, this was the beginning of something that would change my perspective about how coaches can be deceptive and sometimes lie to get you to do what they want you to. The University of Kansas had hired Coach Matthews to join Pepper Rodgers's coaching staff, in large part to help recruit me. I was Billie's ticket out of the high school ranks and into college.

I knew why they hired him at Kansas, but I wanted to believe it was on his own merit and not because of me. I got a hint of the reason for his being hired the day before the signing deadline for the national letter of intent when he took me golfing with him. I'd had surgery on my ankle and still had the cast on my leg, and I had never played golf in my life, but it was the best place to hide me from the other college recruiters.

I don't begrudge anyone for wanting to further themselves to have a better life. However, I felt this secrecy was at my expense because I trusted him. I didn't receive all the letters that colleges and universities sent to me. I was told by Coach Matthews that I had hundreds of scholarships offers, but I took only five trips: to North Texas State, UCLA, the

University of Oklahoma, the University of Houston and the University of Kansas (KU).

North to Kansas

The first recruiting trip I took was to KU, and it also was the first time I had flown. I had a first-class ticket. As we entered Kansas air space, the flight attendants stop serving alcoholic beverages, because that was the law. During the flight, occasionally I would look out of the window, and as far as I could see was flat land covered with snow.

Flying into the Kansas City airport, you had to fly over the Missouri River. As we started our descent, the plane started to shake. It hit several air pockets. I didn't have a clue about air pockets! I was not aware that things like that were ever an issue. You can imagine the thoughts that were going through my head. I was scared, and that's putting it mildly. I looked around me, and everybody in first class was acting as though nothing was wrong. I tried to do the same, but I had a firm grip on my seat's armrest. They were reading newspapers and finishing their drinks. I was trying to be cool and sit there, all the while thinking to myself, "We're going down."

I hadn't been in snow for a while. The last time it had snowed, Wayne and I were walking down Kirk Street coming home from school. I think it had snowed twice in my lifetime, but now was snow was everywhere, and it was cold.

Coach Don Fambrough and John Novotny from the athletic department were waiting for me at the gate. Coach Fam was a Texas native and had been the defensive line coach at KU for quite a while. At the time, John was the assistant athletic director. They recruited me, and both were good men. The ride from the airport seemed long because they were selling me on the university the whole way.

Lawrence is a college town, which means the university is the city's anchor tenant. John took me up to the highest part of the campus, up by Snow Hall. He handed me a lunch tray, told me sit on it, and then I was sliding down a hill in the snow. I said, "This is great!" They let me know that as fun as it was, sledding would be off limits to football players because of the injury risk.

As we were pulling into the hotel parking lot, John pointed to its marquee. Under the name Virginia Inn it said, "Welcome, Delvin Williams." I couldn't believe it, and all I could say was "Wow!" after flying first class and leaving Texas for the first time, which was heady stuff for an eighteen-year-old from the Kelly Courts housing projects. Here is how John remembers it:

"We wanted him really badly. We put his name on every marquee. He got the biggest bang when he went up where he was going to stay at the motel, and there was his name up on the marquee."

When I got home from my trip to KU, I was getting the full-court press from every corner: coaches, parents, friends, you name it. The calls and letters continue to flow in from colleges and universities around the country.

Making a Decision

My decision would come down to the University of Houston and KU, although I only told one person how I was leaning, my mother. No one in my family had ever gone to college, and I felt the weight of the choice I had to make. Although the recruiters, coaches, teachers, and any responsible person I talked to each had an opinion, they all said the same thing: it was my decision. It would be a tough decision! They all had their idea of where I should go.

I had felt the sting of irresponsibility when Kathy got pregnant. However, this would be the start of making personal decisions responsibly, and there would be more to come. My mother was lobbying hard for me to go to the University of Houston, as were several friends. There was immense pressure for an eighteen-year-old in that situation. Donald Charles reminded me of something I had forgotten: the head coach at the University of Houston was Bill Yeoman, who was the father of the Veer T offense that we ran at Kashmere. I had visited the campus before, and my hosts were Robert Newhouse and Elmo Wright.

This time, however, D. C., Leon Strauss, Chucksey, Samuel "Teddy Bear" Rutherford, and I all visited together. We were meeting with Coach Yeoman, and he said that if I signed, he would take all of us, but the condition was that I had to sign along with them. I liked Coach Yeoman, but that didn't go over too well with the rest of the guys. It was designed to pressure me into signing with Houston but an insult to the rest of the guys.

While going through the intense recruiting process, I realized that the University of Houston was not an option. I so badly wanted to leave home, and going there would feel as though I had not left town. I could just see what the pressure for tickets and social requests would be like. KU had done a great job in recruiting me, particularly on my visit (not to mention hiring my high school head football coach). I was getting tired of the intense pressure to decide what school I was going to attend.

It was my decision, but why did I feel like I was letting a lot of people down? Billie Matthews was the difference maker. Going away from home not knowing anyone and to the predominantly white environment was going to be different. At Kansas, there would be at least one person there that I knew.

The one thing that was always in the back of my mind was whether I do it academically. What I heard about college didn't answer the question. If high school was hard, well—college would be harder. Could I do it? Mr. Hendricks was always there for me, but he would only say so much, because he knew it was my decision. My mother wanted one thing, and teammates, family, friends and the hustlers all weighed in with their thoughts. I knew the decision was mine and mine alone to make. When there is no guidance or someone that you can trust to give you the accurate information, it's a tough situation. But it also was a good situation to be in.

The recruiting process gave me an opportunity to tie up a loose end that had long bothered me. I had always been interested in knowing what my father was like. I wondered whether I took after him in reacting to some things emotionally and rationally to others. Though I'd made up my mind to go to Kansas, UCLA had invited me on a recruiting visit, and I knew my father was living in Los Angeles. I told my mother about the visit to UCLA and said that I would like to see my father. She got upset and said, "I don't know why you want to see him. He's never done a damned thing for you." I could understand why she felt that way, but I didn't care what he may or may not have done. He still was my father, regardless of what was between them.

Until I heard his side of things, I would have the same feelings. I don't think some parents understand that. Several times, I wanted to say to my mother, "Maybe you're the reason he's not here." She would've thrown that same iron skillet at me with which she had hit Wayne in the head.

Delvin and Delvin

Through Aunt Mattie, his sister, I was able to contact my father. When I arrived, it was raining, and it rained for the entire trip. I vividly remember hearing Brook Benton's "A Rainy Night in Georgia." It seemed appropriate that it was playing, not just because it was raining but also because of the emotions I was feeling. It had been a long time, and I wondered if we would recognize one another. I knew he was shorter than me. However, the Williams genes are strong and we probably wouldn't differ that much. I was excited about seeing him, but you could say I had some anxiety. I knew he would be proud of me or at least happy for me.

When I arrived, he greeted me at the door. We shook hands, and he put his arms around my shoulder. He smiled, looked at me and commented on how big I had gotten. It was somewhat awkward in that we had not seen one another in years. He asked me how my grandmother was doing, and I said she was fine. They had always been close. We spent an hour talking about things. I knew one of his brothers, Uncle Sonny, although I had not seen him in a while. His oldest brother, Uncle Horace, was there.

My grandmother used to say to young women who were pregnant and misbehaving, "If you keep doing that, you're going to mark that baby," and we used to laugh. However, what she was referring to was genetics, innate factors and cultural makeup. When my mother would say, "You look just like your daddy," she was not lying, because our features did not differ that much. My physical features were on point not only with my father's but with my uncle's as well.

We talked about basic things, and he asked about Wayne and how he was doing. He asked, "What do you plan to do?" He said that with a smile, and in his way he was pushing for me to attend UCLA. One thing was for sure, he would not have been able to tell me what to do. I think he knew that.

The whole visit to UCLA was a wash, because my emotions were focused on my father rather than the school's football program and what it had to offer me. It was an important trip, and it was good to see him.

> *Some of the things I wrestle with in my life were because my father wasn't there. Now I was abandoning my own daughter in the most critical time of her life.*

However, it wasn't long enough and did not satisfy me. To some extent, I don't know exactly what I was seeking or what I had hoped to accomplish. Rather than close the door and move on, it seemed to open a door for more questions. It satisfied some curiosities, but it wasn't enough.

One thing I hadn't planned on at this point in my life was being a father. I had stopped speaking to Kathy, but the one who would suffer the most would be my daughter, Dositheia. She was an innocent eight-month-old child caught in the middle of something she had nothing to do with and didn't ask for it. She did not have a say in the matter, but she would have the most difficult time.

Everybody dreams of becoming a parent and raising their kids without any problems. That was something I had hoped for, but that was not to be.

I was going back and forth with Kathy. She thought I should not go to college but should stay home and take care of my child. It was a hard decision but one I had to make. I asked my mother for her help through this phase of my life, and I knew she would help. This was an opportunity of a lifetime, and my intent was not to let it pass. My mother said she would be there for my daughter in my absence, and that helped ease my conscience some. I have had heated conversations about Kathy's pregnancy, and she knows what happened, but it doesn't make it any better.

After weighing the pros and cons, I made my decision public: I would become a Kansas Jayhawk. As their school chant goes, "Rock chalk, Jayhawk."

The distance from Houston to Lawrence, home of the University of Kansas, is 750 miles up Interstate 35. But for a kid who had failed fourth grade, battled learning disabilities, and came from a family in which no one had attended college, the distance may as well have been infinity.

Kansas, then and now, has always been a basketball school. However, it also has a proud tradition in football, dating all the way back to 1890. It competed in the Big Eight Conference (now the Big 12), which was the best in the nation, with such powerhouses as the Nebraska Cornhuskers and Oklahoma Sooners. Perhaps the all-time greatest KU player was my childhood hero, Gale Sayers.

I arrived on campus in the fall of 1970 as one of the most sought-after high school football players in the country, with accolades beyond my expectations. Being named to All-District, All-City, and All-Regional first teams was recognition for what I had achieved. In eleven games (I missed two because of an injury), I had rushed for 1,806 yards with twenty touchdowns, which at the time were school and city records. When the All-State, All-Southern, and All-American recognition followed, I realized I was one of the best high school running backs in the nation. I was at the top of my position, and it gave me, my family, the school and the neighborhood a sense of pride in the accomplishment.

More importantly I was going to be the first in my family to go to college. I was a step closer to what I wanted, and that was to play in the NFL. However, in the back of my mind the question loomed: could I do the work academically?

I had given my best shot on the tests, but in my heart, as always, I didn't feel it was good enough. Billie Matthews said—as all recruiters do—not to worry, and so I didn't. I carried with me the pride that my family and the community felt about my success. However, what I did at Kashmere was in the past. The hard work both on and off the field was yet to come.

There is an old saying that there are only two sports seasons in Texas: football and spring football. I might as well state my bias and get that out right now: Texas high school football is the best in the nation. There was no better place to be than under the Friday night lights at a Texas high school stadium.

I was part of a Houston exodus to out-of-state schools. The list included Cliff Branch, J. V. Cain, and Charlie Davis, who left for Colorado. Greg Pruitt, Joe Washington, and Billy Brooks went to Oklahoma, and Don Goode, Robert Miller, and I went to Kansas. All went on to play in the NFL. However, we considered the Big Eight to be the best conference around, and I was looking forward to playing against the best teams.

About sixteen thousand students attended KU at that time. The mental load was two or three times more intense than high school, where we had a homeroom teacher and knew what classes we were going to take. In high school, my biggest concern was trying to avoid the difficult instructors. Enrollment at KU was held in Allen Fieldhouse (the school's indoor arena) or one of the auditoriums or both. It felt like all the students were trying to get their classes at the same time. Weren't some of the schedules already set? No! It was mass confusion and chaotic to me. Enrollment alone was enough to make me have second thoughts.

I didn't know what I was going to declare as my major, so I settled on something I thought I knew: physical education. I never thought I would go to college, but there I was and not prepared. The truth of the matter was that physical education was not going to be a walk in the park. To attain a Bachelor of Science degree with a biological science minor, I would have to take several science courses. Prerequisite courses such as human anatomy, physiology, physiology of exercise, and kinesiology were foreign to me. My reason for choosing physical education didn't come after a long deliberation. It was the only thing I knew. I thought, at least I can be a physical education teacher and coach football.

Academic Ineligibility

I knew there were questions about my low grades, but I didn't think I would immediately be academically ineligible. I thought Coach Matthews would tell me if there was a problem—after all, we were a package deal. But in the end, he was just another recruiter getting for himself. The veteran KU football coaches must have known I would not be accepted academically, but they waited until I got there to inform me.

Within twenty-four hours after I arrived, I met with Coach Fambrough, John Novotny, and Billie and was given three choices:

- go to a junior college to get my grades up while playing football;
- work and pay my way through school the first year without football; or
- go home.

This was not the kind of triple option that I had expected. I was a highly recruited high school All-American with scholarship offers to just about every major university in the country, and now I was not going to be able to play major college football. The euphoria of being at KU instantly wore off. After receiving the information, I was consumed by a feeling I was familiar with but couldn't identify. My thoughts slowed down to process what I had been told. What had happened?

The feeling was heavy, and, as I walked from the fieldhouse to the towers, it hit me—I was depressed again. I was becoming familiar with that emotion more than I desired to be. I had just left a ten-month-old baby daughter and had deep resentment toward her mother, but at the time there was nothing I could do about either.

I was hundreds of miles away from home, and the choice I had to make would be the most important decision of my life. I didn't want my mother to say "I told you so," nor did I want to be in the category of "he could have made it, but." I had heard many of those stories before,

My life seemed to be running a familiar pattern with an obstacle course, tests, and hurdles.

and I did not want to be in that category. The rise from the obscurity of having never played organized football to national recognition as a high school All-American faded in an instant. My academic impediments had caught up with me again. If I wanted my dreams to come true—playing professional football and moving my mother out of the projects into a new home, this choice would have to be my line in the sand.

Coach Hendricks used to tell us, "You've gotta believe." Martin Luther King Jr. wrote, "You ought to believe something in life, believe that thing so fervently that you will stand up with it till the end of your days." I accepted that. However, with each obstacle, I was reminded of what it would take.

When I was a kid, living with my grandmother, we said our prayers together every night. She had a family edition of the King James Bible on the coffee table. I asked her one day why some of the writing was in red and the other in black. She said, "The red is Jesus preaching." I wanted to know what Jesus was saying about some things I heard and what he thought about it. Occasionally, I would open the Bible and randomly pick something Jesus was saying. I didn't want to read anything else. One day I opened it up to Mark 11:23–24: "For verily I say unto you, that whosoever shall say unto this mountain, be thou removed, and be thou cast into the sea; and shall not doubt in his heart, but shall believe that those things which he saith shall come to pass; he shall have whatsoever he saith. Therefore, I say unto you, what things soever ye desire, when ye pray, believe that ye receive them, and ye shall have them."

I read that passage so often that I had it memorized, and it became my mantra. However, I had my work cut out for me and had to do what I needed to do. Something else inside of me also was driving this. It was vague, but I could see the end, and it was good.

I played the hand that was dealt to me. I decided to stay at KU and pay my way at least through the first year. I got a student loan and a job at All Star Dairy and began my freshman year of college.

Campus Life

The athletes had good housing at KU, built specifically with athletes in mind. We lived in the Jayhawk Towers apartment complex. The family of Gary Adams, who had been a free safety on the varsity football team, had donated to help build the complex. Bud Adams, owner of the Houston Oilers, was his brother, and Gary had a suite on the sixth floor. Their money came from the oil business. Gary was cool about it and invited us to come up and look at his apartment.

The Towers officially opened for athletes my freshman year, but some of the guys had lived there since the previous January. I liked the living arrangements. The study hall and training table where the scholarship athletes' meals were provided were in the basement of Tower B, the building in which I lived. The first apartment we lived in was 210-B. All the apartments were two bedrooms, with twin beds in each, with KU blue shag carpets. They each had a kitchenette, with one bathroom and a double sink.

I had grown up in an all-black, low-income community in the South. Now I would be in a predominantly white, middle- to upper-class college campus in the Midwest. I was in a different environment, and being around whites daily was a new experience. I had no social reference point to guide me as to what I should expect from people. Both sides had their views and were biased at best. We're creatures of habit and tend to be slow to change. The spring semester of 1970 before I arrived, a Lawrence policeman had shot and killed a young African American kid. It touched off a riot and the burning of the student union. I thought, "What are you getting into?"

The Vietnam War was escalating, and students on college campuses were protesting the war. It was a time of change, rioting, drug use, anti-government sit-ins, and social unrest on a grand scale. Two years earlier, in 1968, Dr. King and Bobby Kennedy had been assassinated. I loved to listen to Dr. King's speeches, and they were an inspiration to me. He had spoken out against the war in Vietnam, and I had been moved emotionally by his death. Bobby Kennedy's assassination washed away the hope that he would continue the work of his brother, President John F. Kennedy. Coincidentally, all of them supported the causes of African Americans. King was nonviolent, and the war was counter to everything he stood for, nonviolence and racial equality. The war was killing Americans, particularly African Americans, while big business profited. Many people thought that was why they were killed.

My first year in Lawrence would be the most agonizing one I would face. All things were new. There were guys from large cities such as

Detroit, Atlanta, Washington, New York, and Chicago. We would talk about what it was like living in the cities where we were from. One day we were playing dominoes, and Lee Hawkins, who was from Detroit, looked at me and asked, "Delvin, do you guys ride horses to school?" We all laughed. Although we never talked about it, I thought everybody in Detroit could afford a car; after all, that's where cars are made. Motown and the automotive industry were all I knew about Detroit.

In the Midwest and particularly in Lawrence, there seemed to be respect for co-existence. Maybe my observations were skewed because it was on a college campus. Students and professors tended to be open to new learning more than locals, but it was different. Although there were more African Americans in the South than in the Midwest, I don't remember seeing cross-cultural relationships of any kind growing up. Consequently, it made our experiences in dating, the classroom, and athletic competition different, whether we were black or white.

I had become an avid fan of Dick Gregory. He was like a mentor. I bought all his albums. My favorite was *The Light Side: The Dark Side*. He talked about the SAT test and how it was unfair. I was on board. It was as though he was speaking directly to me. It reminded me where I had come from and the opportunities that were before me. Listening to him was enlightening, and it raised my cultural awareness. His work became an instrument by which I gauged my sensitivity to social and political awareness. On the album he said, "I'm not here to impress you, only to inform you. No matter when you wake up, this year, next year, you'll always have the one consolation of knowing that at least Brother Greg didn't lie to me." He was right.

Watching and Waiting

I liked Pepper Rodgers, the KU head football coach. He was funny, flamboyant, outspoken, and for the most part a good guy. He had led KU to the Orange Bowl in 1968, which was their first nine-victory season in sixty years. They had struggled the year before I got there, but the future looked bright. Coach Don Fambrough was a mentor. He was a guy I could trust. He believed in me when I was a freshman and hadn't played a down yet.

Watching the team from the sidelines was tough. The varsity had gotten off to a good start and was 5–2 after seven games. I was on the sideline for most of the varsity home games. I didn't see all the freshman games because I had to work.

In high school, we played in city stadiums. Like most colleges, KU had its own fifty-thousand-seat stadium. The stadium was on the street level and the school sat on a hill, which gave the impression that it was in a valley. I had seen the stadium when I was being recruited, but it was covered with snow. To be on the sidelines during the game and look up in the stands and see all the people, you got a different perspective. In Texas, we got good crowds for our high school games, but forty to fifty thousand people was different. The atmosphere fueled my desire to play even more.

There were rumors that a coaching change at the top was imminent. If so, Coach Fambrough was on the short list to become head coach, so there was a good possibility that the coaching staff would remain intact. Charlie McCullers was the offensive coordinator, and I thought he was a player's coach. Future Pro Football Hall of Fame member and native Kansan John Riggins was a senior running back for KU, and McCullers and Riggins got along well, at least from my limited perspective. I liked Charlie. Terry Donahue coached the defensive line, John Cooper was the defensive backs coach, and Dick Tomey was an assistant, and all three eventually became college head coaches.

Despite dropping the last four games, KU still was hosting pro scouts. They were there checking out the seniors and were testing them before the NFL player draft in February, running them through drills and timing the guys in the forty-yard dash.

In the meantime, I had to focus on making passing grades so I would be eligible to play in my sophomore season. John Novotny gave me some excellent advice. "In the beginning, Delvin, I'm going to give you two pieces of information," he said. "If you do these, you will be fine. First, no matter what you do, go to class. Second, if you don't understand something, ask the instructor if you can meet with them and they can show you what to do."

John, to his credit, saw far more academic potential in me than I did:

We were worried about him academically, because a with lot of those kids in the inner-city schools, they just gave them grades and didn't work at improving any of their skills. My job was to go to the high schools to visit with some of the teachers, coaches, and principals and say, 'if we bring this youngster in, we want to be sure we can build a foundation under him academically.' Delvin was the best one to work with. If those teachers at Kashmere High School would have taken time out to understand his situation and work with him, I guarantee he would [have] come in after practice just to learn anything that he needed as a building block for learning. It was an amazing story. If someone would just teach him the right things to work with, he did it. Plus, he had a personality that is out of this world.

I followed John's formula. I went to every class. My English class was an awakening, I was the only person of African descent in a class, a first for me. The instructor said that by the next class we had to read three or four chapters. I had never finished a book in my life, and it was a struggle to read. I also had sleep apnea and would fall asleep in class. In hindsight, I have a better understanding of what helped me in making the transition to college. I was too afraid of failing to be scared of the path I was on.

As Thanksgiving came and went, it was getting close to the end of the semester. I could tell the instructors were pleasantly surprised when I asked for their help. The midterm reports were good, and I was surprised. I wanted to get a sense of where I stood in my classes. The finals were coming around, and I wasn't doing so well in health, of all things. When it was time for my finals, I was nervous. I got reports on some of my finals, and it was looking good. My final in health was multiple choice, and each question had five answers to choose from. You had to know the correct answer, and guessing wasn't going to work. I left the test bewildered and pissed at the professor because of the way he set up the test, although it wasn't his fault how I did.

When I went home for Christmas break, I was depressed. It was a strange feeling. What I mean is that I was anxious to go home like most students, but I was uncomfortable at the thought of it. John Novotny called me over Christmas vacation. He knew I had flunked my health class and what that meant academically. He heard the dejection and questioning in my voice.

Before I could get it out, he said to me, "Delvin, come back for the second semester and see if you can get your grades up to the 2.0 level. If you don't get it done and you want to leave, then I'll understand."

I could have left if I wanted to, but what good would it have done? I wouldn't have been able to play any sport until my grade point-average was 2.0. What else could I do? However, I heard a supportive challenge in his voice. John had earned the right to challenge me, because all he had ever done was support me. How could I explain to family and friends about that first semester and what I had gone through? I was back in the cement jungle, and I seriously thought about not returning to school. I was trying to survive the first semester, and failing health didn't help. There were no adequate reference points that I could call on for the situation I was in. It was quintessential culture shock.

Changing of the Guard

Just before I returned to school after Christmas break, it was announced that Pepper Rodgers and his coaching staff would be leaving for UCLA. Later that day, I heard from Billie. He reiterated the obvious and wished me luck. I thought I would have a support system with Billie and his family, but he was leaving me to fend for myself. Under the hardened exterior, the vulnerability of being human revealed itself. I felt a crack in the armor. I had been betrayed.

When my father left, I was too young to understand the significance. I had more feelings of abandonment when Billie left than when my father left. After my conversations with Coach Hendricks my first semester at KU, and most of all, coming home and seeing what was there for me—nothing—now Billie was leaving. It confirmed for me that I was his ticket out of the high school ranks. He had paid his dues and probably deserved the opportunity, but I thought it was at my expense. It all was starting to make sense.

That trip home was the beginning of a special journey. I started transforming my life by becoming focused on the task at hand. My evolution had started six months earlier, and I was catching up. I went from holding a narrow view about life to mind-expanding awareness about my reality and future possibilities. I had now developed a reference point, and it was there all the time. It was KU.

That's where I would find the answers to the questions that were coming up. I had to face not only the challenges of college and my future but also the issues of the times—race, drugs, the Vietnam War, morality, and more. It was a tall order, because much of this was new to me and gave me a lot to learn.

I had come to Kansas expecting Billie Matthews and Pepper Rodgers to look after me and guide me through the tough adjustment of becoming a student-athlete. Fortunately, another man stepped up to fill the void.

7

Sometimes it's the smallest gestures that have a lifelong impact.

John Novotny, the assistant athletic director who had helped recruit me, was always there when I needed him. On my birthday, he picked me up, and we went to his house. When we got there, my roommates, Don Goode ("Bear") and Emmett Edwards, and John's wife and their two kids surprised me with a party. That was special, and I was touched by his thoughtfulness. It was the first birthday party I'd ever had. I still don't know how he found out that it was my birthday. As John remembers it: "These youngsters are very quiet about things in their private lives, such as their birthday. We accidentally found out it was his birthday, so we planned a little party. But what we didn't realize is that he had never had one before."

I continued to think about it and its significance to me. I had grown up in an environment where the expression of love was subliminal and attached to deeds. Verbal expression was rare. I hadn't done anything to warrant an act of kindness, and there had to be something else, I thought. It was an instinctive response I attached to a gift received. It was a personal experience that was real, a random act of kindness. I was touched, and the emotional impact of my first birthday party was powerful. My response to it was as it should have been. I'll never forget it! Thank you, John.

I finished that semester with a 2.4 GPA, so I would be eligible to play football my sophomore year. It was the first time I'd really had to knuckle down. After doing so, I knew I could do this. Besides doing all the things that John had suggested, I bought highlighted books when

I could, because I was always tired, and it took me longer to read than most students. I always tried to stay ahead. When I looked at what I had done without any direct tutoring, I told myself that I could graduate from college.

I mapped out the next three years of my courses by semester and wrote them in the back of my notebook. I knew that if I passed these each semester, I would graduate on time. It felt like I was seizing the opportunity I had asked for long ago. I knew in the sixth grade I wanted something different from my Houston peers.

Truth is, nobody back home missed following me as a football player because freshmen weren't on the varsity anyway. If I had been on the squad practicing long hours from late August through November, I don't know how I would have survived academically. As it was, I was given a reprieve—one blessed year of school in which I was all student, having lost a season of football but with the possibility of three ahead.

I spent the whole summer working out to make sure I would be in shape. Jerome Nelloms, at five foot ten and 180 pounds, was on the depth chart as the first starting running back for the fall of 1971. I felt that I was a better running back than Jerome, and I think he knew it as well. Steve Conley was the other running back. He would try to sabotage me with teammates by making negative comments about my ability. My athletic ability to run the football was never a question in my mind, and I don't think in anyone else's. He did more to hurt himself than anyone else could have done. I had gone through a lot and waited a long time for this opportunity. In that process, my feelings about school had changed.

This was the first time in my life I felt confident about my academic ability. Getting through that freshman year of ineligibility did a lot for my self-esteem, particularly the confidence I developed about academics. I could also see what was in it for me. I had known that high school academics were important, but then I couldn't see the long-term value to me. Or I could see it, but it wasn't within reach. When I got to KU, what

I already had the potential. It was left up to me to develop it and get somewhere with it.

I wanted was further than I had reached for before. Now the path was clear. There would be no one to blame, and for the first time in my life I felt the future was in my hands.

This probably was the only time in my life that the stakes were so high, with maybe an 50–50 chance of success.

Back on the Field

KU opened the season in 1971 against Washington State University in Lawrence. I was kind of jittery, but being in a real game all started to come back once I put the uniform on. It took a little bit to get used to the contact and pace of the game. We beat them 34–0, and I played sparingly but rushed for fifty-eight yards. It felt good to be out on the field and contributing again. It seemed that spending the whole year away from football made me a little rusty, but there was no question about my ability to contribute.

The next game was against Baylor at home. My contribution was fifty-nine yards on thirteen carries and a touchdown. It felt like I had this pent-up energy that was raging to come out and contribute. I have always wanted to carry my own weight. Local sportswriter Chuck Woodling of the *Journal-World* wrote an article in which he stated that everybody was surprised how fast I was able to pick up the system and contribute. I told Chuck in his interview that I felt the only thing I had lost from sitting out a year was my instinct, and that would come.

Coach Fambrough told Chuck that "the kids" were coming along: "Delvin Williams, a sophomore, is close to winning a starting job in the backfield. We really didn't expect much of Williams until the middle of the season." I thought I had been making progress, and that was encouraging.

The third game was against Florida State in Tallahassee. The good thing was that it was a night game, because at that time of season it would be hot. I was starting to feel comfortable with the system and understanding what we were trying to accomplish offensively. In the middle of the game, I was gang-tackled and lay there on my back underneath the pile. I looked up as one of their players spat in my face. It caught me off guard. He ran back to the other side of the line of scrimmage and into their huddle. That was one of those things where you couldn't do anything about it. Even I knew that if I tried to get even, it would come back to bite me.

Other than the obvious reason, I wondered why he would do something like that. It didn't require any deep thinking—he was a jerk or a racist or both. We ended up losing, but I had my best game to date: fourteen carries for 101 yards. I expected more of myself, and I thought that was just the beginning. After three games, I was leading the team in rushing with 218 yards on thirty-seven carries for an average of 6.2 yards a carry, and it created a buzz around the offense.

Charlie McCullers, the offensive coordinator, said in the newspaper, "Twice he was just an inch away from going all the way. If we had held a couple of blocks just a half second longer, he might have gone."

I was starting to get in a groove and feel good about my position. I seemed to get more confident with each game and practice. There was no doubt in my mind that I could play and be a big contributor to the team. The next day, Coach Fambrough announced four lineup changes, and I was one of them. He was quoted in the newspaper, "You might say with Delvin it is a reward for a job well done." That felt good to hear, because I hadn't contributed much to that point, but things were looking up.

I would suffer some injuries during my sophomore and junior years, a sprained ankle and a torn hamstring, and they hampered my production but were nothing that could end my dream of becoming a professional. I was doing well in school, and I felt good about that. I was beginning to see the opportunity to do something with my life. I always knew I wanted something different, but I didn't know what it was or how it would show up. Most young boys involved with football have dreamed of playing professionally. That was the ultimate, and what it might be was unfolding. How badly did I want it?

Midseason in my junior year, 1972, my grandmother died. Although it was sudden, she had been sick for a while. I flew home for her funeral. The atmosphere was staid, and I remember crying, not only because of her death but because that is when it hit me just how much she had meant to me. The irony is that in death the first flower was blooming from the seeds she had planted years ago. When I think of being loved as a child, I will always think of her.

I remember when I was a little boy and living with her, I got into some trouble. I don't remember what it was, but I do know my mother was coming over to whip me, and I was scared. My grandmother told me to get in the bed. "But mama said—"

She interrupted me and said, "Just get in the bed."

I was lying there scared and waiting for my spanking. When my mother got there, she was coming into the bedroom when my grandmother stopped her and said, "Let him sleep."

My mother said, "But I am going to—"

My grandmother said, "No, just let him sleep."

I started smiling and fell asleep. She protected me. Subconsciously, I had hoped Grandma would be around if all went well for me. I wanted to do something for Grandma to show her that putting up with me was worth it. I knew she loved me, and I will always love her.

Also, during my junior year, I took eighteen units and had a GPA in the high 2s. But after two seasons with injuries, I was worried that my dream of playing professional football might not come true.

My all-time favorite player in high school was Gale Sayers. I wore 40, his jersey number, and I would get to see him quite often. He had come back to KU as assistant athletic director, because he wanted to be a general manager. It was great to meet him and chat from time to time. When I saw him I was stuck for words. I would look at him and smile, and just say to myself, "Gale Sayers!"

Promise of Fall

The arrival of fall term was always special. As the campus filled up with eager young freshmen and we went through the ritual of transitioning out of summer practices, everything seemed new and full of possibilities. But with the coming of classes also came a doubling of our workload. We had to get to practice and classes on time, not to mention preparing for and playing games on Saturdays. Most people have no clue of the commitment and energy it takes to navigate the intensity of a college football season. Just on practices and film sessions, we spent twenty hours per week. If you include the night before the game, game day and day after the game, we spent forty hours a week with football.

Coming into my senior year, in 1973, I got to know Tom Williams, who was a scout for the Oilers. He gave me a workout program to follow. I stayed at KU for the summer and did summer school, worked out, and stretched. He said to do a lot of walking, and I followed him to a T and never had another problem with my hamstring. We were 3–0 going to play at Tennessee, and they beat us 28–27. Losing so closely to a nationally ranked team, we knew we were a good team.

We got off to a strong start, winning four of our first five. We lost a heartbreaking 10–9 game at Nebraska, and the following week we traveled to Ames to play Iowa State University. Ames is like Lawrence, a college town. On Saturdays, outside the stadium, Ames must have looked like a ghost town. On this day, the crowd was rocking, and both sides played a great game of football. The game was coming down to the cliché: "whoever has the ball last will win."

It was late in the fourth quarter, and Iowa State was leading. We had the ball on their forty-yard line, and with a minute left we faced a third and four. We needed a touchdown to win the game, and in this era, unlike today, just about every winning team got a bowl invitation. If we lost, we likely would be staying home in the postseason.

Quarterback David Jaynes called the play. It was a pass, and the moment I heard it I went through my assignment and picked out the man I was supposed to block. Linebacker Matt Blair, who would eventually be a second-round draft choice for the Minnesota Vikings, would be my responsibility.

As David stepped under the center, he started his cadence, which I could faintly hear. "Red 13, red . . ." Suddenly he stood up, and I could see him back away from the center. He was changing the play. He cupped his hands to his mouth and yelled, "Blue 17! Blue 17!"

Instantly, my ears perked up. He was audibling into a draw play designed to spring me open. Instantly, I had to adjust not only my thinking but also my attitude and focus. I wasn't just a blocker anymore— I would have the ball, and I needed to make something happen.

When the ball was snapped, I took the handoff and saw a giant hole open. Without hesitation, I had the first down. I made a step to go upfield and cut left to get away from one player, outran another defender, and then broke into the open field. I knew that I was in a race to the endzone, and there was no way I could be caught.

For a moment, it felt just like it did when I was a kid pretending to score the winning touchdown in the big game. It was joyful and exhilarating, and for an instant I forgot all the difficulties associated with college football. We won the game, were guaranteed a winning season, and earned a bowl game. Kansas had won just a single game the year before I arrived, so the entire senior class justifiably derived a real sense of pride at what we had accomplished together.

We had beaten Kansas State (our intrastate rival), Missouri by a point, Colorado by two points, tied Oklahoma State, and ended the season with a 7–3–1 record, good for third in the Big Eight and ranking in the top twenty in the nation.

We went to the Liberty Bowl on December 17 and played North Carolina State with Lou Holtz as coach. I got speared in the back and couldn't play anymore. That night I got out of bed and took a step and fell to the floor. Our team doctor said it was a cracked transverse process bone. It was just what I needed: another injury!

I rushed for 788 yards that year and finished second in the conference in receiving. We had four guys in the top ten in receiving because of our quarterback, David Jaynes. It was a good year. Out of the eight teams in our conference, three went to a bowl. I was supposed to play in the East-West all-star game on December 29. Coach Fambrough was on the staff, but they sent me back because I was injured. I had been looking forward to the Senior Bowl on January 6, because they paid you to play, but I was still injured. I went back to Texas for Christmas vacation just like always after our season ended.

Soaring Confidence

This time, at the conclusion of the vacation, the drive back to Kansas seemed entirely different. I hadn't graduated yet, but my mind was on the future. The NFL draft was in February. I didn't know how it was going to go for me, but I was excited.

My confidence was high, and for good reasons. I needed to do my student teaching and finish a couple of educational psych courses, and I would graduate. I had never dreamed of going to college, much less graduating in four years. Like most sports-minded kids, I had athletic dreams of scoring the winning touchdown, hitting the game-winning home run, or scoring the winning basket with no time left on the clock. But the thought of being a college graduate was once beyond my wildest imagination, the same as becoming a doctor, a lawyer, or an educator.

The NFL draft was the first step in the league's football factory, although it was not then nearly as sophisticated as it is today. Instead of being a prime-time event broadcast on ESPN (which was still five years from even existing), it was a more informal affair held in an undecorated and modest building, with NFL commissioner Pete Rozelle presiding over events. Most of us were still in school so we didn't show up to hear our names called. There was no strut across the stage to don a team cap and hold up a jersey with your name on it. We just waited to get the telephone call that told us where we were going. What I didn't know swirled about in my head along with what would it mean to be a college graduate. Nobody in my family had ever been one, nor had hardly anyone in the neighborhood where I grew up.

I was twenty-three years old, and now the NFL was moments away. The intense preparation and long hours of conditioning over the summer to carry me into my senior college season was about to bear fruit. I felt excited about the future. As a kid, I had played pickup football games in the sandlots and rocky streets of my neighborhood, imagining that I was Jim Brown or Gale Sayers. The thought that I would have my own name on the back of a professional team's jersey felt overwhelming.

Four guys on our team would be drafted: David Jaynes, defensive tackle Mitch Sutton, Don Goode, and me. We all were projected to be high draft choices. The process we went through to earn that pick, though, was not nearly as exhaustive as what kids today face. Instead of heading off to Indianapolis for a weeklong battery of tests, drills, medical examinations, and interviews, I just fielded a few calls from scouts who wanted to arrange a meeting so they could chat with me a bit and, more importantly, time me in the forty-yard dash.

I'd had conversations with several scouts over the years leading up to this point, but Vic Lindskog had scouted me more intensely and repeatedly than most others had. In fact, I first met Vic during my freshman year when he had timed me in the forty-yard dash. Four years later, he knew a great deal about me and my Kansas teammates. He contacted Don and me to tell us he was coming to town in the next few days and would like to meet with us. The excitement and suspense were building.

When we met, Vic said one of the teams he scouted for was going to draft us. He explained that he scouted for and was paid by a combine that included the Dallas Cowboys, Los Angeles Rams, San Diego Chargers, and San Francisco 49ers. One of them was going to draft us in the first or second round, and he wanted us to sit through the draft with him. The reason Vic wanted us to be with him for the draft was that a fledgling league, the World Football League (WFL), had begun attracting some of the best talent. In fact, the NFL already had lost some of its biggest names to the upstart league. Larry Csonka, Jim Kiick, Mercury Morris, and Paul Warfield had all left the Miami Dolphins for bigger contracts.

Vic would get us a hotel room and pay for our meals, and in return he could keep us hidden from the WFL's scouts and general managers who might dangle contracts in front of us and deprive the NFL of fresh meat. For our part, we thought Vic's plan sounded fantastic. We were still broke college kids, and the idea of eating on someone else's dime was appealing. Although Vic's handling of us reminded me a bit of when Coach Matthews hid me on the golf course to keep other recruiters from getting at me, this at least seemed more up-front. After all, this was the NFL, professional football.

Despite Vic's pronouncement that I would be drafted, I was a bit uncertain because of the back injury I had suffered in the Liberty Bowl. I'd had to withdraw from the East-West Shrine Game and the Senior Bowl, two top showcases for college football talent. On the eve of the draft, I was excited but had reservations stemming from what I had experienced my freshman year. Just when you think everything is okay, something goes wrong. However, I was starting to understand that not all aphorisms are absolute truths. The excitement was a natural reaction that I tried to keep in check. In less than twenty-four hours, my life would change.

Draft Day

The morning of the draft, Vic picked Don and me up and took us to his hotel room. The draft started at 1:00 p.m., and as the first round progressed, we were a bundle of nerves. Then the Chargers took Don in the first round. He was happy, and I was happy for him. He left for the dormitory while I waited nervously, still hoping to be chosen in the first round, but it was not to be. With a second first-round pick, the Cowboys, another of Vic's teams, selected Charley Young of North Carolina State, whom we had played in the Liberty Bowl. Charley was his team's third-leading rusher. He was about my size but an inch taller at six foot one and heavier at 213 pounds to my 195.

The first round had passed, and I was starting to get concerned, but that angst didn't last too long, because I soon got the call that changed my life. George McFadden, director of public relations for the San Francisco 49ers, told me, "Delvin, we have drafted you in the second round."

I was happy. I always wanted to go to a team on the West Coast, because I'd had hamstring problems and wanted to play in warm weather. I was thankful and felt blessed to have the opportunity to play professional football. I left the hotel and tried my best to get on with my day. After all, I still had classes. Even though I followed my normal routine, I was distracted all day. It was just weird to spend the day trying to act like things were normal when I had gotten news that would change my life. In the meantime, even though I knew I would have to report to the 49ers training camp in a few months, I was still a college kid, and I had to adjust.

The 49ers were eager to get our deal done because of the WFL. The new league made our quarterback, David Jaynes, the first player chosen. The 49ers had four draft choices in the first two rounds. They chose running back Wilbur Jackson and defensive lineman Bill Sandifer in the first round and offensive lineman Keith Fahnhurst and then me in the second round. My representative Clifford Paul and I ended up negotiating my contract with Joe Perry. I vaguely knew of Joe as a former fullback, but I didn't know his great history with the 49ers. It was clear that Clifford and Joe had worked together before, because it didn't take long to put my deal together. I think I deserved more money, but in those times no one talked about their contract negotiations. It would be in our best interests if we knew how much the other players were paid, but they had us working against one another. I understood at the time that each team had a certain amount allotted for each round and position. With four players chosen in the first two rounds, this meant the money would be divided among the four of us. Little did I know I was being introduced to Business 101.

I signed a three-year contract for $35,000, $45,000, and finally $55,000. My contract included a $40,000 signing bonus, of which I deferred $20,000. I also had a $5,000 incentive clause for making All-Pro and the Pro Bowl. I used Clifford Paul to negotiate my contract, but that was the end of our business relationship. I was starting to get used to first-time experiences, and this would be another one. I never had that much money in my life, but I did know now that I would have to pay more taxes than I did with my summer job.

Although I wanted a college degree, the number one thing I had in mind when I came to KU was to play professional football. My goals had seemed a little far-fetched at the time: graduate from the University of Kansas, play professional football, and move my mother out of the projects into a new home. Now those goals were right in front of me.

Graduation at Last

Standing in my living room looking out the window at the parking lot of the Jayhawk Towers, I was still worried about graduating. It all depended on not failing one class. I leaped to the phone when it rang, and I heard my chemistry professor say, "I'm giving you a D." That was good enough for me to graduate. I thanked him, hung up, and jumped up with joy, because it was now sealed. After being academically ineligible as a freshman, I would graduate in four years from the University of Kansas with a Bachelor of Science degree in education. I had set lofty goals for a kid from Fifth Ward, but I put the work in and now was reaping the dividends.

I have received many accolades both on and off the field, but no words mean more to me than what John Novotny said:

> The biggest thing that Delvin had going for him was that if he knew what he wanted to do, you weren't going to stop him. He did it, and he always did it right. Delvin never backed off from anything, and he always did the right thing. Coming out of the background he did, how he was able to be such a class act is unbelievable. He came out of the worst situation, but he got the most out of his brainpower and his body of any human being that I ever saw go through KU. Period.

On May 20, 1974, I graduated from the University of Kansas. I was one of the few athletes, black or white, who graduated on time. I later bought my mother the house I'd dreamed one day I'd be able to. Now

> *If you are willing to work hard, one thing is guaranteed: something good will happen.*

I was going to play professional football. I had become a believer that dreams do come true. I learned that if I was willing to expand and grow, I could accomplish my goals.

But as I was also about to learn that when playing football becomes a business instead of a game, you quickly learn to take the bad along with the good.

Football has meant many things to me at different seasons in my life: a childhood game, a place to find acceptance, a ticket to a college education, and finally a big business where I could earn more money than I could have imagined.

All I ever wanted to do was play football and let someone else handle the business side of it. The funny thing, however, is that no one approached us with a plan to help us manage the change in ideology that confronted us as we went from college athlete to professional athlete. I've often thought about how valuable it would have been to have economics courses with an emphasis on professional sports. Even if you didn't make it in the NFL, learning to manage your personal finances and run your household or a business would be useful.

I stepped into this new world thinking I had made it. Everything about this level, the atmosphere of the environment around us, was telling us we had made it. You can call the coaches by their first name, you can smoke in meetings without being lectured, you can curse—all of that was okay. And we were getting paid to play the game of football. All of this meant we were men. I was getting paid to play this game I loved.

I went to sleep one night as a college senior and woke up the next day as a professional football player. All my life, I had been

> *It was a vision I had as a starry-eyed kid, and it couldn't get any better than this.*

searching for my identity as a man. Now I was Delvin Williams, college graduate and running back for the San Francisco 49ers.

Now what?

At the end of December, I had flown to San Francisco for the East-West Shrine Game. We had flown over San Francisco Bay, and, looking out of the window, I'd seen cities spread out on both sides of the bay. Lights shined from the houses in the hills, and the view was unlike anything I had ever witnessed before. As we descended toward the runway, I'd had some fear that we were getting too close to the water. I am not a swimmer, and I was afraid of flying at the time. I had hoped to be drafted by a team playing in a warm climate. My preference was to play for a West Coast team, which meant anywhere from Seattle to San Diego. I remember sitting there on the plane thinking, "Wouldn't it be great to play in San Francisco?"

Drafted and now signed by the 49ers, I returned to San Francisco to begin my professional career. I took a moment to reflect upon playing at Kansas and, before that, Kashmere. I remembered even before that, fantasizing about being Jim Brown during pickup games. Becoming a professional football player had always been on my mind, and soon it would begin. I exited the plane into an adult world, entirely on my own.

History of Futility

I must admit that before joining the 49ers, I knew little about the history of the team or who the owners were. I learned that the team originally was owned by two brothers, Victor and Anthony Morabito. In 1957 the 49ers were involved in an intense game against the Chicago Bears. They were trailing 17–7 when Tony Morabito collapsed from a heart attack in the stands and died. The 49ers stormed back and won, 21–17. They finished the season in a tie in their division with the Detroit Lions but lost a one-game playoff, 31–27, after leading 24–7 at half.

That had been the closest the 49ers had come to playing in any championship game until running into the Cowboys in the early 1970s. Vic Morabito ran the team until he died of a heart attack in 1964. Now the Morabito widows, Josephine and Jane, owned the franchise. Lou Spadia was president, and Jack White was director of player personnel.

The coaching staff, led by Dick Nolan, was a mixture of veterans, most of whom had played on championship teams or were former college players who joined coaching staffs after graduating. In the "us versus them" mentality of players and management, these guys were once "us" and now were "them." Our livelihood depended upon playing well, which for skilled positions typically was measured by statistics. The coaches' livelihood depended on winning. Doug Scovil, a former college quarterback who later coached Roger Staubach at Navy, was the quarterback and running backs coach.

The most notable player to me was Cedric Hardman, a homeboy from Houston. We had met when I was recruited by North Texas State University my senior year in high school. He was then projected to go high in the upcoming NFL draft. He was cocky, flamboyant, and a good player, and I thought, *How he could* not *be good with the nickname "Nasty."* Cedric was going to be the person I was assigned to while on my visit to North Texas State. When I arrived, the recruiter took me to Cedric's apartment, and he was barely awake. The way he talked to the coach was shocking to me. "I don't want to do it now," he said. "You should've called earlier. I don't want no damn recruits." It looked like he had been up half the night.

It was like how some athletes are in high school, not wanting to be a part of the programs. Once your senior year in the sport is over, you're done with your commitment to the athletic program. At that point, the coaches don't have any say in what you do. You were under their control, did what they said, and did it the way they wanted it. But when you become a senior, you're not bound to take part. Because of my relationship with Coach Hendricks, there was no way I would let him down by not taking part. Cedric was having none of it. However, when he told him I was from Houston, he was more accommodating, although I only spent that one day with him.

Longtime 49ers quarterback John Brodie had retired after the 1973 season. The 1966 Heisman Trophy winner Steve Spurrier was expected to finally be able to start, backed up by Joe Reed of Mississippi State, in his third year, and rookie Tom Owen, drafted out of Wichita State.

Jimmy Johnson, Dave Wilcox, Tommy Hart, and Mel Phillips were on defense, and they were the veterans I was most impressed with. There is a strong and weak side of both offense and defense. Teams tend to favor the strong side of their offense, which is where the tight end lines up. It was no coincidence that Johnson, Wilcox, Hart, and Phillips were all on the strong side of the defense. They were well respected by the coaches and every guy on the team.

Jimmy Johnson was a perennial All-Pro cornerback and was selected to the Pro Bowl five times. There were many occasions when he was the last player to join team meetings and the first one to leave. When practice was over, he would run off the field and into the locker room, take a shower and be the first to leave. At the time, he had played fourteen seasons in the NFL, and he would go on to play two more. I would overhear the other players talking about how good a cornerback he was. They said that opposing quarterbacks threw to his side of the field only once or twice a game.

I heard a story about how one guy quit the team because Jimmy would not allow him to catch a pass in practice. He felt that if he couldn't beat Jimmy in practice, he didn't stand a chance to play in the NFL. Cedric told me that Jimmy was the only player on the team who didn't give out his address or telephone number, just a P.O. box.

Dave Wilcox had a lawn chair in his locker instead of a stool. He didn't say much, but he would sit there and smoke a cigar. Dave was about six foot three and 235 pounds with a scruffy beard and was very unassuming, soft-spoken, and quiet. He reminded me of Clint Eastwood. But when he put a helmet on, you didn't want to piss him off. Dave had a bad knee and practiced only once or twice a week. He would get his knee drained and start on Sundays and play the whole game. He was a vocal guy on the field. Dave would finish his Hall of Fame career in style at the end of the 1974 season, returning an interception for a touchdown in what was his final game, the first and only touchdown of his career.

I remember seeing an ashtray of top of a locker. College football was authoritarian, with a quasi-wholesome image, but this was going to be different. Finally, after all those years in college hiding from the coaches, I could smoke in the open. As far as playing with injuries, the bar was set high by Mel Phillips. Mel played half the season with both forearms broken. It was thought he would be out for the season, but he was out one week. He then started and played with a cast on each arm. After about a week, he had to take one of the casts off. As Jimmy tells the story, with both casts on, Mel couldn't go the bathroom alone and depended on his wife for help. Mel and his wife Ann were elementary school sweethearts. As I write this today, they are still happily married.

Boys to Men

What I would come to realize is that we were considered men. At twenty-three, legally I had been an adult since the age dropped to eighteen in 1972 (when I was twenty-one anyway). But around these older guys, I realized I had some growing up to do. These guys had kids and called the coaches by their first names. How do you tell grown men what to do? They knew how to do their jobs and knew what happened if they didn't perform. If there was anything that symbolized being a professional and mature, of all things, it was smoking. I thought that was the damnedest thing. You could sit next to your coach in the meetings smoking, and they wouldn't say a thing about it. I had arrived, but the expectations were high. There were no excuses. You had to be prepared to do a lot of work on your own, with no complaining. I thought I would fit in just fine. I hadn't shied away from working to get the things I wanted. I had gone through a lot to be a part of this, and I was ready.

No one needed to hand me a job description when I started my new career at a position I had played all my life. Running back is considered one of the more glamorous positions, and we usually are the most versatile athletes on a team. A good running back will have a combination of speed, quickness, agility, and good hands. We also take the most punishment. On a good game day, the offense will run sixty to seventy plays. A starting back will be featured by either running or receiving the ball in a third or more of the offensive plays. If not involved directly, we're blocking solo or helping a lineman.

Sometimes as a running back you break through untouched, but often you take the punishment if a linebacker sheds a block or shoots the gap to nail you. It's nothing to be assaulted on one play by several tacklers, usually much bigger than you. Football is a violent sport, and there's no other way to describe it. Running the ball into the teeth of a defense is like being in one car wreck after another. Let's not have any illusions that routine player contact is the same as getting hit with a hard tackle while going at full speed. It's not.

A running back gets hit more than players in any other position. The best way I can say it is that we're at the point of the spear. It should come as no surprise that the average length of an NFL running back's career is two and a half years, compared to three and a half years for all NFL players. The heavy physical contact is to blame.

CHAPTER 8

A running back must have great instincts and broad peripheral vision to see things unfolding and sense things before they occur. He needs the ability to read defensive players' reactions while on the move and intuitively evade tacklers to gain the necessary yards, all in a matter of seconds. Often it's obvious who is going to get the ball to get that short yardage for a first down or touchdown. And that person cannot be faint of heart.

No matter what the other ingredients are, one intangible quality can not be measured in yards gained or lost. It's the heart of a running back. You might question my desire, but never question my heart. To do so would be the ultimate insult to me as a running back.

Plethora of Running Backs

There was a logjam at my position. Wilbur Jackson of Alabama was their top draft pick, and they also had drafted running backs Sammy Johnson of North Carolina, Manfred Moore of USC, and Kermit Johnson of UCLA. (Kermit Johnson would sign instead with a WFL team.) A total of sixteen running backs were in camp, and the competition was going to be stiff. Vic Washington had led the team in rushing. Larry Schreiber had backed up fullback Ken Willard, who had been with the team since 1965 but then was traded to St. Louis. Seven-year veteran Doug Cunningham, two-year veteran Randy Jackson and second-year man Dave Atkins were all competing against us rookies.

The 49ers held a rookie camp in May 1974 at their facility in Redwood City, some thirty miles south of the city. It would be my first time viewing an NFL playbook. There was a lot to learn in a short period of time. We spent more time in the classroom than on the field. On the second day, Cedric Hardman dropped by the training camp just to work out before the veterans had to report. He had on a jean jacket with Bugs Bunny and the Warner Brothers logo on the back. I thought it was cool and asked where he got it.

Cedric informed me that he would try to get me one. He let me know that he had been doing some acting and was involved in Hollywood. I got the feeling he was placating me, and, for the record, he didn't get me one, but he also had said I could always buy my own. My thrill was connecting with another guy from Houston who was also playing for the 49ers. I felt a kinship with him even if I was a rookie trying to make the squad and he was an established veteran. It eventually would be the beginning of a long friendship. May he rest in peace.

I came to camp with no illusions. Wilbur Jackson was ahead of me, I knew, but when I got the opportunity, I wanted to be ready. The playbook was complex. Because it was clear that athletic ability alone would not be enough, I was prepared to do what it took to make the team, including being a quick study. Because I was a second-round draft choice, management and teammates had high expectations.

During a morning practice not long after two-a-day practices started, I got poked in the eye. It was hard to see out of it, and before our second practice I went to see the head trainer. Chuck Krpata was a soft-spoken guy and had a good relationship with everyone. We would become good friends and still are today. I told him that my eye was bothering me. After he examined it, he thought for a second and asked me if my sunglasses would fit under my helmet. I smiled and asked him if he was serious. He replied, "You got hit in the eye and can't see out of it. Plus the sunlight is bothering you." I thought, *Okay, he's the trainer* and tried them on. He helped me adjust my helmet, and I headed out to practice. Several guys were looking at me and smiled. Some asked if I was sure about the glasses. "Chuck told me I could wear them," I said. I looked behind me, and there was Coach Nolan. He saw the sunglasses and grabbed me by the arm, saying, "Where do you think you're going with those on?" I started to tell him that Chuck had told me I could wear them, but he was all over me before I could finish.

"Where do you think you are? Did they let you do that in college? I don't care what Chuck said. Get your ass back in there and take those things off!"

I was pissed off at Chuck. I was a rookie, and he'd set me up. I think Coach Nolan was in on it. He looked like he was laughing at the end of his diatribe. I couldn't stay mad, and I had to roll with it, because there would be more of it coming my way if I didn't. Welcome to training camp, rookie.

There had been a strike as of July 1, 1974, by the NFL Players Association. Eventually some veterans came into camp. The usual first-stringers were immediately listed at the top of the depth charts as full team practices began. Some of the rookies were disappointed to not begin the season as starters, but clearly the veterans were superior. The pace picked up, because there wasn't a learning curve with them as with the rookies. I can understand when one of us missed an assignment and why the coaches would say "damn rookies." Two weeks into training camp, tempers got short. It was always full gear and competitive.

Enduring the Grind

With players carrying those wet and heavy pads in the afternoon heat, tired from lack of sleep and not enough water, it didn't take much to set someone off. There were squabbles and threats, pushing and shoving. Offensive linemen hold on just about every pass play. The defensive linemen didn't like it, especially Bob Hoskins. He would grab one of the linemen, telling them how he was going to kick his ass if he kept holding him. For us rookies, all this was eye-opening.

I was having a good training camp. I didn't have trouble picking up the plays and learning my assignments. After ten days, it felt like we had been in camp for a month. After a week of two-a-days, we'd get a day off. A day off meant no evening meetings, and we'd go to a local bar and have beers. Some of the players' wives came down to visit them, and they weren't drinking. If they were with their wives, we didn't tease them. However, if they weren't married, we'd tease: "Watch out, he's gonna be real light tomorrow now that he's gotten the weight off!"

Practice was my opportunity to express myself, and physically it didn't feel any different from college. But something was clear: superior talent was on display at every position. Contrary to the group consciousness I felt in high school, this was the opposite. This was a job. I had this feeling from the beginning of training camp. The revelation hit me while I was getting dressed. There's no one to blame for your mistakes and no one to rescue you. I was accepting the reality of being on my own again, because I would need to find my way when the season started.

Everything in my football life—from the streets of Houston to Kashmere High School and then the University of Kansas—had been preparing me for the moment I would step onto the field as a professional football player.

After the long grind of two-a-day workouts, every player is eager to play in front of a crowd and against another team instead of beating up on team-mates. As a rookie, I was eager to show the world what I could do with a football in my hands.

Our first preseason game was at night against the San Diego Chargers. During practice that week, Wilbur hurt his ankle, and it was unclear if he would be able to play. I was second- string running back. All week long I was preoccupied with Wilbur's injury. Sure enough, he couldn't play, and so I would start.

It was Saturday night, and I was sitting in the Chargers' visitors' dressing room. It was my first game as a professional, and I was aware of starting. It was much different than I thought it would be. In my dreams of being a professional football player, I was always in the game. There were no two-a-day practices, no complex playbook, and no veteran line-backers drilling me.

In high school we talked about our positions as if they were our job. Now football literally was a job. These were grown men I was going to be playing against. At first it seemed unfair, because these guys were older. It wasn't their ability so as much as their knowledge of the game.

In my imagination, pro football was all excitement and glory. That was a dream. This was a job.

We were a team only in concept. Within the team, we were men fighting for a job. Everybody, coaches included, was for himself, and understandably so. Emotionally, you were detached from the need to win, especially in preseason, which doesn't count toward any championship. There were no rah-rah motivational speeches of any kind. Just get your job done.

I had never doubted my ability as a running back. However, the butterflies were fluttering. Our locker room was full of nervous rookies, free agents, walk ons, and veterans who crossed the picket lines. It was our first make-or-break opportunity in a real game. I was waiting for the pregame speech, wondering what it was going to be like. As he addressed the team, Coach Nolan said, "There will be cuts next week. Some of you won't be here, and this is a chance to show what you can do." Just get your job done, and you might last another day. That was it! There were no motivational speeches of any kind.

Walking through the tunnel and running on the field had a different meaning for me than in either high school or college. I realized that I had arrived at the uppermost level and was on my own. It helped that I saw Bear, my University of Kansas roommate, who was playing outside linebacker for the Chargers. The last time we played against one another was in high school when Kashmere beat Booker T. Washington two out of three, and I had never let him forget it. Now we were in opposing professional camps.

After the kickoff, I took the field with our offense as starting halfback. Immediately, I found the pace faster and more intense than it was in scrimmages during practice. It took a few series, with contact and short drives, to me to settle down. During our next possession, I had carried the ball several times and was starting to feel good about my contribution. The Chargers stadium was shared with the Padres baseball team, still in season, and so the infield was left as dirt. I didn't know the infield of a baseball diamond could be so hard.

The dust and dirt got in my face. On short yardage, carrying the ball felt like I was caught in a cattle stampede, with bodies were flying around. It was hard to discern by the jerseys who was winning the engagement, my guy or theirs. When you are winded and getting tackled by someone, the last thing you want is dirt in your eyes and mouth, which already is dry enough from anxiety. You have to take what you see, seize every opportunity.

We reached the Charger ten-yard line. I ran off the left tackle where the outside linebacker was Bear, whom the tight end was assigned to block. After being tackled while gaining three yards, I could hear him laughing while the pile on top of me unstacked.

"Is that you, Bear?" I asked.

"Tell them not to run to this side," he said as he helped me off the ground.

The next play was an incomplete pass. Then our fullback, who was an unsigned walk-on, ran a quick trap up the middle and was stopped on the goal line. Now it was fourth down and still goal to go. Our fullback got the call to go up the middle again. Taking the handoff, he tried to jump over the linemen. When they hit him, the ball popped out. A defensive tackle picked it up and started running toward their goal line. Having blocked my man, I got up to chase him.

I almost caught him when one of the Chargers blocked me. As I was falling, I put my hand down to brace myself and landed hard. When I rose, I had pain in my right wrist. Standing on the sideline, it got worse. Not wanting to complain about it, I went back in the game for a few plays. I ran a sweep to the left and stiff-armed one guy and collided with Bear at the sideline. Once again we broke out laughing and talking to one another. But this time when I came out of the game, I told Chuck, the trainer, about my wrist.

During his examination, it hurt even more. Still early in the second quarter, Chuck took me inside to get an X-ray. When the photo came back, he told me I had broken my wrist. I hoped he was playing another prank, but it was too painful not to be true. I couldn't believe this. I was injured while not even carrying the ball or blocking. Furthermore, I was told it would take six weeks to heal. They put a splint on it, and I sat out the rest of the game. The only high point for me was meeting with Bear after the game ended. He sympathized with my injury, and we parted company.

Playing through Pain

Back in Santa Barbara at training camp, my arm was placed in a long cast. After two weeks, Coach Nolan approached me and asked, "When are you going to take that thing off?" I looked at him and thought, *Is he crazy?* I told him it was broken, and he said, "I know."

I had played with pain before but never with anything broken. In the NFL, there are unwritten rules, such as one distinguishing pain from injury. You can play with pain, but you can't play with an injury, because playing injured can hurt your team's performance, I thought. But all the veterans played with injuries, and the peer pressure was nuanced. I was a running back and handled the ball. I had to use my hands. That was a double bind, because the worst thing a running back can do is fumble the ball.

Coach Nolan said I could talk to the doctor, but he thought my wrist was okay. This was my welcome to the business side of NFL, Inc.

I talked to 49er team doctor Lloyd Milburn about the long-term ramifications and treatment of my injury. I decided to give playing with a cast a try. The competition in camp was tough with seven other running backs all competing for one position. It was going to be a long summer. I wore the cast for approximately six weeks and then started wearing a wrist brace.

I wanted to do what I could to help the team, and I didn't want to miss the 1974 season. After sitting out for two weeks, I started to play on the special teams' punt and kickoff coverages. After the final cuts are made and the season starts, the team goes from eighty players in camp to forty-five on the final roster. If you didn't start, you played on special teams.

Our first two regular games were away, first at New Orleans and next close by at Atlanta. Instead of traveling back to San Francisco between games, we had to pack for two weeks. We beat both teams and came back to the Bay Area 2–0. I played some on offense but more on special teams. We started out strong, but the offense sputtered. Our defense kept us in the games, but we lost our next seven games in a row, including a defeat to the across-the-bay rival Oakland Raiders and twice to our longtime in-state rivals, the Los Angeles Rams, both at home and away. We also lost to our longtime nemesis, the Dallas Cowboys. I was able to make a small contribution offensively, which some said was a glimpse of what I had to offer.

We had played the Raiders at Candlestick, and it seemed like they had at least as many fans as we did. During a timeout, I looked in the stands and saw Raiders and 49ers fans fighting! The level of intensity was not just about winning, it was about survival and validating the franchise. The Raiders were in their heyday back then, having lost the AFC championship to Miami the year before. Here were these guys whom I had seen on television: Ken Stabler, Bubba Smith, Jack Tatum. I had respect and even a sense of reverence for those guys, but I didn't fear them. I wanted to be on the same field with them.

When I entered the game in the third quarter, the Raiders were up 14–10. Quarterback Tom Owen called Flow 38 Sweep Right, a hand-off to me. From high school, you're taught to carry the ball in the hand on the side to which you're running, thereby keeping it farthest from would-be tacklers. But with the cast on my right hand, I had to run right with the ball in my left hand. It felt odd, but I made sure I had a solid grasp as I took the handoff and followed my key blockers, fullback Larry Schreiber and the pulling guard Woody Peoples. The play as diagrammed was for me, the halfback, to follow the blocking and outrun everybody to the endzone.

Aside from the short yardage situations for a first down, every offensive play is designed to score a touchdown, and sometimes they do. As they made their blocks, I read them and turned upfield. I had heard Skip Thomas was the fastest player in their secondary. Seeing him out the corner of my eye, I outran him to the endzone, going seventy-one yards for the touchdown. After spiking the ball, I saw a sea of red jerseys coming to congratulate me, led by Dave Wilcox and Cedric Hardman.

However, the next time we got the ball, I fumbled on my next carry, setting up a Raider touchdown. Although we were still ahead, the momentum shifted, and they scored twice more. The mistake I made sealed our fate and was the deciding factor in our 35–24 defeat. After the game, I couldn't take much pleasure in my long touchdown run. Because of the fumble, I was the goat.

Early Contributions

Late in my career, several sportswriters would tell me that seventy-one-yard run showed my potential as a running back. I had a long way to go, and one touchdown run cannot determine a career success. Getting to play my rookie year and contributing what I could went a long way in my development and confidence as a pro. My anxiety decreased about playing with a broken wrist, which helped raise the bar for me on pain tolerance. In football, the ability to tolerate and play with pain creates a false sense of invincibility. But I learned that if you are going to play, that's what you must do. For me, pain was the alpha and injury the omega of football.

Wilbur Jackson would lead the team in rushing with 705 yards and was the NFC rookie of the year. Larry Schreiber at fullback had 634 yards. Sammy Johnson and I split time as the other rookie running backs. Sammy carried forty-four times for 237 yards and two touchdowns. I had thirty-six carries for 201 yards and three touchdowns.

After spending the football season in the Bay Area it was clear to me that it was where I would spend my offseason as well. I went home to Houston for the Christmas holiday, which would become an annual sojourn. I was getting back to my roots. I saw most of my high school teammates, plus some of my family and friends in the neighborhood. They expressed happiness and pride in my success, having made it to professional football. There were naysayers who never expressed direct cynicism, but I could tell they had doubts about how long my career would last. It was grounding as well as humbling because my injury had limited my performance.

That year was very important because I learned what it was going to take to make it in the NFL—playing with pain *and* injury. Although my wrist never healed that season, I had passed the ultimate test for a professional football player. And others' opinion of my ability was the last things on my mind since I was preoccupied with my upcoming wrist surgery.

Pain was the alpha and injury the omega of football.

My ability to come back from the surgery as a player was not in doubt, but I worried about whether the pain would go away. Would it distract me and hinder my performance? I also was concerned about the damage I might have done by playing with the wrist not healed. During the season, Dr. Milburn's periodic X-rays revealed failure of the scaphoid fracture to heal.

I had broken the right carpal navicular bone. For around two and a half weeks, I had worn a cast from my knuckles to the middle of my upper arm, and after that I played the whole season. Protecting it, I had pain just shaking hands or rising from a reclining position. Eventually

I was scheduled for surgery in early 1975 and was admitted to St. Mary's Hospital in San Francisco. A bone was grafted from my left ilium to the break in my right wrist.

The surgeon was Dr. Lloyd Taylor, with team physician Milburn. I didn't know many people yet, so I decided to drive myself to the hospital. I didn't feel like I needed anyone to help me. That was part of the macho athlete mentality, equating emotional needs to physical expression, either stoically or, in some cases, angrily. I figured that I could have the surgery and be home before sundown the next day. With that mind-set, I drove myself to San Francisco from Foster City, where I lived during my rookie year, and checked into St. Mary's Hospital.

In 1975 you could drive yourself from a hospital after surgery without someone being with you. You could even smoke in the hospital. Today they wouldn't let you in the hospital or have the surgery performed if you didn't have a responsible person with you.

Post-surgery was a time for rest, relaxation, and recuperation.

Putting Down Roots

About half of the team made the Bay Area home. The natural beauty of the area was irresistible and spoke to me. Foster City at the time was a relatively new community in San Mateo County. It's like an island, with three ways in and out, and I thought, *What happens if there's an earthquake?* Living on the mid-peninsula, I wasn't far away from some of the most beautiful sights in the country. It was twenty minutes from San Francisco and thirty from Half Moon Bay and the Pacific Ocean. It was a two-hour drive to the wine country of Napa Valley and Sonoma. You couldn't ask for much more in terms of outdoor activities, and it didn't get much better than the San Francisco Bay Area.

When you're in San Francisco going down Columbus Avenue in North Beach, you see strip joints, peep shows, and fine dining on the same street. I hadn't seen this type of openness before. Landmarks from movies such as *Dirty Harry* and television shows like *The Streets of San Francisco* made it come alive. It was different from the stroll of Lyons Avenue in Fifth Ward and Club Matinee in Houston. Seeing movies made in the city where I lived was something I had never experienced.

I didn't realize how close Alcatraz Island was to San Francisco. Looking at the city from the Alcatraz, it didn't seem so far away. However, I could see that with the cold water and heavy waves someone wouldn't likely make it to shore.

Come to think of it, sinking or swimming is a good metaphor for players as training camp and a new season draw near.

10

Change is a constant for everyone, including NFL teams, from the Super Bowl champion to the bottom feeders. Bad teams hope an influx of new talent will change their fortunes, while good teams try to keep their momentum going as they replace aging veterans with rookies who are younger, faster, stronger—and cheaper.

After eleven seasons, all with the 49ers, Dave Wilcox retired. In the last game of the 1974 season, he had returned a pass interception for a touchdown, the first time doing so in his illustrious career. The Hawk was gone, but otherwise the defense was intact. The offensive line would miss two veterans, though: Forrest Blue was traded to the Baltimore Colts, and Len Rohde retired after fifteen seasons, all with the 49ers. There was a definite change-of-the-old-guard feeling in camp.

As the team's leading rusher in 1974, Wilbur Jackson would start. After spending the spring with my arm in a cast, I had it removed a month before training camp started. I was told that the bone graft would speed up the healing, but even after six months I don't think it had healed.

Ever since leaving high school, I had gone into training camp concerned about one injury or another. Breaking something affects other parts of the body as well. I didn't have time to do much strengthening or

I was just starting to recognize the discrepancy between expectation and outcome.

increase my conditioning. I worked out and did as much as I could, but it was hard for me to run outdoors and do football-type sprints.

I wasn't concerned about the football aspect of playing. In fact, I was excited and motivated to start my second season under the same coaching staff. I asked permission to report to early training camp with the rookies. All the equipment that I had been using at the 49ers Redwood City facility to strengthen my wrist had been moved to our training camp in Santa Barbara.

With plenty of running backs, the 49ers drafted mostly linemen that winter, until selecting Notre Dame fullback Wayne Bullock in the fifth round. But the team also added running back Kermit Johnson, who had been drafted out of UCLA in the seventh round the year before but had signed with the World Football League, as had his college running mate, James McAlister, drafted in the sixth round by the Raiders.

Besides Wilbur, the backfield competition included the team's second-leading rusher, Larry Schreiber, and second-year men Manfred Moore, Sammy Johnson, and me. John Wesley Saunders III was my roommate that year. He was born in Toledo, played for the University of Toledo Rockets, and was drafted by the Rams in 1972 but wound up with the Buffalo Bills. He missed the 1973 season but was signed by the 49ers for 1974, appearing in four games. He was six foot three, weighed about two hundred pounds, and played free safety. Soft-spoken, he moved with a certain ease and seemed never to be in a hurry.

During preseason, he did not like to play in the fourth quarter when coaches would insert all the free agents who were on the bubble, giving them a fleeting shot to show what they could do. When asked about his reluctance about getting in the game at that point, Saundo would say, "Judge, there's no telling what a desperate S.O.B. will do." We laughed. He was one of those on the bubble as well. We shared a two-room apartment and similar social activities.

In 1974 after the season started, there had been a rumor that Coach Nolan was going to be fired. I understood why there had been pressure for me to play despite my wrist injury. The quarterback position had also been a problem for most of the year. Personally, I liked all our quarterbacks, and they all had something to offer.

I was then a rookie and didn't know the nuances of the quarterback position. Steve Spurrier ("Spur") had arrived at the 49ers in 1967 with the highest college football honor, the Heisman Trophy. The University of Florida alum had been the heir apparent to long-time quarterback John Brodie, who finally retired after the 1973 season. Spur had a gunslinger mentality, with a good ol' boy persona, but he also was smart. The way we saw him later as head coach of South Carolina's football program (2005–2015) is how he was as a player. He had an edge about him. Some would call it cockiness, but he knew the difference between common sense and confidence. He knew the game of football. His finest hour would be turning Duke from perennial losers to conference champions. I liked his style.

When Spur dislocated his shoulder in the last preseason game in 1974, he had been out for most of the season. We had then played musical chairs with country and western guitarist, singer, and quarterback Joe Reed. Joe was a nice guy, and as far as I know he had a good relationship with everyone, but it was a tough situation to be in. Wily veteran quarterback Norm Snead had joined the 49ers late in the 1974 season and knew the position. When he had to warm up before going into the game, he'd throw a couple of passes and move his arm around and around as though he were making a circle, then would say, "I'm ready."

Quarterback Tom Owen and I were kindred souls. We had been drafted in the same year, and both of us had a connection to the state of Kansas. He was young, confident, and had the ability to be the quarterback. Late in the 1974 season, when Tom started to play more, there was some production at the position. The defense kept us in the games we won but didn't get the credit they deserved, and our 6–8 record may not have reflected their contributions.

A New Season

We opened the 1975 season against the Minnesota Vikings on the road . Their defensive line was known as the Purple People Eaters. Three of the four, Jim Marshall, Allen Page and Carl Eller, all had been multiple All-Pro selections in various years since 1968. The fourth, Doug Sutherland, had recently replaced former starter Gary Larsen. This team had lost the two preceding Super Bowls.

Late in the fourth quarter, the Vikings were up 13–10, and I was in the game. We had been moving the ball. Now it was third down with short yardage, and we were going to pass. I was a designated secondary receiver coming out of the backfield. All I was thinking about was making a first down to keep the drive alive. Coming out of the huddle, I knew I could get the ball. While in my stance, I caught a glimpse of where the first down marker was, and by that time the ball was snapped. There was no blitz, so I was in the pass route thinking I could get the ball. Carl Eller was engaged with our tackle, Cas Banaszak.

As I got next to them and into my route, Carl stuck out his arm, clotheslined me around the neck, and took me out of the play. I got a jolt down my arm as it stretched the nerve. I threw my arm up, complaining to the official, but to no avail. Then it dawned on me that this is what assistant coach Doug Scovil had been telling us the last two years: to be aware of things like this when playing against smart, veteran defensive linemen. They will wait until the most opportune time, a critical time in the game, to take you out of the play. When they do, it's our ten against their eleven, advantage defense. We lost the game 27–17. It took getting clotheslined, but it was a lesson learned.

We played the Rams twice a year and had heard the speech many times about watching out for ourselves. Perennial All-Pro lineman Merlin Olsen was the anchor of their defense. He was a man among boys. Playing them twice a year, there was a history of repeated squabbles, particularly in the line play. Their defensive ends were All-Pros Jack Youngblood and Fred Dryer. Youngblood was verbal and tried to intimidate you.

Whenever something broke out between one of our linemen and Youngblood, Olsen was the peacemaker. He would step in and separate them. He'd put one hand in the chest of one player and his elbow in the other and yell, "Knock it off!" It was as though he was separating two kids. That was the respect he had on both sides of the ball. I wouldn't discount our defense, because we had some guys with bad attitudes as well. We had Cedric Hardman, Cleveland Elam, Tommy Hart, Mel Phillips, and a sometimes out-of-control Ralph McGill. Any time we played the Rams, there was tension. Southern California versus Northern California, Lala Land versus fruits and nuts, however you want to characterize it, we were rivals.

Wilbur had been playing hurt and made a couple of mistakes. One was a fumble that led to a field goal. I was told to go in the game. I entered the game and contributed a thirty-eight-yard touchdown run. Free safety Bill Simpson hit me on the ten-yard line, but I didn't go down until we were in the endzone. That touchdown gave us the lead, 14–3. It was short-lived, however, and the Rams won the game, the first of our two together, giving us our second loss.

We did have a scare during the game. The Rams kicker, Tom Dempsey, had no toes on his right foot and wore a squared-off boot, and he was one of the better kickers in the league. The Rams had lined up for a field goal, and, when the ball was snapped, Ralph McGill laid out to try to block the kick. He barely missed the ball, but Dempsey followed through with his special boot and hit Ralph in the head.

The game was delayed, and Ralph's wife, Janice, left the stands to come on the field. They took him off in an ambulance, which is a scene that always gives players pause. Dempsey made three field goals that day, which was the difference in our 23–14 loss. Ralph, who had been taken to the hospital, was back the following week, playing defense as well as still returning punts. This was the era without an established concussion protocol. In today's climate, he would not have played the next week.

Getting the Start

That third game was away against the Kansas City Chiefs in a battle of two winless teams. Coach Nolan was looking for a combination that could result in points, because the offense had yet to score either in the first quarter or the second half. I learned from reading the newspaper that I would start in place of Wilbur Jackson, who had gained only eight yards on six carries against Los Angeles. Because we had been friends since being rookies the year before, I felt bad for him but also knew now it was my ass on the line. I had sixty-six yards on fifteen carries, including an eighteen-yard run to set up a touchdown as we beat Kansas City, 20–3.

Wilbur and I split carries the following week in a home loss to Atlanta. Against New Orleans at home the next week, after two touchdown passes from Norm Snead to Gene Washington, I reversed field during a sweep and ran twenty-five yards for a touchdown without being touched. We won, 35–21. Next, Wilbur and I both had miserable games in a road loss to New England. Our rushing game was stifled, and I gained only nine yards on six carries, and he gained a single yard in his only rush. Larry Schreiber, our fullback, got twelve yards on seven carries.

Back home against Detroit, I had a fifty-two-yard run that set up a touchdown and wound up with seventy-two yards on nine carries. But we lost once again, this time 28–17. Not only that, our opening quarterback from 1974 season, Joe Reed, started for Detroit and outplayed Snead, who threw two interceptions and eventually was pulled for Spurrier.

Rollercoaster Ride

We got a little winning streak going as we beat the Rams, with Steve throwing a touchdown pass to me, followed by wins over the Bears and the Saints, evening our record at 5–5. At home against Chicago, I outgained rookie Walter Payton, and barely—106 yards to his 105—but on only twelve carries to his twenty-three, which at the time was a solid measurement for me.

But then our nosedive began, and we lost our last four games. My season low was minus four yards on nine carries against my hometown Houston Oilers in a Candlestick loss, as our rushing game was totally stifled. Wilbur and I both bounced back against the Falcons in Atlanta, as I had 104 yards on ten carries and he had 80 yards on eight carries, both of us having long gains of more than forty yards. But Spur, having replaced Norm, threw two interceptions, and we narrowly lost.

Tom Owen finally got to start our last game against the New York Giants, Coach Nolan's former team, on December 21. We had the lead at 23–20 but lost the game on a final Giants one-yard touchdown. Both teams finished 5–9. The Giants had improved their record from the previous season, and their second-year coach kept his job. But it would be Dick Nolan's final season with the Niners.

I ended the season with 631 yards rushing and 5.4 yards per carry, second in the league only to O. J. Simpson's 5.5 average. But he had gained 1,817 yards, just short of his 2,003-yard mark set in 1973. My per-carry mark didn't mean as much, but it was significant. On our team, I had emerged as a solid running threat. Hurt for much of the year, Wilbur had 303 yards with a 3.9 average, and Larry, used for a lot of short-yardage gains, had a 2.5 average and 337 yards. Sammy Johnson was the only other back with significant carries, gaining 185 yards, with 3.4 yards per carry.

I was glad that my broken wrist from the previous season had not caused my benching. At the time, I thought Coach Nolan was unfairly pressuring me to play. From his standpoint, both of his top two running back draft picks were hurt, and all the other experienced halfbacks had gone on to other teams. Ever since going out for football in high school, I had said that I would do whatever I could to help my teams win. When we lost to Hebert in the state quarterfinals my senior year, I was driven not to ever feel like that again! A championship defeat is a big motivator. As it turned out, playing out 1974 with my wrist in a brace and nursing it during the offseason didn't hurt my 1975 output.

I liked and respected Dick Nolan. I appreciated the fact he took a chance, drafted me in the second round, and made me a 49er. He was the head coach for eight years and was credited with developing the defense that helped the 49ers win three consecutive NFC West division titles. But he left the offense to others who were less capable. It was his nudging that gave me the impetus to play with a broken wrist. He was challenging me, although at the time I didn't see it that way. It allowed me to take the question "What are you prepared to do?" to the next level. Anytime his name came up around Cedric Hardman, I would tell him he was Dick's favorite. May Dick and Cedric both rest in peace.

Welcome, Monte Clark

As is in most cases in the NFL when head coaches are fired, the players are concerned about who will be the next coach. There is uncertainty about your position and the type of offense and defense you will play. It can influence everybody. The defensive unit would probably stay intact because they were solid. By contrast, in 1975, our run offense finished twenty-fifth out of twenty-six teams. If we were going to generate more offense, it would have to start with the running game. We needed offense. It was just that simple. Management didn't waste much time replacing Dick Nolan, and they made a good choice. On January 16, 1976, they hired Miami Dolphins offensive line coach Monte Clark.

Monte had been the Dolphins' offensive line coach for six years. He was the architect of the offensive line that enabled both Larry Csonka and Mercury Morris each to rush for one thousand yards in a single season. During his tenure, he orchestrated what many consider to be one of the best offensive lines in NFL history. Larry Little and Jim Langer are both in the Hall of Fame, while Bob Kuechenberg gets nominated every year.

When I heard that Monte Clark was going to be the head coach for the 1976 season, I couldn't believe it. It was like a dream come true. I was excited, motivated and looking forward to the upcoming season. One thing he did was to move Wilbur to fullback and open the halfback position to competition. When he did that, I thought he was the real deal. People had forgotten Wilbur was rookie of the year. I had visions of both of us having thousand-yard seasons. If anybody knew how to set the dominoes for that to happen, it would be Monte.

Instead of competing against one another, Wilbur and I were playing together as a tandem. Monte put the backs in the right positions. Wilbur was around six foot one and 215 pounds, a little light for fullback and more of a hybrid. However, he had the power to run over you. In two seasons, I had averaged 5.4 yards per carry and led the team in rushing in 1975. Monte would have to build an offensive line, but as far as the running backs went, the skills were there. He put the icing on the cake when he changed training camp from Santa Barbara to San Jose State, which was twenty minutes from my house. The nights we were off, and I could go home and sleep in my own bed.

Monte had played for the 49ers and Cleveland Browns and had blocked for Jim Brown. He was a big man at six foot six, 260 pounds—an imposing figure. He had a work ethic unlike anything we had seen. He named Floyd Peters defensive coordinator. We had all the pieces, or, if not all, we certainly had the foundation for a solid team. He made all the right moves as far as I was concerned. I'm sure there are some who would not agree with the decisions he made.

Each player's situation is different. What I liked the most about what Monte was doing, strictly from my perspective, was putting the right players in the right positions. It felt as though he was giving us a real opportunity to win. I can't speak for the whole team, but the energy was high, and we were focused. It was the first time my bullshit detection antennas didn't beep over something I was being fed.

I dropped by the training facility to pick up my playbook before minicamp. I stopped by Monte's office, and we talked about offensive football and the possibilities we would have running the football. I expressed my excitement about what we could accomplish. Before I left his office, I made a pledge to him. "Coach, if you want me to play the whole game, I will," I said. "If you want me to come out, I will. Whatever I need to do to help us win is what I want to do."

He talked about wanting to create an environment of fun. We had to develop a learning attitude, which in turn would create a winning atmosphere. He went on to say, "The only time that success comes before work is in the dictionary." As we talked further, he said, "Success equals the peace of mind and self-satisfaction of knowing you have done your best!" He talked about a lot of things. I was trying to figure out how to get out of there, because my head was starting to reel, and I think he sensed that.

Whenever there's a new coach, the whole offensive philosophy can change, and in this case it did. The numbering system, play calling, and the names of the plays all changed. He drew up some plays that were more complex than what we had run before.

Commitment to Winning

I don't think there was any question in Monte's mind about my commitment to winning. I have always been a team player, but also, more importantly, simply a player. A player to me is someone you don't have to worry about on Sunday. You can count on them to do what is necessary to help the team win. I worked to have that level of respect for my teammates and coaches. When I left his office, I'm sure he understood my commitment, but only time would tell.

When minicamp started, there was a normal level of confusion, particularly for the backs. In the old system, the numbers for the backs always stayed the same. For example, the quarterback was 1, the halfback was 2, the fullback's number was 3 and the numbers never changed. In the new system, our number changed from play to play, depending upon what side of the center we were running. It was all incidental confusion that comes with a new system.

This is the type of thing that impedes the team's learning curve in all three phases of the game. When you hear a coach say, "We didn't get to put in all of our offensive system," especially if you're rebuilding with a lot of rookies, this is the type of thing he could be referring to. Even so, there was excitement on both sides of the ball.

Defensively, Floyd Peters had put a scheme in the new system that freed the defensive linemen to rush the passer more aggressively than before. Floyd also had been a player and knew the game of football. There are very few coaches who can make the adjustments from player to coach and succeed on both levels. The year before, the team had drafted defensive tackles Cleveland Elam and Jimmy Webb. Both would become mainstays and integral parts of the 49ers defense.

Monte had been in the Miami heat for years. Getting in shape wasn't a problem there. However, when he came to San Francisco, we were introduced to the vehicle for conditioning called "gassers." We found out what he meant by working hard and to be in top condition. Gassers were after-practice conditioning workouts. One gasser was a sprint across the width of the field over and back two times, and we had to do three. And during two-a-days, we had to run them twice a day. I can tell you that I did not like running them, and I can't tell you anyone who did.

When Monte moved the training camp to San Jose State, it was huge in the attitude-adjustment department. It was great to have training camp in the Bay Area, especially for the players with kids. Now we could do other things on our days off, such going to a movie or see friends. Sleeping in your own bed, even if it was for one night, was a big thing. Coach Clark was making all the right moves. The head coach's job is to lead, and that is what he was doing.

The first meeting in training camp, we didn't know what to expect. When the coaches change, so does the philosophy. They are in control, and they will put their imprint on the team. We had gotten a preview of what things were going to be like in minicamp. I was anxious and excited, probably more so than the others because of his offensive pedigree. He started by reintroducing the coaches, trainers, and equipment manager to the team:

> These people are important people to me. They are the leaders, your bosses, who will help me run the football team. These are the men who will help me decide on your lives. . . . The trainers, equipment men, and scouts are also important members of my staff. The things they ask you to do are to be understood as an extension of my policies. . . .

I want you to feel you can contribute. Suggestions are welcome. You are invited to talk to your assistant coach or me at any time. No matter how busy I am. I will make the decisions, and I will run the team. All we want is your very best. Your best is good enough! Remember our criteria. What is expected of you is no longer simply how you think or feel about it, or what your own personal desires are. We have a responsibility to each other that is bigger than serving only ourselves. Think of your team first, then yourself.

Then he paraphrased author Elbert Hubbard: "If you must growl, condemn and eternally find fault, resign your position and when you are on the outside, damn to your heart's content. But if you are part of the institution, do not condemn it. If you do, the first high wind that comes along will blow you away, and you will probably never know why."

The Full Monte

He gave us the Full Monte, as he would later call it. There was the normal disagreement or a smile here and there, with maybe a sense of defiance behind it. However, in that meeting it was clear who was in charge. There was no doubt the direction of this organization was moving, our level of inclusion and decision-making. It was a great job of coaching, and we hadn't even put on our uniforms. I bought what he was selling. We were back to being a team, in the way I had envisioned it. That was the first time, professionally, I could say we were a team.

The previous two years, a lack of a consistent offense had been a problem. As with most offenses, to be productive, there must be a leader on the field. That starts with production from the quarterback. Spur was too smart and independent for the NFL. It's my opinion that he didn't last because of restrictions on his capabilities and the lack of creativity allowed to him. He was traded to the expansion Tampa Bay Buccaneers in April 1976 and in 1978 went into college coaching where he belonged. Norm Snead retired.

Also gone were Larry Schreiber, who had been the starting fullback, and starting defensive tackle Bob Hoskins. Larry was the elder statesman of the backfield and well-liked. Both he and Bob would be missed.

One of the hard things about professional football is the friendships. You are torn when one of your teammates and friends is traded, and it's even worse when one is cut.

The quarterback question was answered in April 1976 when the 49ers traded Tom Owen and four high draft picks (two in 1976 and two in 1977) to New England for Jim Plunkett, who had played in the Bay Area in college. The team hoped a change of scenery and a return to the Bay Area would be good for Jim. That remained to be seen. I've always said that I would never want to play in my hometown. It would be hard to perform because of the distractions from my friends and family. Jim had won the Heisman Trophy at Stanford his senior year and been the first player drafted in the first round of 1971 by the Patriots.

As in most cases, the first pick had gone to the team with the worst record. Jim had then struggled with the Patriots as they were trying to rebuild their team, winding up with three coaches in his first three years, the last being Chuck Fairbanks, who was then fresh out of the college ranks. Jim had taken a lot of punishment on losing Patriots team—and ridicule after losing his starting job to rookie Steve Grogan in 1975, and I thought being on the 49ers could be the best thing for him.

A new quarterback, a new coach, a training camp closer to home—perhaps these changes off the field would bring more success on it.

11

Even seemingly small changes can go a long way toward creating a positive attitude as a new season approaches.

Having training camp locally at San Jose State University was great. Monte worked his magic with the offensive linemen. Our defense had always been ahead of us, but the defensive linemen had also taken their play to a higher level. They were so disruptive in practice that it made it hard to run our plays. Floyd Peters was vocal and very active. Sometimes it seemed as though he wanted to suit up. Tackle Cleveland Elam had progressed faster than anyone thought possible. He and Jimmy Webb, both in their second years, would be the starting defensive tackles.

The 1976 preseason was getting ready to start. The first game was against the Seattle Seahawks. They were then a first-year expansion team, and it would be the first professional football game ever played in the Kingdome. There were other firsts as well: Monte's first game as a professional head coach, the first time Wilbur and I would be in the backfield together, and the debut of a revamped offensive line that Monte had pieced together. Wide receiver Willie McGee was sure to contribute. Wilbur and I had a good training camp, and we were clicking.

Jack Patera was the Seahawks head coach. He was the long-time defensive coordinator for the Vikings. Monte for Miami and Patera for Minnesota had squared off before, when the Dolphins won Super Bowl VIII. It was going to be interesting.

Going into the game, we knew Monte was going to play a lot of people, and the starters would play only the first half. We won the toss and elected to receive. The offense set out on a fourteen-play drive that took eight minutes. It was a textbook ball-control drive. I touched the ball on twelve of those fourteen plays and had the privilege of scoring the first touchdown ever in the Seattle Kingdome. Before this game, if someone had said our offense would put together a fourteen-play drive, I would have said they were crazy.

The defense played like hell and got after it, sacking Seattle quarterback Jim Zorn seven times in the first half. It was the metamorphosis of our pass rush into the Gold Rush (drawing on our team colors of red and gold plus the 1849 Gold Rush history). We led 17–0 at halftime. With our starters on the sidelines, the Seahawks fought back, but we held on and won 27–20. In honor of Monte's first victory, he was given the game ball. It was a good test for both teams, and we would meet again in the third game of the regular season.

In our third preseason game against the Kansas City Chiefs, a 21–13 win, our running game was starting to click. Everybody on offense was blocking and contributing something to help us win. The offensive line had taken a lot of abuse over the last two years, but now they were doing well. We surprised ourselves, averaging 232 yards per game rushing in three games. We averaged five yards each time we ran the ball. A lot of credit needed to go to the offensive line. Monte was a great offensive line coach. We saw him take players off waivers (after being cut by one team) and in three days start them on Sunday. Jim Langer, Larry Little, Bob Kuechenberg were perennial All-Pros. The Lineman Whisperer (Monte) whipped them into shape and built their confidence.

Against the Chiefs, I had gained ninety-nine yards on sixteen carries for a 6.2-yard-per-carry average and a touchdown. However, in the beginning of the fourth quarter, I was hit in the head, and my helmet was knocked off. I was dazed and had double vision, and it took me a while to gather myself. I didn't play the rest of the game. It was a concussion. If that happened today, I probably wouldn't play the next week. Oakland and Los Angeles beat us in the next two games, but they were close. Then we beat the Chargers 17–16 in Hawaii. We finished the preseason 4–2, and I led the NFC in rushing.

Starting the Season

The offense had played well in preseason. The defense had dominated opponents and set the tone for what was to come, but now came the real test. The night before a game the team had a mandatory snack time and afterwards watched films of our opponents. It was an unofficial meeting with an edge to it. Monte had instituted another change, which I thought it was a good one. It was more like a meal for some of us than a snack. We sat and had hamburgers, beer, and chips, talked football, and then went to our position meeting. I had a burger, or two while I was there and took a double hamburger to my room for later. I didn't eat a pregame meal but would have a couple of eggs sometimes. Wilbur and I were roommates, and anyone who put up with my snoring is a patient person. There was never any animosity between us. We were competitors, friends, and now a tandem.

We opened the regular season in Green Bay, which with its storied history was the Mecca of professional football. Their head coach was none other than Bart Starr, a disciple of the legendary Vince Lombardi. Starr had led the Packers to victories in the first two Super Bowls ever played. We flew into Green Bay on Friday night and stayed in a downtown hotel. Looking around on our way to the hotel, I was reminded of a college town. It was as though I had been there before.

As usual the morning of the game, I got to the stadium two hours before kickoff. Several of us—Tommy Hart, Willie Harper, Frank Nunley—took a taxi to the stadium. It was important to take my time getting dressed, to get taped without hurrying, and most of all to get my mind right, with the help of a little solitude. It would have been easy to get caught up in nostalgia, this being my first game in Lambeau Field. Players and coaches started trickling in from the first bus arriving, with the second one not far behind. The intensity began to build as the players got into their game-day rituals, doing whatever was necessary to get ready for kickoff.

Facial expressions changed. Is he Jekyll or Hyde today? Which one will show? There was no hitting the walls, no kicking-in of bathroom doors or shouting obscenities, just subtle intensity. We had come to accept the changes of feeling that one goes through before a game. The nervous twitch, sweating, and cottonmouth all were called pregame jitters but were all symptoms of fear. You've prepared, now the media are

> *Maybe it was starting my third season*
> *as the number one halfback, along with*
> *the two additional years of maturation,*
> *that now was driving me. Whatever it was,*
> *I was ready to play football.*

around, and there's a reckoning on game day, all of the parts coming together for a crescendo before kickoff. I winked at some and smiled at others to connect. I checked in with Chuck, our trainer, the only person I let tape me. Since the sunglasses prank two seasons before, we had gotten close. Tommy Hart was a quiet assassin. You knew where Ralph McGill and Frank Nunley were, because you could hear them.

Monte's pregame speech was a reminder of what it was going to take to win: know the details of your assignment, execute, minimize mistakes, and have fun. You can be damn sure we were prepared! Playing football sometimes called for motivation other than simply winning. From time to time you must play for something outside of yourself and use that something as a motivator. It was one of the times in my professional career that I felt prepared to play and compete. I had broken my wrist my rookie year and alternated at my position the second year.

Injured Again

Less than a minute into the first quarter, the Packers intercepted a screen pass and ran it in for a touchdown, and were up 7–0. That kind of early mistake is not easy to overcome. It rattles you and can change your mode of thinking, and we were shaken. The next series, we settled down and got into a groove. We put together a fifty-eight-yard, fifteen-play drive. I was running to my left toward a first down, was tripped up by one of the Packers, put my left hand down to break the fall, and a pile of humanity fell on top of me. My hand was under my body. I felt something give, and I couldn't feel my left thumb. I got up, started walking to the sideline, and looked at my thumb. It was dangling, which shocked me. When I got to the sideline, I showed Chuck my thumb and told him what had happened.

I had dislocated my thumb and torn the ligaments. Damn it, what was I going to do? Chuck secured it with some tape for the time being, then looked at me and said, "Okay, try that." I thought, *How will I hold onto the ball?* The pain was delayed because my adrenaline was flowing, but that wouldn't last much longer. Once again, I had to decide to stay in the game, but unlike with my wrist injury two years before, I didn't have much time to think about it. I was more concerned about fumbling than the stability of my thumb. I paced the sideline with ice on my hand. I had played through all the previous pain and injuries to be in this situation. This was the opportunity I had worked for, and I couldn't let it pass.

The Packers fumbled a punt, and we recovered it. I was on the field before I could think about my thumb. We struck quickly when Jim Plunkett hit a wide-open Willie McGee across the middle for our first touchdown. Between series, I put ice on my thumb to keep the pain and swelling at bay. Adrenaline and nothing else could help me when I was hit on it. The defense held, and I was back on the field. Jim called a play to me off left tackle. The hole was wide open, which left me one-on-one with a linebacker. I froze him with a stutter step move and ran toward the sideline of the field. Struggling for twenty yards to stay inbounds, I outran the rest of the defenders to the endzone for a fifty-nine-yard touchdown. McGee scored another touchdown, and we finally put them away, 24–17.

We left Lambeau Field with an opening-day victory. The defensive line would start off their year with four quarterback sacks. It was good to begin the season with a victory, particularly on the road. Normally that would make for a pleasant flight home, but I was in a lot of pain because of my thumb.

The Chicago Bears were our next opponent and home opener. I had my thumb wrapped and taped with foam underneath it. I didn't know if I would play and had only practiced during a walk-through of the offensive plays. I started and struggled with pain and discomfort throughout the game. The Bears beat us, 19–12, and it wasn't close. We didn't score a touchdown until I caught a thirteen-yard touchdown pass late in the fourth quarter. Their defense dominated and shut us down offensively, and they scored enough points to win comfortably. We had regressed and would have to correct our mistakes, concentrating on game films. Practices were more focused than the week before and corrections were made. We went back to Seattle for our third regular game and this time beat the Seahawks, 37–21.

The winless New York Jets with Joe Namath at quarterback came to Candlestick Park for our fourth game of the season. Broadway Joe had a tremendous career and had predicted a Super Bowl III victory and delivered in 1969. However, Joe's ability to maneuver was now limited because of bad knees. Our offense sputtered during the game, and it looked as though we were falling back into losing mode. What we forget sometimes is that no matter the other team's record, our opponents are getting paid to beat us. We were in a battle with the Jets, and they were holding their ground.

In the heat of the battle, one of my shoes came off. I ran to the sideline near Monte to put it on. As I was doing so, he said to me, "If you don't start running, I'm going to take you out of the game." As I headed back onto the field, I looked at him like, "What did you just say?" His comment had come out of left field, because I had been working my ass off and had taken some good hits.

I couldn't get that out of my mind and wondered where it was coming from. I was giving him 100 percent, my best, and I knew it. The longer the game went on, the more I thought about it. I couldn't get rid of it from my consciousness, and it was a distraction. We won the game, 17–6. In the locker room after the game, I asked Monte if I could come by tomorrow and talk with him, He said yes. I had made some mistakes during the season and preseason but never anything to warrant my being taken out of a game. I thought we had a good relationship, not something that would cause him to question my effort. The next day, following our practice, I went in to see Monte.

An Apology—and a Hug

When I walked in his office, he stood up and reached out to shake my hand. I was focused on the issue and was about to start the discussion while we were standing. He suggested I sit down. I began to speak about the incident, but before I could get very far he said, "I was caught up into the heat of the game" and apologized for the comment.

His apology defused the energy around the issue. In fact, I don't think I've ever heard a coach take ownership like that. We talked about several other things, and after about five minutes, the conversation ended. As I was leaving, we shook hands, and he hugged me and said, "I still love you."

It was 1976, and men did not tell men they loved each other. I embraced the concept, but immediately my bullshit detector surfaced. Up to that point, Monte and I had had a good relationship. I had been set up by coaches before, and I had a heightened sensitivity to what they were saying. Monte had been straight with me and made all the right moves to put us in a position to win. I had to accept that this was just a blip on the radar, and it was just that.

After that meeting, Monte never said another word to me about how I was doing on the field. Even though I later fumbled and of course made mistakes, he didn't say a thing, not a word. Aside from Coach Hendricks in high school, it was the beginning of the best player-coach relationship I ever had, particularly in professional football. The fact that you can go out and play with freedom of choice and feel as though you can take chances without being yelled at is the best feeling as a player you can have. One game, I was walking off the field after having made a mistake. I can't remember what it was, but Monte came walking over to me as I was sitting on the bench. I was waiting for him to ask, "What were you thinking about?" Instead, he asked me what plays I liked and what I wanted to run. I took his comment as a demonstration of his trust in me. Although I couldn't tell him what play to call, he freed me up to run.

We were 3–1 and feeling pretty good about ourselves. Next up were the Rams in the Los Angeles Coliseum. The game would be nationally televised on *Monday Night Football*. We were in uncharted waters, tied for first place in our division. A victory Monday night would put us in sole possession of first place in the NFC West. We played the Rams twice a year, and this time something was on the line other than our pride.

The Rams were solid at all positions. Seven of the defensive starters at one point or another in their careers were named to the Pro Bowl. They were Youngblood, Olsen, Dryer, linebackers Isiah Robertson and Jack Reynolds, defensive tackle Larry Brooks, and cornerback Monte Johnson. However, our defensive linemen—Hardman, Elam, Webb, and Hart— came into the game leading the NFL in quarterback sacks as a team.

CHAPTER 11

That night was a game for our defense to shine. Rams quarterback James Harris was sacked ten times by our defensive line. Underrated and often unnoticed Tommy Hart sacked Harris six times.

We held our own offensively and outscored the Rams, 16–0. The big play was a touchdown pass to Willie McGee, after which he tap-danced on the back of the endzone line. It was a great catch! That meant a lot to Willie. The Rams had traded him to the 49ers during training camp. It was good to see him make plays against his former teammates and his idol, Harold Jackson. Our defense was clearly a force to be reckoned with. It was a great win for the team and especially for Monte.

Still More Injuries

I'll always remember the sixth game of that season, against New Orleans. Early in the contest, a pass play was called. Jim was going deep to McGee, and the backs had given him max protection. After blocking my man, I landed on the turf and looked down the field. I saw Willie lying with a leg up in the air and what looked almost like the apex of a triangle. He had broken his femur, and it was not a pretty picture. I ran to where he was. He was just lying there, and it had to be extremely painful by the look on his face. He was gone for the season, which would be a big blow to our offense. Willie drew a lot of attention because of his speed, which opened the secondary. Opposing defenses could not double-cover Gene Washington, our veteran receiver from Stanford. The injury would have a domino effect on our offense.

Later in the game and not long after Willie's injury, I made a cut that put pressure on the big toe on my right foot. The Candlestick artificial turf wouldn't give, and the big toe popped out of joint. We called the stadium "Candlestone" because it had the worst artificial turf in the NFL. Imagine a sidewalk with a thin piece of worn-out rug over it. That's what it felt like when you landed on it. I had what is commonly called turf toe. We beat the Saints, but the bad news was that I was out of next week's game against the Falcons. With the damned injuries, I essentially would miss a game and a half. I hated missing the Atlanta game, but I didn't practice for about three days, and the rest would do me good two weeks later in St. Louis.

But first, after winning the Saints game, we beat the Falcons, 15–0, and we were 6–1 at the halfway mark, just ahead of the 5–1–1 Rams. It was the best start a 49ers team had had in years. The stage was set for a show-down with the St. Louis Cardinals. Our defense had forced nineteen turnovers. The press had named our defensive line the Gold Rush, and they were on their way to a record-setting year with thirty-seven sacks. Jim had thrown ten touchdown passes, and our backfield had run for more than nine hundred yards. We had a good week of practice, prepared well, and were ready.

The Cardinals came into the game with the best offensive linemen in the NFL. Dan Dierdorf, Conrad Dobler, Tom Banks, Bob Young, and Roger Finnie had only a few times picked quarterback Jim Hart up off his fanny after a sack. Their offensive weapons were Mel Gray, Terry Metcalf, and J. V. Cain, and they all were dangerous. J. V. and my roommate, Don Goode, had been high school teammates. Both were chosen in the first round, fifth and fifteenth respectively.

After sitting out against Atlanta, I was champing at the bit to get to play. It was one of those games that didn't require any effort to get up for. CBS was broadcasting it on national television as game of the week.

Against the run, the Cardinals defense was the best in the NFC. Our offensive line, blocking for Wilbur and me, was having a good season. I was looking forward to this one. We were going to be challenged on both sides of the ball, and we were ready! We won the toss, so the first series of the game would be ours.

While I stood on the sidelines waiting to take the field after the kick-off, the damnedest thing happened. The deep backs receiving the ball, Paul Hofer and Bobby Farrell, must have each said to the other "You take it." Both ran past the ball, and the Cardinals recovered it. Right away, we were in a hole. Three plays later, Jim Hart dropped back to pass. Cedric had beaten Dan Dierdorf and had the sack, but he tried to take Hart's head off and missed him. Hart, a crafty veteran quarterback, saw him coming, ducked, stood up, and then hit Cain in the end zone for a touch-down. They took advantage of the gift and struck first: 7–0.

We proceeded to run the ball, and it seemed like we were doing so at will. Before I knew it, we were at the goal line. The next play was to Wilbur. He was stopped at the goal line, and I helped push him into the end zone. It was called back for unnecessary roughness by me. We argued to no avail, and I couldn't believe it. The next play, I ran a dive and scored. It was a new game, 7–7.

The game seesawed back and forth. We had just acquired wide receiver Jim "Whip" Lash, in a trade for Sammy Johnson, to fill Willie McGee's position. He made a couple of great catches that put us in a position to score. He told me, "The next time you run the sweep, give an outside fake to the defensive back, and I will block him."

Sure enough, we set up Cardinal defensive back Roger Wehrli for a twenty-three-yard 49ers touchdown. Our kicker, Steve Mike-Mayer, missed the extra point, so it now was 13–7. Later in the third quarter, he would miss a forty-yard field goal, and in the fourth he would miss a twelve-yard field goal. At the end of the fourth quarter, the score was 20–20, and we were going into overtime.

The Cardinals won the coin toss and ran fullback Jim Otis three times. Our defense held. Standing on the sidelines, I was excited, because I didn't believe they were going to stop us from scoring once we got back on offense. The Cardinals punted the ball to Tony Leonard. As Leonard headed to his right, one of the Cardinals hit his arm, and the ball popped out. The Cardinals recovered and commenced to march down the field and kick a field goal to win the game, 23–20.

Record-Breaking Performance

The defense had played great all day and sacked Jim Hart four times. They won the battle against their offensive line, and offensively we had won the battle against their defense. Kudos to our offensive line and the job they did. I knew I'd had a great game. Unbeknown to me then, I'd had the best day of any 49ers running back in history. I set the single-game record for most yards, 194, and carries, thirty-four, in a game, and scored all three touchdowns.

Someone came over and mentioned the records to me. I was surprised and impressed for a moment. I had no idea that I had that many yards or carries. I was wrapped up in the game and the fact that we lost and should have won. It was my best day ever as a pro running the football, but none of it mattered to our season.

If we had made one field goal or the extra point, things would have been different. As they say, "Would have, should have." The press was all over kicker Steve Mike-Mayer after missing the extra point and the two field goals. We all were looking for someone to blame and hoping it would make us feel better. However, Monte put all of it in perspective in the locker room. Simply put, he said, "He could have won it for us, but he didn't lose it." And he was right.

A reporter asked Monte his thoughts about my achievement. He paused to reflect for a moment and said, "The 49ers have had some great backs over the years, and some of them are even in the Hall of Fame. Delvin has swept past some of them with his performance last week. I think he did a great job. I would just like to see what he does when his foot isn't sore. I had a special feeling about him from the first day we met. He's a winner; he has everything it takes—great speed, good blocking, and fantastic hands. He could be a wide receiver."

Monte later shared with the press about how I had come into his office and told him to feel free to bench me if I didn't do all the things he asked me to do. That was nice of him to say, but the Cardinals still won the game. What an empty feeling!

In the NFL, however, coaches talk about the twenty-four-hour rule. Win or lose, put the game out of your head, strap on the pads, and begin preparing for the next opponent.

12

The NFL season never gets easier as the weeks go on. Little mistakes, if not corrected, can lead to breakdowns on offense, defense, or special teams. Nagging injuries are compounded after repeated blows, with never enough time to heal. Winning and losing both become ingrained.

Washington was our next opponent. We were coming off a close but heavy loss and were picked to win. George Allen and his roster of assorted veterans were coming to Candlestick Park. Our whole team knew we had played well on both sides of the ball, but we needed to bounce back. After my performance against the Cardinals, I was now a marked man. We spent the early part of the week trying to correct what went wrong in the Cardinals game the week before. There were four obvious things you could point to: the opening kickoff debacle, two missed field goals, a missed extra point, and the fumbled punt in overtime. By the end of the week of film and practice, we had licked our wounds and were ready to play.

It was a beautiful day at Candlestick, without a cloud in the sky. Coach Allen had no patience for rookies and the mistakes that came with them, so I knew they were a veteran-laden team. Their job was to stop our running game, including me. I could tell on certain plays that they were not going to let me get outside. It appeared that every time we lined up in the formation, they were reading the toss sweep play. Veterans are smart, but sometimes they're a step slower, and they were positioning themselves to be able to stop the sweep. As such, they were overplaying it.

In the second quarter, we struck first. Plunkett called I-formation toss right. When the ball was snapped, it was as if they knew the play. Three or four of their players had clogged the hole and push our guys into the backfield. I stopped and reversed my field. I got by Chris Hanburger, cut up field, picked up a couple of blocks and by then I was in the open and outran the field untouched for an eighty-yard touchdown. I thought that seemed easy, but by no means would it stay so. We were up against a team that was playoff-bound, as it turned out.

Seven points was a lead that we knew wouldn't hold. Joe Theismann threw back-to-back touchdowns of eighteen and thirty-three yards to Jean Fugett to take the lead, 14–7. A while later it was third down, and we were on our own fifteen-yard line. Jim called a pass play, and I was the safety valve. My assignment was to pick up a linebacker if he blitzed, otherwise find an open spot and be ready. Jim was flushed out of the pocket and rolled to his right, away from me. I was uncovered and ran to an open spot, and nobody picked me up. Jim saw me. It was just me and Redskins linebacker Harold McClinton, and I was hoping no one else was around. I could beat him in open space. That was the scenario, and when I caught the ball, I gave him a move. Pat Fisher and Kenny Houston couldn't catch me. It was an eighty-five-yard touchdown pass that tied the score at 14–14 before halftime.

In the third quarter, the Theismann-to-Fugett combination connected again for a three-yard touchdown to make it 21–14 Redskins. In the fourth quarter, we put together a drive to Washington's twenty-two-yard line. I was thinking first down, but tackle Keith Fahnhurst, Wilbur at fullback, and Tom Mitchell—the best blocking tight end I played with—made their blocks, and I could have walked in for the touchdown that tied the score, 21–21. On our next possession, we had a good drive going. Jim threw a short pass to me, and when I turned around, it was just Kenny and me destined for a collision. Before I could get my head down, he got just enough of his elbow through my face mask to hit me in the eye.

I left the game seeing double and thought it would be all right, but it got worse. I went back in the game, thinking I could work through it, but it was not to be. With a little over eight minutes left. I was done. The next series we were three and out. Time was running. Theismann had been evading the rush all day and had already thrown three touchdowns. They were set up for a long field goal, but Theismann faked it, ran around the right end and picked up the first down. With less than two minutes to go, Mark Mosley kicked a field goal to make it 24–21 for a Redskins win.

It was frustrating to be on the sidelines with nothing I could do to help my team. We had battled another NFC contender and lost again. There were no missed field goals, and there was no one to blame. There was still time on the clock as I met Kenny on the field. He wanted to know how I was doing and apologized. I teased him about our earlier collision, but it was all in the game. That was football.

Missed Opportunities

It was those two games with Washington and St. Louis that fueled my desire for my team to win it all. I would think thought about those two 1976 games over the years, wondering what happened, how we lost, and what we might have done differently.

The Falcons, whom we had shut out three weeks earlier, were our next opponent. We flew into Atlanta and hadn't finished licking our wounds. They seized the moment and beat us, 21–16, after we led 10–7 going into the fourth quarter. If there were ever a time when "On any given Sunday, anybody can be beaten in the NFL," it was that day. Mr. Hendricks used to tell us all the time, "You take a sledgehammer to kill a gnat!" When you have someone down, put them away. Although Wilbur and I had respectable games, the offense sputtered, while the defense held their own. Atlanta to San Francisco was always a long flight, and having lost the game made it even longer.

> *When two teams play at such a high level with something on the line, it consumes you.*

The Rams were the reigning NFC Western Division champions. They were a proud bunch and an All-Pro-laden team. We had previously dominated them on *Monday Night Football* in their house. We knew they were coming to Candlestick Park with chips on their shoulders. Chuck Knox, their head coach, one of the best to ever coach in the NFL, personified intensity. All coaches tried to work the officials, but he had a lot of success with it. Sherman White played defensive end for the Buffalo Bills when Chuck was their head coach. He talked about how he would get in the officials' faces, and I won't repeat their conversations. He also said Chuck was a veterans' coach and treated them like men. All he asked was to be professional and ready to play on Sunday.

There was no doubt they were ready to play. They held us to eighty-eight yards total offense and beat us 23–3. It wasn't close. The loss to the Rams was another blow to our pride, and we lost Cedric Hardman for the season. Cedric was the consummate defensive end and at that point was the team leader in sacks. The emotional leader of the defensive lineman who were leading the League in quarterback sacks broke his ankle. A consummate football player, instead of using the ambulance to get him off the field, he told the doctor, "Get a couple of the boys to come and get him."

The Minnesota Vikings, who already had clinched the NFC Central Division title and were in the playoffs with a 9–1–1 record, were our next opponent. It was our second Monday night game, but we were playing this one at home. In each of my two years on the team, we played the Vikings and lost. In my rookie year, Carl Eller had taught me a lesson: backs should look out for defensive ends when going out for a pass.

Jim had struggled during our four-game losing streak because of injuries. He was playing hurt, but no one really knew how much punishment he was taking. He took injections in his rib cage before games and never complained. During the Washington game, I missed an assignment on a blitz pick-up. Jim was blindsided by outside linebacker Brad Dusek, the guy I was supposed to block. All I could do was help him get up. I told him it was my fault, as if he didn't know that, but he didn't say a word.

Clash with the Vikings

The Vikings mirrored the Rams with a stable organization and experienced players at each position. They had two players on defense who had made the 1975 Pro Bowl—Jeff Siemon and Alan Page. Jim Marshall and Carl Eller had made previous Pro Bowls. Although Doug Sutherland and Wally Hilgenberg had not, they were good enough as well. Their defense had been great for a long time. However, Monte was the offensive line coach when the Dolphins beat the Vikings in the 1974 Super Bowl. With rookie Scott Bull as our starting quarterback to give Jim's cracked ribs a chance to heal, we figured the Vikings would be going after him and try shaking him up. With its bend-but-don't-break philosophy, their defense was known to be vulnerable to the run.

Our plan was to establish the running game, stay away from their intelligence, and run right at them. We had our first three plays set up before the game. Today they call that scripting. As a matter of fact, some teams script up to the first fifteen plays. Wilbur and I, along with the offensive line, accepted the challenge and were up to the task. In the locker room before the game, Monte reminded us we were not out of the playoffs. He invoked character in his speech, challenging us.

The Vikings won the toss and elected to receive. Our defense did its job and forced them to punt. We followed the game plan and ran right at them. Our first series, we drove fifty-one yards on eight consecutive run plays, and Wilbur scored the game's first touchdown from the one-yard line. By the end of the second quarter, we were leading, 10–0. It would end up being a night to remember for the offense. I knew going in that I needed 141 yards to reach 1,000. Cas Banaszak, our offensive tackle, who did not play, said he would keep track for me on the sideline. I didn't think too much about it until the fourth quarter, with us ahead 17–16. The measurement for good running backs is one thousand yards in a season, then fourteen games long (it would be expanded to sixteen games in 1978). Every running back dreamed about reaching that plateau, and I was no different.

We had a second and six at our own fifteen-yard line. Alan Page got penetration at the snap of the ball, and I had to cut back, and I then ran straight upfield. It was a twenty-four-yard run that put me over one thousand yards. I was the first 49er to do that since J. D. Smith in 1959. Wilbur and I would both rush for over one hundred yards that game. The last time two 49ers had rushed for more than one hundred yards in the same game had been in 1971 (Ken Willard and Vic Washington). With our rookie at quarterback, we ran on fifty-four of our sixty-two offensives play for 317 yards rushing. At game's end, we had won 20–16 against the Vikings, who would go on to win the NFC. I couldn't say enough about our offense—wide receivers Gene Washington and Jim Lash; tight end Tom Mitchell; guards Andy Mauer and Steve Lawson; center Randy Cross; linemen Jean Barrett, John Watson, Cas Banaszek and Keith Fahnhorst; and my roommate and running mate, Wilbur Jackson.

Scott didn't have a good game at quarterback, completing only three of his eight passes while being intercepted once, but he was good enough, even running twice, including scoring a touchdown from the one-yard line. The best part of my reaching one thousand yards was that we won the game against a quality opponent (who would lose to the Oakland Raiders in the Super Bowl at season's end).

Wilbur was back in form and posted his best game of the year, with thirty carries for 156 yards and a touchdown. I had twenty carries for 153 yards. It was only the third time in NFL history that two running backs on the same team rushed for 150 yards or more. The others were Jim Brown and Bobby Mitchell in 1960 with the Browns, and John Riggins and Emerson Boozer in 1972 with the Jets.

When Monte was interviewed, he said, "We felt we had to get the pressure off our young quarterback, so we stressed the running game all week in practice. Plus, we didn't make any mistakes. We didn't have any costly fumbles or interceptions. I have never been prouder of this team than I am right now. They played as good of a game as they have all year, but it makes me wonder. Del and Wilbur did an outstanding job running against the Minnesota defense, which is one of the best areas, and I can't help but think if we had been able to run this way all season things might have been a little different."

We took our 7–5 record to San Diego in a must-win situation. Jim tried his best and was seven of thirteen passing with an interception when he came out for Scott Bull. While completing only three of eight, Scott hit rookie Paul Hofer to tie the low-scoring game at 7–7, which went into overtime. The game was decided when Mercury Morris, after seven seasons with the Dolphins, now twenty-nine years old and in his final year, went thirteen yards for a touchdown on only his second carry of the game. I got 104 yards and even completed an eighteen-yard pass, but it wasn't enough. Steve Mike-Mayer missed three field-goal attempts that let victory slip away once again in overtime, and now we were surely out of the playoffs at seven wins and six loses. This was another loss that could have been a victory, and once again it was a desultory loss.

Off to New Orleans, we had one last game to have a winning record. Starting for the injured Plunkett, Scott played well, completing fourteen of twenty-eight passes, with a touchdown to Gene Washington, as we won handily, 27–7. I got eighty-seven yards, closing out my season with 1,203 rushing yards in thirteen games with an average of 4.9 yards per carry, finishing second to O. J. I averaged 92.5 yards per game, including that minus-nine-yard game against the Rams. My total yards of 1,203 and game average of 92.5 yards per game beat Joe Perry's 1954 club record of 1,049 yards and 87.5 yards per game, set when the season was twelve games.

As a team, we had squeaked out an 8–6 record in 1976, with two losses coming in overtime. But as we had set the bar high by starting off 6–1, the second half of the season ended in a disappointing 2–5. On top of my record year, Wilbur Jackson had gained 792 yards, with an average of 4.0 yards per carry, which was better than his rookie year of 705 yards. Wilbur and I had a combined 1,995 yards rushing for the season. Our rushing offense was fifth in the league, but the passing offense was twenty-third in yards and twenty-second in interceptions. The defense had been solid, finishing second in the NFL in combined yards allowed and leading the NFL with sixty-one quarterback sacks. Although the offense still had a way to go to measure up, we had closed the gap to other teams with the running game.

It turned out to be a great year for me. My accomplishments matched those in my dreams. I broke and set the team's twenty-two-year-old single-season rushing record while having missed one game, as well as single-game records of most yards and carries in a game. I finished third behind O. J. Simpson and Walter Payton in rushing and second to Walter in rushing in the NFC, and I made the Pro Bowl, to be played January 17, 1977. I would finish in the top ten in ten NFL offensive categories. It was a breakthrough season for me, and I was all of twenty-five years old, prime time for a running back.

But in two out of my first three years in the NFL I would need surgery. I had bone grafted out of my hip to repair a break in my wrist. I dislocated the big and small toe on my right foot and tore the ligaments in my left thumb. When I injured both, I had a choice to make. I chose to continue. If I hadn't played, none of my accomplishments on the field would have happened. However, there was one piece of unfinished business.

Welcome to the Pro Bowl

I walked in the NFC locker room at the Pro Bowl and saw Charlie Sanders and Lem Barney of the Lions talking to one another. I looked to my left. and there was Conrad Dobler. Roger Staubach made a motion as though he was explaining a pass play to Ron Jessie. I waved at Kenny Houston, and at that moment I saw O. J. Simpson talking to Chuck Knox. Knox was the head coach of the Los Angeles Rams and was serving in that capacity for the NFC. Chuck Knoll of the Pittsburgh Steelers was the head coach for the AFC. Chuck Knox had a cigar between his fingers when he saw us, the 49er contingent of Tommy Hart, linebacker Dave Washington, Cleveland Elam, and *me* walking into the locker room.

The game was going to be played at the Kingdome in Seattle. It was the first year for the Seattle Seahawks, so they would get to be the host of the Pro bowl. Chuck asked O. J. if he knew us, and he said yes and shook our hands. When he got to me, he said, "Delvin, you're having a good year up there in my town," referring to San Francisco, his hometown. It was my first time meeting Juice, but the conversation was as if I had known him all my life. It was indicative of the charismatic person he was. There he was in the NFC locker room talking to the head coach and on a first-name basis with everybody. He cracked a joke with Chuck and left smiling.

After Chuck finished talking with O. J., he walked back over to the four of us. Smiling, with the cigar in his mouth, he said, "Yes, the 49ers. You guys had a good year . . . you came down to L.A. and kicked our ass on *Monday Night Football*." We all smiled as he continued, but his smile was replaced with an intense look when he added: "But I told my guys, there's nothing wrong with getting your ass kicked . . . but the test of a man is: will he get up?" I knew right then I liked Chuck Knox and would have enjoyed playing for him. We all laughed, and I responded by saying, "You guys came up there and kicked our ass, and it wasn't close." He appreciated my response, and it was true. They beat us 23–3, and I had minus-nine yards rushing.

It was an honor to represent the NFC in the Pro Bowl ending the 1976 season. I was chosen by my peers and the coaches, which made it special to me. The respect of peers is the highest recognition I could ask for. In 1976 O. J. Simpson led the NFL in rushing, Walter Payton was second, and I finished third. My dreams were coming true and falling like dominoes. By playing in the Pro Bowl, another dream would come to pass. The other running backs were Mike Thomas of the Redskins and Lawrence McCutcheon of the Rams. Walter Payton and I would be the starters.

Playing with and being around these guys at this level of talent would elevate my game and understanding of the responsibility that came with being there. The same observations I had about professional athletes my rookie year were evident in my first Pro Bowl. One day in practice, I was thrown a pass out in the flats. Kenny Houston and Isiah Robertson were defending. I was about to turn upfield when Kenny came up to take away the cutback. In doing so he shouted to Isiah, "Outside, outside, outside!" It was an alert to Isiah that he had the outside—the sideline—covered as they closed in on me. The on-field communication made it clear that these guys had been there before.

It was a small thing, and some might say, "So what?" But to me it spoke volumes about their experience and communication, especially because it was our first practice session, and these two weren't ordinarily teammates. The people who play their positions can appreciate it and the value in their communication. It reaffirmed the importance of being a student of the game. About not guessing what you should do but *knowing* what to do. What I had been studying and trying to learn was the right thing to do. Finally, it confirmed Monte's mantra of knowing the details of your assignment.

I hadn't seen Ron Jessie since he left KU. He had been there during the John Riggins days, when we didn't do a lot of passing. Jessie overcame the setback of being a receiver on a running team at KU, but now he was playing in the Pro bowl. We talked and reminisced about our time at Kansas.

Most of the players socialized with their teammates, but I spent some time with Lem Barney. He was upbeat, and we laughed a lot as we connected. He knew Marvin Gaye and shared a story with us. After the death of singer Tammi Terrell, Marvin fell into a deep depression. Lem and other friends would stop by to try and get him out of the house. One day he got a call from Marvin, and he asked Lem and other friends to come over. When Lem arrived, he told him what he'd been working on—the album *What's Going On*! The rest is history. It was a transcendent album ahead of its time. As I write today, the album is more than fifty years old and still relevant. It was quite revealing of Marvin and his experience of love, loss, and pain, all from a spiritual perspective. That was how it came about. Lem contributed background vocals on the album and received a Grammy for it.

What's Going On. What was about to go on for *me* was a change of owners, then coaches, and finally teams.

13

The NFL rumor mill was working overtime as the new season began in 1977, with the 49ers at the center of many of the rumors.

The one that would affect me most directly said the team was being sold, with former Oakland Raider owner Wayne Valley being mentioned as a possible buyer. Once a general partner with the Raiders, he had struggled with Al Davis for control and lost after a bitter court battle. As it turned out, Davis had worked behind the scenes to stall Valley while contacting Joe Thomas, who recently had been fired as general manager of the Baltimore Colts. Thomas in turn contacted Ohio developer Edward DeBartolo Sr.

As the story goes, Thomas, the former director of player personnel for the Vikings and Dolphins, after being fired by Miami in 1971, arranged for Robert Irsay to purchase the Los Angeles Rams. Irsay then swapped ownerships with Carroll Rosenbloom of the Baltimore Colts, and in 1972 Thomas became general manager of the Colts, who had won the Super Bowl V in January 1971. Thomas fired Super Bowl–winning head coach Don McCafferty after five games in the 1972 season.

That winter, in January 1973, he traded Johnny Unitas to San Diego and drafted Bert Jones, a star quarterback out of LSU. Thomas then went through five head coaches over five years, including himself, going 2–9 in 1974. In 1975 Jones came into his own, and he was the NFL MVP in 1976. The Colts made the playoffs three seasons in a row (1975–77), only to run into the Pittsburgh Steelers twice. When Thomas moved to fire coach Ted Marchibroda after 1976, Irsay let Thomas go.

On March 7, 1977, one month to the day after my surgery, the widows of the Morabito brothers sold the 49ers to the Edward J. DeBartolo Corporation of Youngstown, Ohio, for roughly $20 million. DeBartolo Sr. turned over the team to his son, Eddie Jr., then thirty. In one sense, the ownership went from one family to another, but it also went from two sisters-in-law to a multimillion-dollar corporation.

Eddie Jr. wanted to hire Thomas to take over some of the general manager duties, including director of player personnel, which Monte had been handling, as well as other duties. Monte was offered more money and an extended contract if he gave up his player personnel duties to Joe. Monte and Joe had both been on the staff together with the Miami Dolphins when Joe handled personnel and Monte coached the offensive line.

Hearing all this, Cedric and I stopped by Monte's house to discuss the situation with him. He said he was not going to give up the player personnel responsibility. Though he had not really had a good relationship with Joe, he was willing to work with him but not without having control of who was on his team. Several days later, on April 6, 1977, the newspaper announced that Monte was gone—"resigned" was the word—and that Joe Thomas was the new general manager.

Everybody was surprised, especially me. Monte had put an offense together that had bolstered the running game, allowing me to maximize my abilities. The team was better than when I had joined in 1974 because of what Monte had brought to the organization. We had established a great player-coach relationship.

Now, after a single season with a new coaching staff, the entire upper level administration had been swept clean, although many of the assistant coaches would be retained. What would this mean for me? Thomas's Colts had featured more than Jones's prolific passing. They had a running game that featured Lydell Mitchell.

I had always been told that NFL stands for "Not for long."

Mitchell had been drafted by the Colts in 1972, before Thomas arrived, and he'd had back-to-back thousand-yard seasons in 1975 and 1976, with 1,193 and 1,200 yards. (He'd make that three straight years, with 1,159 in 1977.) Also, in 1975 Thomas had drafted

Roosevelt Leaks, the first great black fullback for Texas, who had rushed for 342 yards against SMU before a knee injury ended his senior year. (It would limit his production in pro ball too.) Leaks inspired Tyler, Texas, high schooler Earl Campbell to attend the University of Texas.

Ken Meyer Takes Over

Thomas hired Ken Meyer as the new 49ers head coach for 1977. Unlike Monte's lineman build of six foot six and 260 pounds, Ken was five foot ten and weighed 160 pounds. That he didn't have Monte's size or pro experience was a message to us regarding the dominance that Joe must have wanted to exert.

Ken did have a deep coaching background, although not as a head coach. He had been an assistant under Bear Bryant at Alabama, where he worked with quarterbacks Joe Namath and Ken Stabler. Dick Nolan had hired him in 1968 to help coach the offensive backs. The following year, Ken moved to the Jets in the same role, earning himself a Super Bowl ring. After four years, he became the offensive coordinator for the Los Angeles Rams.

Elijah Pitts, the former Packers halfback, was the Rams running backs coach, but Ken had installed the Rams offense. We thought it was methodical and predictable. Around the league, head coach Chuck Knox was known by the nickname "Ground Chuck." But the Rams kept winning the division with it, and Lawrence McCutcheon kept topping one thousand yards each season, which was fine with me.

Because Coach Knox had brought along his staff to the Pro Bowl, I already had met Ken. He seemed personable enough, as well as knowledgeable and likeable. I had reason to still be optimistic about the upcoming season despite the coaching change. We were coming off a good season, and most of the team was returning. Of the starters, star defensive back Jimmy Johnson had retired after the 1976 season, just before his thirty-ninth birthday. Frank Nunley, the Fudgehammer, who at age thirty-one had been our starting middle linebacker, also retired.

The 1976 season was my last under the three-year rookie contract I signed out of college. Having set the team's rushing record for most yards in a game, plus being a major contributor to the team's first winning record since 1972, I didn't think negotiating a new contract was going to be difficult. Joe Thomas was known for being shrewd but could be fair when it came to salaries. I had talked myself into feeling good about a new contract with its promise of significantly more money and was looking forward to getting it behind me so I could get past the transition from Monte and concentrate on the upcoming season.

Assuming I would be rewarded, I started looking for a new home that was not quite as packed into a neighborhood as was my house in San Carlos, and without all those steps. I needed an agent for my new negotiation and was introduced to Maurice Shaw. I felt confident about his ability and hired him. Because Maury also was a real estate agent, I asked him to start looking for another home for me.

Maury found a house in Los Altos Hills. Like my home in San Carlos, it was a three-bedroom, two-bath house on about a quarter-acre, tucked away in the hills with only a couple of other homes nearby, unlike where I'd been living. It also had a swimming pool, which would not have made sense in San Carlos, situated in the wind corridor blowing from the fog bank that often sat on the ridge to the west. I bought it and moved in during the beginning of the summer.

Playing Hardball

Meanwhile, negotiations weren't going well. One day before training camp started, I was sitting on the steps in front of the pool, thinking about my financial decision to buy the house and concerned about the $1,135 monthly mortgage payment. Though times have since changed dramatically with the price of Bay Area real estate, my salary was only $55,000 a year before taxes. I had been counting on getting a raise and now was fretting over getting it done and how much it would be.

Frustrated with the process, I decided to cut off negotiations and was prepared to play out my option at the already established price so I could concentrate on getting ready for the season. In two out of my first three years in the NFL, I had played hurt and had delayed double surgeries until the off-season. I hadn't missed many games and felt that Joe wasn't serious about getting me signed to a fair deal. I was starting to get the sense that he had no concern about what was in both of our best interests.

I had thought the organization would reward those who did what it took to help the team win, even to the point of playing through injury.

I was naïve in thinking that management cared about what was important for the player.

In the last week of camp, we finally agreed to a two-year contract, worth $285,000 for two years. It was more money than I had ever had in my life, and I felt comfortable with it. In my rookie year, I was just happy to be there and was anxious about making the team. The money then was more than that I ever had, but it wasn't as important as it was to establish myself. However, this time around I had earned my salary and had physically paid a price for it.

In our negotiations and before I signed a contract, Joe verbally agreed with me to make this year's preseason pay retroactive to reflect my new salary, because I already had received my preseason draw. Pleased it was all over it, I was eager to move on to football and get to work. New head coaches often bring a new system with them, which means having to spend time studying and learning new schemes and terminologies. Instead of installing a new offense, Ken adjusted to the system we were using. I give him credit for making the transition as smooth as possible.

There was one additional change: our head trainer, Chuck Krpata, had left the 49ers to start his own physical therapy business. His assistant, Fred Schwaky, now was in charge of the training room.

During the 1977 season, I had this feeling that I was not being used properly. I was taken out of the games for no reason. It was beyond my understanding. I knew then that something was afoot. I thought something was going to happen.

There were rumors that the 49ers were going to trade for O. J. Simpson. At first, I didn't think too much about it because O. J. had turned thirty and had knee surgery the previous year, appearing in only seven games. Beat reporters started calling me, asking me about the rumors and how I felt about them. I once commented that we were both halfbacks, so who was going to block? A running back needs to stay in the flow of the game to be productive.

By season's end, I had gained 931 yards, down from 1,203 yards the year before. Wilbur had 780 yards, just below his mark of 792 yards the season before. Our rushing offense was still in the league's top ten though we had fallen from fifth to tenth. Each of us had scored seven rushing touchdowns, and I'd had two touchdowns on pass receptions. O. J. had gained 557 yards in half a season with Buffalo, not bad, but with no touchdowns.

Our 1977 season had begun with five straight losses followed by four straight wins, then a split of two games, and then three straight losses at the end, leaving us 5–9. Not good.

After the season, the trade rumors persisted. From one standpoint, a trade of O. J. Simpson would make sense. O. J. could be valuable as an attendance draw, because he was the league's most famous running back still active. Also, he had been a local hero both at San Francisco's Galileo High School and at City College of San Francisco for two years before attending USC. But would they really trade me for him? Based on my past record and being at my peak, they could rebuild by getting young players and draft choices by trading me instead of acquiring a running back who might have little left. I had one more year on my contract, and they would not have to pay my salary if I were traded, but they would have to pay O. J. something substantial.

I had figured I would end my career in San Francisco. I owned a new home in Los Altos Hills. I didn't want to be traded, even if it meant going to a better team. When they finally did deal for O. J., I knew it was only a matter of time before I was traded. The price to get O. J. was steep: second- and third-round picks in 1978, a first-round selection in 1979, and second- and fourth-round picks in 1980. It wasn't hard to figure out that when the team made the deal for him, I was history. I heard that I was being shopped around, and it disappointed me.

Traded to Miami

On April 17, 1978, my twenty-eighth birthday, Joe Thomas called to tell me I had been traded to the Miami Dolphins. In exchange, the Dolphins would send two players, wide receiver Freddie Solomon and safety Vern Roberson. In addition, the 49ers would get first- and fifth-round draft choices, a four-for-one deal. I didn't have time to think of the ramifications, and I said to him, "Joe, if you were a woman, I would kiss you!" That was for sending me to a top-notch team.

I put on a good face, and there was some happiness about the prospects of being traded to Miami, but I didn't want to go. I would have to leave my friends, teammates, and the other connections in my life of the preceding few years for the unknown. Sitting on the steps to my pool, not knowing what to make of it, I spent a few hours that day sifting through the changes I would face, wallowing in sadness.

The DeBartolo Corporation came in and made it clear in their first press conference that pro football a business. I remember Eddie saying, "We're not here to placate to anyone. We are here to run a business."

Joe never did come through with the prorated pay increase for my 1977 preseason play based on the salary that we agreed upon as the regular season started. When Joe later didn't pay that increase, there was confusion about it from the NFL management council as to whether he would or not. In a letter dated March 12, 1978, from the owners' lawyer Sargent Karch to Ed Garvey of the NFL Players Association states, "Now that Del Williams has been traded to Miami, Don Shula has called to ask about the status of Williams' grievance against the 49ers. I advised Shula that the Players Club Relations Committee (PCRC) decided at its meeting in San Francisco that Williams lost the grievance, but [New York Giants owner] Well Mara agreed to talk to Joe Thomas to see whether Thomas would voluntarily pay the difference for the sake of relations with the player."

The letter went on to say, "Apparently, the O.J. trade and consequent Williams trade were already in Thomas' mind and he therefore chose not to make the voluntary payment. Shula's only concern was that Williams know of the PCRC's decision." My thanks to the Mara family for the patriarch's compassion for the position I was in. It started an intimate, but conflicted relationship between the NFLPA, NFLRB, and forty years later, it's still unresolved.

The Hard Reality

What we were being told as kids and bought into was a different game than what we were playing as professionals. It's like trying to put a round peg into a square hole. When it comes to the game, we're like toddlers trying to make sense out of it. However, when you tell us it's a business, that's like an adult telling their toddler, "keep trying, it's going to fit!" It's incongruent, and we can't reconcile it and make it fit.

All the emotion, passion, and craziness that we go through in retirement I believe is because we're being forced to try to put a round peg into a square hole. It does not work. We didn't think about the game as a business. We are not robots. You can't industrialize emotion, passion, and the sheer joy of the competition. I thought what I had done for the team mattered and was valued by the organization. It did, but only for the good of the organization. But like many of my peers, I didn't know that then. Everybody I knew who played was drawn to it because of the game. But some were drawn to the industry because of money.

> *You can't industrialize passion.*

I know it's a business, but we're still locked into the game, and being part of a team is hard to let go of. We don't think about the business side of it, and so we have a false sense of what our value is to the organization. I thought those 49er rushing records set in 1976 under Monte were valued by the organization. They were, but only for use by the organization.

I found out later that the Baltimore Colts were concerned about their division opponent Miami acquiring me and had offered a package that included tight end Raymond Chester and several other players. Thomas told me that my trade to the Dolphins was a good one for both me and the 49ers. I again thanked him for trading me to a good team and wished him good luck.

After my conversation with Thomas, Coach Shula called me. He let me know that they were happy to get me and were looking forward to my coming to Miami. He said, "Giving up first- and fifth-round draft choices, Vern Robison, and Freddie Solomon tells you what we think of you."

I shared my enthusiasm about being a part of the Dolphins' rich history, and I looked forward to being a part of the organization. Good-bye, Bay Area, and hello, South Beach.

14

I was grateful that Miami, like San Francisco, was a warm-weather city. But that is where the similarities ended.

You can't get much farther away from the Bay Area than South Beach without leaving the country. While the 49ers were an established franchise in the National Football Conference, the Dolphins were a relatively young team in the American Football Conference. They first began playing in the aging Orange Bowl in 1966.

It hadn't taken long for the Dolphins to become successful, however. In 1972 they had a perfect season, with a record of 17–0 and a victory in Super Bowl VII over Washington. No team has done that since (although the regular season since has been expanded from fourteen to sixteen games). A year later, Miami became the first AFC team to win consecutive Super Bowls when they beat the Minnesota Vikings.

Much of the credit for that success went to Don Shula, who would eventually retire as the winningest coach in NFL history. (Shula, who died in 2020, coached the Baltimore Colts from 1963 through 1969 and then the Dolphins from 1970 through 1995.) His high-powered Miami offense for a time featured quarterback Bob Griese, wide receiver Paul Warfield, and running backs Mercury Morris and the tandem of Jim Kiick and Larry Csonka, who were known as Butch Cassidy and to the Sundance Kid.

So, when I hung the phone up after speaking with Joe Thomas, I realized that professionally it was a good opportunity, even if it did not feel that way. The 1976 season had been the only time the 49ers had been close to getting in the playoffs while I was there. We finished 8–6, and we easily would have been 10–4 if we had made two field goals, but the person who got us there was fired. I believed in what Monte Clark was trying to do, and we all felt that way.

Most of the Dolphins coaching staff went back a long ways with Shula. Carl Taseff, the running backs coach, had been Shula's college roommate at John Carroll and the best man at his wedding. They both had played for the Cleveland Browns as rookies in 1951 and then for the Colts from 1953 to 1956. After leaving the Colts in 1956, Shula had played one more season with the Washington Redskins before becoming an assistant college coach for two seasons and then joining the Detroit Lions. Carl had been on the Dolphins staff since Don became head coach in 1970. The offensive line coach, John Sandusky, also had been with the 1951 Browns, as a tackle, having been a rookie the year before. He was an assistant with the Colts when Shula took over as head coach and retained him. Sandusky remained when Shula left and even coached the last nine games in 1972 after Don McCafferty was fired. After moving on to the Eagles, he joined Shula's Miami staff in 1976.

Tom Keane was the defensive backs coach. He had joined the Colts as a cornerback in 1953 for two years, joining fellow defensive backs Taseff and Shula. The defensive line coach was Mike Scarry, known as "Mo Scary." He was the old man of the staff at fifty-eight and had been a pro coach for only three seasons before joining the Dolphins in 1970. He had been a head coach for three seasons in the mid-1960s at Waynesburg College in Pennsylvania, where he played as an undergrad. Professionally, he had played for the Cleveland Rams from 1944 through 1945. When the Rams moved to Los Angeles, he stayed in Cleveland for two years, signing with the Browns of the newly formed All-America Football Conference, where the 49ers and Colts also got their start.

High Expectations

After finishing 6–8 in 1976, the Dolphins had bounced back to 10-4 in 1977, tied with Baltimore for first place in the division. But the Colts got the playoff spot because of a better conference record. The Dolphins were looking for another piece of the puzzle.

I was deluged with phone calls from friends and the Miami press between the time the trade was announced and minicamp began. The press asked me: "What will you bring to the Dolphins? Do you believe you will make a difference?"

Behind each question was an implication that the Dolphins had given up a lot to get me and, accordingly, expected a lot in return. I wanted to make it clear that I was not coming to Miami to lead them to the Promised Land, better known as the Super Bowl. I absolutely knew I wanted to get there with them, but it would take a team effort, and I was just one player.

My first goal was to make sure I fit in. I felt the pressure, which I embraced, but I wanted to dispel expectations that my presence would offset any other team shortcomings or allow others to just sit back and watch.

I arrived at the airport for minicamp and was greeted by an explosion of flashbulbs (I am dating myself here). A Dolphins assistant trainer introduced himself and said the reporters were there for me. I hadn't been warned that a makeshift press conference would take place. I got the same line of questioning that I had been hit with already, and it would continue all the way up to the first game. This was even before ESPN was launched a year later. Unlike the San Francisco Bay Area with its multiple football and baseball franchises as well as pro basketball, Miami had only the Dolphins as a professional team at that time.

My first day in Miami was hot and muggy, the kind of weather you can only get that far south. The Dolphins' training facility was on the campus of a small college called Biscayne, now known as St. Thomas University. I was shocked when I walked into the locker room, expecting at least a modern facility for a two-time Super Bowl–winning franchise. The lockers were run-down, with outdated green shag carpet in the locker room.

Putting my things down, I went to meet with Coach Shula, who welcomed me to the team and said they were happy to have me. We talked football, as I had in my first meeting with Monte. I reassured Coach Shula of my commitment to the team and that I was there to help the team win a championship. Just as I had told Monte two years earlier, I said that if benching me was needed to help the team win, I would not hold it against him.

It was a good meeting. He asked me if there was anything else pending he needed to know, and I said no, there wasn't. About to walk out of his office, I thought about the grievance I had filed with the NFL Players Association (NFLPA) against the 49ers regarding the salary matter. So far, I had not heard the outcome but figured that, with his prestige and contacts, Coach Shula could get an answer for me. I explained the situation and asked if he could find out if there was a decision in my case. He said he would check on it and let me know.

"Getting him is going to make us better," Shula said later to the press. "I wouldn't have made the trade if I didn't think so."

I didn't want to let him down or disappoint Monte, who had recommended me to the Dolphins. It also was the second and final year on my 49ers contract that Miami had acquired. If I had a good year, the next contract would take care of itself. Along with everything else, I wanted to stay healthy, both so I could make my mark with the team and bolster my own career.

The only player I knew on the team was middle linebacker Steve Towle, who had been a year behind me at KU. A good guy, he had set a Dolphins team record for tackles in 1976, his second year, and had been voted team MVP.

Meeting the Team

Once in the locker room, I began meeting my new teammates, such as veterans Bob Griese, Jim Langer, and Larry Little. Defensive back Norris Thomas, a rookie the year before, would become one of my closest friends. I also met tight end Andre Tillman, who I learned was from Dallas; veteran safety Tim Foley; running back Don Nottingham; and fullback Leroy Harris, who presented himself as one not lacking in confidence. Everybody I met was cordial. Although I didn't hear anything directly, I was told that there were questions and doubts about my touted ability as a running back, particularly among the existing backs. I didn't blame them, because I probably would have felt the same way about someone new reputed to be taking over a starting role.

Harris would be the starting fullback, having started five games in 1977, his rookie season, gaining 417 yards, including a seventy-seven-yard touchdown run. He had rushed for more than one thousand yards during his senior year at Arkansas State. The other fullbacks were older: Norm Bulaich, age thirty-two, from Galveston, and Don Nottingham, twenty-seven. They had broken in with Baltimore in 1970 and 1971, respectively, after Shula left after the 1969 season for the Dolphins.

Bulaich had come to the Dolphins in 1975 after two seasons with Philadelphia and after Larry Csonka jumped from Miami to the fledgling WFL. Nottingham, nicknamed "The Human Bowling Ball" because of his short stature and thick torso, had been traded to Miami during the 1973 season. Csonka had been the man, gaining more than one thousand yards in 1971–73, and carrying thirty-three times for 145 yards and two touchdowns in the Super Bowl VII victory over the Vikings. In 1977 Bulaich had been a sometime starter at fullback, gaining 416 yards to Nottingham's 214.

One halfback was Benny Malone, age twenty-six, from Tyler, Texas. He had been drafted out of Arizona State University in 1974, just two ahead of me. The other back, Gary Davis, twenty-four, from Cal Poly, San Luis Obispo, was drafted 174th in 1976. I was a little taller at six feet, compared to each of them at five foot ten. Malone, who was drafted forty-seventh overall in 1974, didn't become a full-time starter until 1976. In 1977 he had started eight games and carried 129 times for 615 yards and five touchdowns. Davis had started the other six games, gaining 533 yards on 126 carries with two touchdowns.

With the 49ers in 1976, I pretty much had matched their combined totals, carrying 268 times to their 255 and equaling their seven rushing touchdowns. My total yardage of 931 was less than theirs added together, but the year before I had gained 1,203 yards to Benny's 797 yards, while rookie Gary had hardly run the ball. The circumstance was not created for competition, production was expected.

Monte Clark had been Miami's offensive line coach from 1970 to 1975. He was quoted as saying, "Delvin's gonna think he's gone to heaven once he runs behind that offensive line." These guys were all experienced veterans still in their early thirties. Tackle Wayne Moore had been a Dolphin since 1970. Mike Current had joined the team in 1977 and, like Moore, was thirty-three. Guard Larry Little, known as Chicken Little, also was thirty-three and had been a five-time first-team All-Pro since joining the Dolphins in 1969. The other guard, thirty-one-year-old Bob Kuechenberg, called Kooch, had made first team All-Pro twice since joining the Dolphins in 1970. Also with the team since 1970 was center Jim Langer, thirty years old and a six-time All-Pro first team. All members of the starting line had been to at least one Pro Bowl, with Kooch topping out at six.

Bob Griese, thirty-three, was the proven quarterback. Along with the experienced coaches, these guys were the veteran status quo. Except for Mike Current, they all had Super Bowl rings and had played in the Dolphins' perfect season of 1972.

The day after I asked Coach Shula to investigate my salary dispute, he told me that I lost the decision. I couldn't believe it and said, "I lost it? Nobody ever told me." He said it had been finalized some time ago, with the vote being 4–2. That meant one of the player representatives had voted against me. Stunned, I thanked him for finding out for me.

I had a vivid memory of my conversations with Joe Thomas regarding my retroactive increase. Because the preseason is part of the entire season, it made sense to me that those six games would be included at my new salary. When I had spoken to him about it, he had assured me that I was not asking for anything that was not due to me. I had been one of the team's most productive players. It then felt like the 49ers were trying to slip off the hook.

Later in the year, I talked to Gene Upshaw who was at the Dolphins training camp for player representative meetings. I asked him, "What happened, and how did I lose it?"

Gene told me, "Delvin, you gotta get these things in writing."

That blew my mind. Neither Joe nor I had regarded it at the time as a separate negotiation. If Gene was looking at it that way, of course, I didn't have it in writing. Joe was my general manager. If it should have been in writing, why wouldn't he have done so right then and there? To this day, I still do not know why I was denied the money. I find it hard to believe that Joe would have purposely deceived me.

For some reason, he must have been unable to deliver on what he agreed to do for me. If so, he would have had to admit to me that he had overstepped his bounds in offhandedly agreeing to the retroactive pay. Not getting what I felt was due me was one thing, but his reneging without any kind of explanation was something else.

On top of that, the 4–2 vote by the grievance council must have meant that Gene had voted against me, because he told me that I didn't have written proof.

Not making it a 3–3 tie denied me an opportunity to at least have the arbiter hear my case. That gave me doubts about the NFLPA having the players' backs.

Howard Schnellenberger had returned as offensive coordinator, a position he had held during the 1970–72 seasons before coaching the Colts in 1973 and briefly in 1974 following the McCafferty dismissal under Joe Thomas. So Shula was supported by yet another longtime associate and friends, in this case someone who had recently been a head coach.

Howard's wife, Beverlee, would sell me a Miami townhouse. The season wound up being his last with the Dolphins because, when the season ended, he was hired to coach the University of Miami. I got to know him a little bit because of my real estate relationship with Beverlee and spoke with him about why he was leaving the pros for the University of Miami, then a lackluster program. He told me that there were a lot of good high school players in South Florida, including the Miami area. If he could recruit those guys and get them to learn a pro system, he felt that there was no telling what they could accomplish. As it turned out, he produced a national championship for Miami in 1983, and the Hurricanes have been a powerhouse ever since. Howard left to pursue a leadership position with a USFL team that didn't pan out and then went back to college coaching, turning around the program at the University of Louisville.

Learning the Offense

I had no trouble picking up the offensive system, because it was the same that we had in San Francisco under Monte. I had a good mini-camp, accomplishing the things I needed to and feeling pleased with my performance.

While in Miami, I looked at places to buy instead of renting. Beverlee Schellenberger stayed in touch with me after I returned home to the Bay

Area for a brief stay after the camp ended. I was told by one of my friends still with the 49ers that Freddie Solomon, for whom I had been traded, was around and would be interested in getting together and swapping information about our new teams and cities. I eagerly accepted, and we visited at my Los Altos Hills house and talked about many things, not just football. I came away from our wonderful conversation with a better understanding of the Dolphins and who was really in charge.

Getting injured in the past had reinforced for me that you could work hard to get in shape and learn your position but still have the unexpected pop up at any time. My options in Miami were to find a local Cheers type of bar or go to school, study, stay home, and focus. I wanted to get a master's degree, but I wasn't sure in what area. If I were going to attend graduate school, this would be the best time to do it, because I didn't know anyone in Miami and would have spare time in my evenings. I enrolled in the sports administration master's program at Biscayne College. I knew going to school wasn't going to be easy, but I wanted to give it a shot.

Consequently, however, during the season I ended up being tired and fighting through bouts of depression, injuries, anxiety, and loneliness, battling internal and external forces of which I was unaware. Some of that was of my own making., but I was trying to make sure I didn't fall into any traps and doing what I could to avoid unforeseen mishaps.

Beverlee found a townhouse in Miami Lakes for me to buy, which was better than renting since it was an investment. It got rather complicated, but I learned that I could not deduct the mortgage interest on my second home (I still owned the house in Los Altos Hills), because I owned it as a professional athlete. It was in my interest, therefore, to rent it out for more than my mortgage and meanwhile rent something else myself, which I could deduct as a business expense.

Although I didn't live in the Miami Lakes condominium, Melanie and Gary Levine, who sold it to me, would be my first Miami friends away from football. Melanie was pregnant at the time with their first child, Lani, whose first spoken word (or first spoken name, at least) would be "Delvin." They eventually had a boy named Justin. I would become lifetime friends with their families as well.

In setting up my contract and how I would receive my payments over the now sixteen-week season, I had to talk with Jim Steeg, the Dolphins' business manager, who was about six months older than me.

Our conversation turned into a friendship, which was unusual for a team administrator and player. It would be one of the most mutually respectful relationships I've had with anyone in management.

We talked about personal issues and kept business on the side. We both are jazz enthusiasts and would visit Les Jardins on Le Jeune Road in Miami. The first time I first met jazz musician Joe Donato was in 1978 at Les Jardins. He was a hot act around the airport district, which then was the happening place in town. When I had surgery on my shoulder, Joe brought a wooden flute to me in the hospital. I thought that was cool and let him know that I appreciated it.

Before our last visit to Les Jardins, Jim was hired by the NFL to head its Special Events Department, which included annually organizing the Super Bowl setup. I hated that he was leaving but was happy for him. He worked for the NFL in that capacity until 2004, when he became executive vice president of the San Diego Chargers. We've stayed in touch over the years.

The Miami practice sessions and schedules mirrored those in San Francisco. Though the locker room wasn't great, the practice fields were always manicured and kept in good shape. Practices focused on running game in the morning and passing in the afternoon. They were well-organized, and every practice we were getting better. We did the repeat sprints that Monte Clark had introduced in San Francisco, called "gassers" because you ran hard, across and back, always nearly running out of gas. The Miami heat made gassers even more challenging. I remember losing eight pounds a practice, and many of the linemen were in double figures. There was new learning every day. Having played under Monte two years before, I had no problems with understanding what we were trying to do offensively. In a morning meeting before practice, Coach Shula mentioned a third practice for the day. I thought I had misunderstood, but, as I looked around at the other players, I got my answer: I had heard him correctly.

On several occasions we had three-a-day practices. The first time, I thought that we were going to go out there in full pads for the third round, as we had for two earlier ones that day. But after dinner, we dressed in shorts and T-shirts, with no pads. If there was something new to learn, we'd have a walk-through. Those were very beneficial for me, because I could pick up my blocking assignments and see my responsibility. In film study and running plays at full speed in practice, you miss where a hole could be. I also was surprised to see the coaches put in an unbalanced line in training camp. My experience had been only dealing with that during the season. When you think about it, it made sense to install it in training camp. If you put it in during camp practices, it won't be difficult to run it in a game during the season. There also was an emphasis on not beating yourself with penalties. I found all the nuances of mindfulness helpful and keys to winning or losing.

But then I got injured again. I was running a pass route out of the backfield, caught the ball, turned to run, and slipped. I put my hand down to break my fall and slid with my arm behind me. As I was sliding with arm down, I heard something pop, and I felt it in my arm. I got up and ran back to the huddle, but my bicep was sore. When the session was over, I started my after-practice exercise program. I started doing chin-ups, but I couldn't finish the first one. I told the trainer, Bob Lundy, what had happened. He checked it and told me I had torn the "long head" tendon of my biceps. Damn it!

There was nothing that could be done about it at the time. I was told it would not keep me from playing, although in the off-season I would probably need surgery to fix it. The one thing I had been hoping wouldn't happen, had happened. The coaches were not about to have me sit out, nor did I want to, especially with all the fanfare and hype around my arrival. The good news was that I could play with the injury, but it wasn't going to be pain-free. I also lost strength in my arm, but I could work with it.

I was adjusting to my new home in Miami. I also was learning that as a high-profile athlete, it usually is best to *stay* home.

15

Athletes are only human. Like everyone else, we need to get away from the pressures of our "office" and relax now and then. If you're not careful, however, the experience can be like being surrounded by sharks in Biscayne Bay.

Gary Levine had offered to take me out for a drink to celebrate buying his townhouse. Being in camp all summer and having started school, I just didn't have time to do it. I told him I would after our first game, which was in New York. As little as I went out at night, I already had learned about the allure of professional athletes. Some guys claim to be athletes to get women. Other guys like being around a professional athlete, just to feed off the attention. Gary was no different. Finally accepting his offer after our regular season opener and flying back to Miami, I hoped to go out Monday night to some place quiet, have a nice dinner and drinks, just the two of us. We ended up at the Mutiny, a classy hotel in Coconut Grove.

Back in 1978, there was no South Beach nightlife, only high-rise condominiums. We sat at the bar in Coconut Grove to have a drink and talk. A couple of guys walked up, and Gary introduced them to me. I have always been wary of walking into a bar or a crowded room, feeling that people knew more about me than I did about them. Often, there's not much you can do about that as a public figure when you go out. One guy offered to buy me a drink, stating that he had won some money on the Jets game that we just lost. That didn't bother me, because I was used to people occasionally mentioning a bad game I'd had or a loss, just to see how I would react. I never gambled other than dice games as a teenager back in Houston. We stayed long enough to have a couple of drinks. Then I thanked the pair for the drink, and we left.

Outside, Gary asked me if I knew who those guys were, and, of course I didn't, having just met them through him. He told me that one was a bookie. I exclaimed, "A bookie?" I told him that I couldn't be around bookies. If I were seen around someone like that and fumbled the ball or dropped a pass in a case where we didn't cover the spread, I could be implicated. Even if nothing was proved, doubt would always remain every time I fell short of something or screwed up. Checking up on the Mutiny, I was told that it was a place where athletes shouldn't go because of reports of bookmaking and loan-sharking around the establishment.

It was a wake-up call for me to be more aware of my surroundings. I knew the story of Joe Namath's Bachelors III, which he had been forced to sell back in 1969 because it was an underworld hangout. Even if an athlete doesn't actively associated with gamblers, just informal talk about anything regarding the team could set off a flurry of betting, as well as ill will felt by those who might have lost on such hunches. Having the loan sharks circling was a whole other danger, whether for an athlete temporarily in a bind or for an associate seeking to get out of debt by passing on an unintended tip. As much as the league emphasized no gambling, it's ironic they have a team in Las Vegas, the Mecca of gambling.

Later that night, we wanted something to eat, but every restaurant was closed. At the last place we tried, I ran to the door desperate to use the restroom. Finding it locked, I ran around to the back of the building and took a leak against the dumpster. Just as I had finished and started to walk away, I saw a man coming, he looked at me and said, "Hey, you're Delvin Williams!" I couldn't believe someone recognized me so late at night in the dark and under my frantic circumstances.

After that, I limited my evening appearances but did attend team-sponsored events, such as going to Dolphins booster clubs. At a Fort Lauderdale booster club meeting, I sat at a table with Joie and Bill Tipmore, who were an older couple with grown kids. We hit it off and would become friends, going out to dinner several times during the season. Anytime Joie read something negative in the newspaper about me, she would call to see if I was okay with the criticism. There also was a young lady at our table to whom Joie introduced me.

One night, I was scheduled to make an appearance at Gary Fronrath's Chevrolet dealership in Fort Lauderdale. Gary had let me use a Corvette for promotional purposes during football season. It was the first time I had a car given to me for my own personal use. Because I was to be in their town anyway, about thirty miles north of Miami, the Tipmores asked me and the young woman I was with out to dinner. Afterward, I spent the night at the lady's house, and in the morning my car had four flat tires. To this day, I wonder if it was racially motivated because the woman was white or because it was a nice, new Corvette.

Because I would be late for the team meeting that morning while getting my car fixed, I had to call Coach Shula and relate all that had happened, including the possible racial overtones as well as having been given the car, which was not against the rules but good for disclosure. I had to get the car towed back to Fronrath's and then get a loaner to make it to practice. It was the first time I was late for a meeting, and it wouldn't be my last, but it was due to these unusual circumstances, none of which I was pleased to have to tell my coaches. After the incident, I decided to spend my nights at home, where I at least felt in control of my surroundings. Even so, isolating myself may have worked against me.

I had met Raiders defensive back Neal Colzie two years before during the off-season while playing in a 49ers charity basketball game versus the Raiders. Later that year, we played against the prison inmates at Soledad Correctional Facility in California and were on the same team. When I was traded to the Dolphins, Neal's family got in touch and invited me to dinner. I eventually would meet Neal's godmother, Bertha Hamilton. She would become my surrogate godmother. We called her and her husband Mrs. and Mr. Hamp. There were several kids, and the youngest, Kenny Hamilton, was a contractor. I got to know him very well, and we're like brothers. There were great cooks in the Colzie and Hamilton families, and I never lacked for a good home-cooked meal.

A New Season

Before 1978, the NFL played a mind-numbing six preseason and fourteen regular-season games. The league and players' association agreed to change that to four preseason and sixteen regular-season games. That meant two additional regular-season games counting toward season and career statistics. Most players who put their bodies on the line each week would prefer to do so in games that count.

In 1978 we opened the preseason schedule in the annual Hall of Fame Game in Canton, Ohio, and lost to Philadelphia, 17–3. Like most starters, I didn't like playing in the preseason. However, because this was my first year with the Dolphins, I wanted to be in the mix. I played only the first quarter and did well. Former 49er guard Woody Peoples now was with the Eagles, and we had an opportunity to talk after the game, just like the veteran he already was and I had become. We agreed that we missed San Francisco and the Bay Area but were glad to be away from Joe Thomas's management.

After losing to the Eagles, we beat the Cardinals, Saints, Vikings, and the Buccaneers for a 4–1 record (playing in the Hall of Fame Game extended our preseason to five games). I played more but was glad that the preseason ended earlier than before. All the training would be over, and we could strap on our Riddell helmets a little tighter and to get to the real action. The AFC East was a strong conference, with three competitive teams: Baltimore and Miami had tied in 1977 with 10–4 records, and New England was a game behind at 9–5. The New York Jets and Buffalo Bills were tied at the bottom with 3–11 records.

Joe Namath had played the 1977 season for the Los Angeles Rams, and O. J. Simpson of the Bills had gone out injured after seven games. Now he had taken my spot with the 49ers. The Colts still had Bert Jones at quarterback, and the Patriots had been doing well with Steve Grogan as the full-time starter.

When I was traded to the Dolphins, I didn't ask to renegotiate my contract for the 1978 season, which was the last year of the contract I had negotiated with the 49ers. I felt that if all things went as expected and I had a good year, a contract for next year would be the least of my worries.

The New York Jets were our first game and in the Big Apple. Bob Griese had sprained his knee in the last preseason game would be out for several weeks, and Don Strock would start. He had been with the Dolphins five years and could run the team. I had never played in Shea Stadium. I wasn't fond of playing on multiuse fields, but today was different. It was the maiden voyage. The Jets' top guys on defense were Greg Buttle and Joe Klecko, but as a unit they were young. The offensive line would have their hands full dealing with Klecko.

Richard Todd and Cal's Wesley Walker were their offensive weapons. After we were stopped on our first series, the Jets scored on a forty-seven-yard, Todd-to-Walker pass. Strock threw interceptions in the next two series, but the defense held them to a pair of field goals. We were behind 13–0 before we knew what hit us. We passed the ball for much of the first quarter and up to that point, I had one carry.

I was patient, and it gave me time to get in the flow of the game. In the second quarter I had one reception for 19 yards. We put a play in specifically for their aggressive defense. We figured the youthful Jets would try to deny us the sweeps. We put in a reverse play off our sweep: flow 39 reverse, the play was called. I started the sweep left, reversed and picked up a block from Don Strock and turned the corner upfield. Everybody did what they were supposed to do, and I ended up with a fifty-eight-yard touchdown. After a missed extra point and another Jets touchdown, the score was 20–6 at halftime. Guy Benjamin came in the game and made a strong showing at quarterback. I ended the game with eleven carries for 119 yards, and I felt I had delivered. We had been favored but lost, 33–20.

I began the season with a signature game as I had hoped. The measuring stick for running backs is one hundred yards in a game. However, I didn't think I would have a fifty-eight-yard touchdown run. The expectations were high, and I wanted to answer some of the questions, even my own. Playing for Monte Clark in 1976 allowed me to showcase my ability. Now I was with the guys he shaped and molded into one of the best offensive lines in the NFL. After the game, I think we all exhaled, but we were 0–1.

Then we beat the Colts 42–0 and the winless Bills 31–24, a game in which I scored my first Dolphins touchdown in the Orange Bowl. After more games and beating Baltimore again on October 29, we were 6–3.

As a running back, I had to run a designed play—but if it is not there, you take what you see. I was open to what my linemen suggested, but I considered the source. You can create what you want by setting a play up for an alternate path. Through tendencies we create, the defenses know where I'm *supposed* to go, but I know where I'm going. There's a high probability that they're right. I felt the wrath of Don Shula for the first time. Kooch was suggesting I take the inside route all day on a play we were running. I listened to Kooch and deviated from what I had been

CHAPTER 15

working on. When I took the inside route, his guy beat him and was waiting on me. It was third down, and I'd missed the first down.

Walking off the field with my head down, I could see Coach Shula. When he was angry, he threw his hands up as if he were signaling a touchdown. He had that "what the fuck are you doing" look on his face! And that was exactly what he said to me. I was trying to explain what Kooch suggested, but he would have none of that and chastised both of us. I learned a lesson: to go with what I knew. That way, the success or failure of the play would surely fall on me. That was the only time he said anything critical to me, other than, "Delvin, did you see that?" to wake me up.

Game for the Ages

Miami's venerable Orange Bowl Stadium has seen more than its share of electrifying moments since it opened in 1937. There has never been a bigger game for me than the Miami Dolphins versus the defending Super Bowl champion Dallas Cowboys on November 5, 1978.

The stars were aligned for an unforgettable game, and local and national fans—as well as the media—knew it. The coaches didn't have to worry about keeping us focused in the week leading up to the game. Local newspapers and radio talk shows were filled with hype about the matchup between two heavyweight contenders for division titles in our opposing conferences. If everything went just right, the teams could be on a collision course for a rematch of the 1971 Super Bowl game in which the Cowboys beat the Dolphins. (I must admit that as a Texas kid, I had rooted for Dallas.)

The individual matchups could not have been scripted any better. Don Shula of the Dolphins and Tom Landry of the Cowboys would retire as two of the most respected and successful head coaches in history. Miami's Bob Griese and Roger Staubach of Dallas were both Super Bowl–winning quarterbacks and two of the league's marquee names. The great Cowboys running back Tony Dorsett, who had run for more than one thousand yards in his rookie season of 1977, was battling Walter Payton of the Bears for the NFC rushing lead, while I had more yards than any running back in the AFC.

What could be better? The game was nationally televised, and my mother was in the stands to watch me play professional football for the first time.

We practiced hard on Wednesday and Thursday, eased up on Friday, and only did a walk-through on Saturday. I arrived at the stadium two hours before kickoff on Sunday as usual ritual. Some teammates sat alone in a corner, while others quietly huddled and discussed strategy. I wanted to take my time and make sure I was prepared in every way.

Every game day is special, but you could feel that something different in the locker room that day. After warm-ups on the field, several players were starting to talk about the game. Players made eye contact with each other and winked or smiled.

An official knocked on the door to alert Coach Shula that kickoff time was approaching. He called everyone to the middle of the locker room, where we recited the Lord's Prayer. Before taking the field, he shared some last-minute thoughts. He talked about what this game meant to both teams and the Dolphins in particular.

"We've prepared for this, done all of the things we needed to do, and we are ready," he said. "Go out and play the way that we know we can play. Don't make mistakes to beat yourself."

The temperature was a perfect seventy degrees, without a cloud in the sky, when we took the field for the 4:00 p.m. start. The stadium announcer would introduce the Dallas defensive starters and our offensive starters. Linebacker Thomas "Hollywood" Henderson from Austin, Texas, stood next to me. We shook hands and laughed, as opposing players often do when they know each other.

Then it hit me: these were the Cowboys, the team I rooted for as a kid (if they weren't playing my hometown Houston Oilers). I had played against them the previous season when I was with the 49ers, and they beat us on their way to the Super Bowl. This game felt like the playoffs to me.

The announcer introduced the Cowboy starters first and, of course, the Dolphin fans booed lustily. The boos turned to thunderous cheers as the announcer turned his attention to our offense: "Now ladies and gentlemen, the starting lineup for your Miami Dolphins." Eighty thousand people started to roar. The noise was deafening. I couldn't hear when my name was called, but I was overcome with emotion. As I ran

That game undeniably was one of the greatest highs of my professional career and, indeed, of my life. Trying in vain to recapture that feeling would cost me untold time, money, and pain.

onto the field, chills went through my body; it was electrifying. It was the highest I had ever been for a game on any level. I never felt that way again before a kickoff.

In the first quarter, I scored a touchdown to put us ahead 14–0 and a Garo Yepremian field goal then put us up 17–0. We kept our lead into the fourth quarter when a Staubach touchdown pass cut it to 23–16, which was the final score. Their defense held me to twenty-six hard yards, half of which I got on one of my fifteen carries. But I also caught three passes, one a forty-two-yarder. It was by far my best emotional football experience, and we won the game.

We beat Buffalo on the road the following week. I opened the scoring with a twenty-five-yard rushing touchdown in the first quarter and then had a twenty-six-yard rushing touchdown in the second quarter. We won by a point, and I finished with 144 yards, my highest total so far that season. It was my fifth game of the year over one hundred yards, along with three games over ninety yards. But I was injured in the game—ribs and neck—and spent four nights in a hospital, sleeping in traction.

Back Home in Houston

Needless to say, I didn't practice much that week. My hometown and boyhood team, the Houston Oilers, were next, with us playing there. Out of all the weeks to be hurt, it would have to be this one. I was looking forward to playing before the hometown crowd. It was a special game, because family and friends would be in attendance. It also was a Monday night game, and I was leading the NFL in rushing.

When asked about potential records that I might break, Coach Shula was quoted as saying, "We don't go into that sort of thing with a game like this coming up. If we win the Super Bowl, then we will rehash all the things that happened in the season. You can break all the records, but if you don't make the playoffs, then it doesn't mean anything." But, he conceded, "I've never been around anyone who is as complete a back as Delvin Williams."

Hearing Don Shula saying that was beyond my wildest dreams.

I took shots of painkillers in my ribs before the game. We took the lead with a Bob Griese ten-yard touchdown pass to Nat Moore. Earl Campbell went in from the one-yard line to end the first quarter 7–7. Houston quarterback Dan Pastorini threw a touchdown pass, and then I scored from the one-yard line to tie it at halftime, 14–14. In the third quarter, Earl scored from the six, and our fullback Leroy Harris from the one to tie it 21–21. A. J. Duhe started off the fourth quarter tackling Pastorini in the endzone, putting us up 23–21. Then Earl scored his third touchdown, this time from the twelve-yard-line, putting them up 28–23.

Later, our defense had them bottled up with a third down on their own nineteen-yard-line with two minutes left when Earl broke loose for one of the most-remembered plays on *Monday Night Football*, turning the corner and outrunning our defensive back for an eighty-one-yard touchdown, his fourth of the night.

Bob Griese threw for the last touchdown, closing the score to 35–30. He had one of his best games, completing twenty-three out of thirty-three passes for 349 yards. Injured as I was and wearing a neck collar, I gained 73 yards on eighteen carries. Leroy Harris, our other halfback, got 51 yards on twelve carries. Earl Campbell had 199 yards on twenty-eight carries and became the talk of the league. Washed out by the loss was the fact that I had set a team season rushing mark of 1,130 yards, breaking Csonka's fourteen-game mark in only twelve games. But our whole locker room was down after a big-time defeat we had suffered on national television. However, it was Earl Campbell's coming-out party. Many say it was one of the best Monday night games ever played.

Maybe that loss took some wind out of our sails. We lost for the second time that season to the Jets, this time at home, 24–13. We dropped to 8–5, while the Jets improved to 7–6. My performance declined further as I still was unable to practice much and gained forty-one yards on twelve carries.

But our regular season ended with three straight victories, including shutting out Washington on the road, 16–0, then beating the Raiders, 23–6, and Patriots, 23–3, both at home. I barely played in those last two games, getting seven total carries. Our 1978 record of 11–5 wasn't as good as the Dolphin's 1977 record, but this time we made the playoffs.

I had left my heart in San Francisco, as the great Tony Bennett sang, but I was proud of what I had accomplished on the field in my first regular season with the Dolphins. Even more importantly, I was thankful that my new teammates had accepted me.

16

Paying attention to your own press clippings is a recipe for disaster. Although I wasn't concerned about what the media thought of me as a player, I was pleased to read about how my head coach and teammates felt about me.

- "I've never been around anyone who is as complete a back as Delvin Williams."—Don Shula
- "We've become a more explosive team. We break Delvin and he'll go all the way, but when we broke Csonka, he [would] get 30 yards or so at most. We can still control the ball, but we are more a quick-scoring team [than before]. Where we [would] run 10 plays with Csonka, we can run two now with Delvin."—Jim Langer
- "At the time, Csonka was the most important part of our offense. Now it is Delvin who is our catalyst." —Bob Kuechenberg.

I also was excited to be in the playoffs, especially because it once again would be against the Houston Oilers. We had one week to prepare for our playoff game against the Oilers, which would be a home game on Christmas Eve. It was a classic South Florida Christmas, with a temperature of seventy-seven degrees and 78 percent humidity at kickoff.

Bob Griese and Houston quarterback Dan Pastorini matched touchdown passes in the first quarter, and the first half ended at 7–7. Houston got a field goal in the third quarter, and then big Earl Campbell pushed over from the one-yard-line, and we were down 17–7. We failed to get any more points. Pastorini ran into the endzone for a safety near the end, and we lost, 17–9. I had forty-one yards on thirteen carries, and Leroy got forty-three yards on nine carries as they checked our running game. Bob threw two interceptions, and Don Strock threw one. The excitement of making the playoffs turned into deep disappointment. Nobody wanted the season to end this way, and it made for a blue Christmas the next day.

Back to the Pro Bowl

We had five players chosen to play in the Pro Bowl, and all were offensive players: Quarterback Bob Griese, left guard Bob Kuechenberg, center Jim Langer, kicker Garo Yepremian, and me. I was having surgery on my bicep and knee in mid-February. I considered not playing, but my injuries weren't going to get any worse so I decided to play in the game. Given the great experiences I had in 1976, I did not want to miss it. Furthermore, we were playing in the Los Angeles Coliseum. It was the same venue where Jim Brown was Pro Bowl MVP in January 1966. Another dream was coming to pass.

The Pro Bowl was played on January 29, 1979, a Monday night game and the last professional football game in the Coliseum for many years as the Rams moved to play 1979 in Anaheim (and then on to St. Louis for twenty-one seasons before returning to LA and the Coliseum in 2016). It also would be the last Monday night Pro Bowl game. We had played the first sixteen-game regular season and some of us postseason games too. Most of us who were used to fourteen games were extra tired, particularly yours truly. The other running backs chosen for the AFC team were Earl Campbell, Franco Harris, and Sam Cunningham—not bad company.

Ray Malavasi of the Rams was the NFC head coach, and Chuck Fairbanks of the New England Patriots coached the AFC. When Fairbanks was head coach at the University of Oklahoma, he had recruited me. The first letter I received from the university was from him. I didn't know any of my AFC teammates personally but had met or knew of them through other friends. Cedric Hardman from Houston and Joe Greene from Pittsburgh were teammates at North Texas State, and we shared some laughs about their time together. Cedric spoke of Joe as though he were an older brother, and Joe was one year ahead. It was fair to say that Joe was his role model. He respected and revered Joe. However, the three of us had one thing in common—we were from Texas.

Lynn Swann and I had met before and we talked about that. He attended Serra High School in San Mateo County, not far from the 49ers headquarters (and the same school attended by Barry Bonds and Tom Brady). We were named in *Parade Magazine's* 1969 High School All-American team. The magazine named one hundred players from all regions of the country. Out of one hundred, only three of us went on to play in the Pro Bowl. I am pro–Texas high school football and obviously Lynn felt strongly about California players.

My second year with the 49ers, we had played the Houston Oilers. Emmett Edwards, my college roommate, played wide receiver for the Oilers. He introduced me to Robert Brazile, also known as "Dr. Doom," one of the top outside linebackers in the NFL. He was about six foot four and 245 pounds, ran a 4.6 forty, and loved being on the field. He played on all the special teams and only came off when it was time for the offense. When I played against him, he seemed to be laughing and having fun while he chased me down. Because of his athleticism and size, he was a difficult linebacker to block.

I met Denver Broncos outside linebacker Tom Jackson. He was intense, and on the field knew only one speed. Rick Upchurch and I indirectly had a longstanding relationship. When he was at the University of Minnesota, we played against one another and we both ran track.

There was no difference from when I played in the Pro Bowl for the NFC in 1977. Most of the players had been there before. But my left knee bothered me all week before the game. In fact, some of the guys asked me why I was there with a bad leg. I would not start at running back. Earl Campbell and Sam Cunningham were the starters. It was an honor to be alongside the likes of Mike Webster, Joe DeLamielleure, Leon Gray, Terry Bradshaw, Curley Culp, Mike Haynes, John Jefferson, Riley Odoms, Lynn Swann, and Lyle Alzado, not to mention my teammates Garo, Jim, Kooch and Bob Griese, but I was a Dolphins rookie to them.

The NFC took a 6–0 lead with 7:06 to play in the second quarter when Archie Manning of the New Orleans Saints engineered an eleven-play, seventy-yard drive, and Eagles running back Wilbert Montgomery carried it in from the one-yard-line on fourth and goal. The point after was missed.

We responded by moving sixty-two yards in nine plays. The touchdown came on an eight-yard pass from Griese to Seattle's Steve Largent. Both Largent and Manning were playing in their first Pro Bowl and were their respective teams' first representative since the merger. Following a sixteen-yard punt by Oakland's Ray Guy and with 3:43 remaining in the third quarter, Cowboy quarterback Roger Staubach hit his teammate Tony Hill with a nineteen-yard touchdown pass. The drive covered forty-five yards in five plays. Neither team scored in the fourth quarter. The final score was 13–7. Largent and Ahmad Rashad of Minnesota each had five receptions. Earl Campbell led all rushers with sixty-six yards on twelve carries.

The victory marked the fourth NFC win in five years. I happened to be on the NFC team in 1977 that lost. Rashad was voted the game's MVP. Although everyone was glad to see the season come to a conclusion, Rashad said of the Pro Bowl, "Egos get involved, your pride kind of takes over. The best kind of comes out. . . . Once the game starts, you want to play your best football and win."

Trying to Get Healthy

Going into the 1978 season, my main concern had been to stay healthy, which I did for two-thirds of the schedule. Although I played with injuries and in a lot of pain, I missed only parts of the last two games. The season had begun after four preseason games instead of the normal six games. Had it been a fourteen-game schedule, I probably wouldn't have gotten beaten up as badly. It would have been nice to end the season as I had started, but it didn't happen. My neck didn't get any better, but the upside of it would be that I got some rest those last two games before going into the playoffs. Although we accomplished one of our objectives by reaching the playoffs, we had lost in the first round.

I had been able to stay focused and accomplish the things that I knew I could for my new team. I was considered one of the best running backs in the NFL, having finished fourth in rushing behind Walter Payton, Earl Campbell and Tony Dorsett, guys who were twenty-three (Earl) and twenty-four years old (Walter and Tony) to my twenty-seven.

My most gratifying accomplishment was being named the team's most valuable player for the 1978 season. That award is the highest team honor a player can receive.

With more games, I finished the season with 1,258 yards rushing, which was a Miami Dolphins team record (and just above my 49er record of 1,203 yards in fourteen games).

Being named the Dolphins' most valuable player for the season meant a lot more to me. It was an affirmation that I had gained my new teammates' respect, after all the fanfare that had come with my arrival in Miami. That had made me uncomfortable. The last thing I wanted to be was a distraction. I wanted to blend in and be a part of the team. At the presentation of the award, Coach Shula said, "We traded for Delvin on his birthday. It looks like we were the ones who got the birthday present."

The 49ers, meanwhile, finished 2–14 that year. O. J. Simpson started ten games and gained 593 yards on 161 carries, leading the team in both categories. Wilbur Jackson missed all season with an injury. Freddie Solomon led the receivers with thirty-one catches and 458 yards. He also got to play quarterback in the last game when Steve DeBerg and Scott Bull were injured, completing five of ten passes but throwing an interception in a loss to Detroit. Pete McCulley was fired midway through the season, and Fred O'Conner, the offensive coordinator, was named coach for the last seven games, beating only Tampa Bay in the next-to-last game. After the season, team president Eddie DeBartolo Jr. took more command of his franchise, firing Joe Thomas and hiring Bill Walsh, who had been head coach at Stanford the two preceding seasons.

You could feel the Dolphins' potential going into the 1979 season. In 1978 we had finished second in offense in the NFL. One big loss was right tackle, where Wayne Moore, a nine-year Dolphins veteran from Beaumont, Texas, had hurt his knee and retired. Also, unfortunately, run-blocking specialist Andre Tillman at tight end broke his femur during the preseason, ending his four-year career. But when you add fullback

Larry Csonka, re-signed with Miami after spending the three preceding years with the New York Giants, along with returning receivers Nat Moore (forty-eight catches) and Duriel Harris (forty-five catches), we didn't lack for offensive weapons. If anything, there was concern about how to best deploy our wealth of talent.

Bill Arnsparger was the defensive coordinator, having returned to his old coaching position in 1976 after the Giants let him go as their head coach. The Dolphins made an off-season trade that brought free safety Neal Colzie from the Raiders back to his hometown of Miami. Neal's presence at free safety gave our secondary more speed. We already were friends and now would become closer. I had gotten to know his family and would be invited to have dinner with them more often. After dinner, I had a comfortable chair in the living room to sit in, and it was without question that I would fall asleep in that chair. If I wasn't asleep yet, I could hear Mr. Colzie laughing, saying, "Connie, we're losing Delvin. You better get him!" "Neal" was short for Cornelius, but his family called him Connie.

Contract Hassle

Meanwhile, I was deep into contract negotiations, and we weren't close to an agreement. It was a distraction that neither the team nor I needed. Perhaps I was still naïve as a five-year NFL veteran, but I figured that if you put yourself out totally on the field, you would get appreciation back from the team in the form of fair compensation. I didn't see it, however, and was disappointed by the front office.

Having suffered through injuries while still producing a record-setting year and then paying the price in the off-season with shoulder and knee operations, I wanted the team to care more about me than they demonstrated. Discovering the front office was all business at contract time was like a slap in the face. Very few of the players thought in those purely business terms or were around anyone who was business-savvy. We didn't have the time to learn about business. We'd hire someone to handle our business affairs, which was mainly taxes and strategizing, so we didn't get stuck with paying the government more in April. However, that mentality could come back and bite you in the ass.

Despite no contract, I still participated in practice, and I could tell that Csonka—"Zonk"—was a hell of a football player despite being so soft-spoken, at least when I was around. It's a small thing, but when we broke the huddle and before we got in our stance, he would repeated the snap count and play. At first, I thought he had forgotten the play, but I quickly realized he was reminding me, perhaps as well as himself. When the offense breaks the huddle, a lot of things are going through the running back's mind: whether the play is designed for you or not; the down and distance left for a first down; time left on the clock; what your assigned linebacker is going to do—blitz or drop back in pass coverage; whether it is a zone defense or man-to-man. I thought Csonka's repeating the snap count and play was great, very professional, and was looking forward to learning from him.

In our fourth and final preseason game, against the Philadelphia Eagles, we sputtered offensively and didn't play our best football, but we still won. The defense was playing great, and we finished the preseason undefeated. I was thankful for having made it through the without getting hurt or reinjuring my shoulder and knee. Still, being still unsigned at the beginning of the season, as all players know, is a tough position to be in. The local press was there every day asking the same questions over and over: "How do you feel about not having signed a contract?" "What about playing with Csonka?" Not having a contract was a distraction, and I was getting upset.

In a general conversation with a reporter, I was asked if I had considered not playing. My response was, "Sure, I've considered not playing. You have to think about your own well-being and what's in your best interests." It appeared in print that I was threatening not to play. Coach Shula pulled me aside and asked if I was going to play or not. I assured him that I had no intention of not playing and that my comment was taken out of context. Yes, I had considered not playing but had dismissed the notion. When I was on the field, I always gave it 100 percent, even without a contract.

Going into the season without a contract had happened with the 49ers when Joe Thomas arrived, and being in that situation a second time, in 1979, didn't make it easier. If I were hurt, the result would be different than if I were to be injured while under contract. I wanted to focus on football. On the one hand, I felt the team wasn't concerned about my well-being, as demonstrated by allowing me to play without a contract. But on the other hand, I still held deep down the naïve belief that a pro football team is a family, just as it was for me in high school, and that self-sacrifice is required. I didn't know about my own family's history of anxiety and depression at the time, but I was familiar with the feelings. At the time, there were things I was dealing with that I unknowingly had been struggling with all my life.

I signed a three-year contract with Miami for $275,000 a year, three weeks into the 1979 season against the Bears. But in the third quarter, I had a concussion and sat out the rest of the game. Csonka scored from the one-yard line in the fourth quarter, giving us the win, 9–7, the first of four consecutive wins. Then we lost four out of seven, and two weeks into November our record was 7–4. The following week I scored to put us ahead of the Cleveland Browns, 24–17, but they came back to tie and then won in overtime 30–24, making us 7–5. The next four games were critical for us in terms of making the playoffs.

After winning the first two games, we faced the Lions in Detroit, with Monte in his second year as their coach. The Lions had won only two games all season. We won handily, clinching the AFC East. We finished at 10–6, one game behind our previous year's 11–5, but for the second year in a row we were in the playoffs.

That meant we had to play the defending Super Bowl champion Steelers in Pittsburgh on December 30. They had been 14–2 the season before, when they beat the Cowboys in Super Bowl XIII, and they had just finished 12–4 in 1979. On game day it was cold, with a windchill of eighteen degrees. The Steelers jumped out to a 20–0 lead in the first quarter as they bottled up our running game. Zonk had a long run for the game of six yards, and my longest was three yards. Our team total was twenty-five rushing yards on twenty-two carries. Csonka got our only rushing touchdown near game's end.

The Steelers wound up winning 34–14, and they continued on to the Super Bowl again, and again they won, prevailing 31–19 against the Los Angeles Rams in Super Bowl XIV.

Behind the Numbers

During the regular 1979 season, I had rushed for 703 yards, compared to 1,258 yards the previous season. I wasn't as disappointed by my numbers as I was about how the season went for me. Only by comparison to my previous team-record season did my numbers suffer. At midseason I had been leading the team in rushing with 505 yards, but in the ninth game of the season, against the Packers, I broke three ribs and missed the next two games. My first game back, against the Browns, I had seventy-nine yards, two touchdowns and lots of pain. For the season I sat out thirteen quarters and had 184 carries, compared to 272 carries in 1978. With fewer breakaways, my average fell from 4.6 yards per carry to 3.8. With Csonka at fullback, we had a more balanced attack. Zonk overtook me in yardage with 837 yards on 220 carries, which also was 3.8 yards per carry. Because Csonka played fullback, he got more goal-line carries, scoring twelve touchdowns to my three. We each caught one touchdown pass.

Coach Shula let the papers know his thoughts about my numbers' decline: "At the beginning of last year [1978] he was healthy, and he became the first running back in the league during the season to gain 1,000 yards. He got pretty well banged up in last year's December 3 game against the Washington Redskins and, really, he's only been full speed periodically ever since."

I had sustained knee, rib, and shoulder injuries against Washington and couldn't walk for a few days without a cane. Limping into the play-off game with Houston, I had managed to gain forty yards. In 1979 I was even more banged up but figured I could contribute as a decoy if nothing else, knowing that opponents would have to watch me.

A reporter asked me if I had learned to play in pain, and all I could do was laugh. I said, "I've been playing in pain ever since I've been in the NFL. The thing to understand is that when you're a running back, you attract a lot of attention. You are going to get hit, and there is not much you can do to avoid it."

There would be no Pro Bowl, awards, or accolades of any kind for me, unlike the previous season but, more importantly, also no surgeries. Over the winter, my neck and ribs got better—I felt spared by the injury gods and felt relatively healthy. The money I was paid as a professional athlete represented, to me, my value to the team and what they thought my contribution, but I had learned the unforeseen problems that came with money. Hiring lawyers, accountants, and investment advisors seemed urgent, and I knew nothing about any of it. In reaching out for help, I quickly discovered how difficult it was to find a supportive network of professionals I felt were trustworthy.

The perception of the Dolphins' lack of production drew criticism from the fans and media. In their view, I'd had a mediocre season in 1979. Given the makeover of the team, 703 yards, and missing thirteen quarters, I called it respectable but far below the benchmark I had set. When I broke my ribs, I had been leading the team in rushing.

Running backs coach Carl Taseff commented publicly, saying, "You can't coach what Delvin has. That quick change of direction. The instinct to follow blockers. Running isn't just grabbing the ball and . . . sprinting. It's seeing the hole, reading the blocks and accelerating. Delvin is a natural at all three." This was the public stance, but in film meetings I often heard, "Delvin, did you see that?" Sometimes I would smile, but, if we had just lost, the comment had a little bite to it. The combination of injuries and criticism made the physical and mental challenges I wasn't consciously aware of even more difficult.

Growing Frustration

Near the end of the 1979 season, I had felt that the focus of criticism of the team's offense was on my production, rather than the offense as a whole. I felt wrongly blamed. At every level of football, I had been a team player and never a prima donna who might demand more carries or complain about the efforts of teammates.

At the time, I didn't know the severity of my sleep apnea. During the 1978 season, Coach Shula had made a comment in jest to the press. "I'd like to see him stay awake in those classes," he had said, referring to me, and we all smiled and laughed it off. However, in 1979, by midseason he was starting to fine me for falling asleep during team meetings. I didn't understand why, because, as I looked around the room, a lot of guys were falling asleep, especially after lunch. During film study, wide receiver Nat Moore would sit right next to Coach Shula and fall asleep. Nat's head would damn near hit Coach Shula on his shoulder. Coach Shula would take his elbow, nudge him, and say, "Nat, Nat, did you see that?"—at which we would laugh to ourselves.

Near the end of the season, I stopped Bob Lundy, our team trainer, in the locker room. I asked him if he knew where I could find somebody to talk to. He looked at me and said, "Delvin, you are one of the sanest guys on the team. What do you need to talk to someone about?" I played

Everything that was happening to me and going on around me had an external focus. But I was beginning to realize that I had been drawn to football as a kid to fill a void left by the loss of my grandfather.

it off and told him I had some things going on back home, which was true. I wanted independent confirmation that the thing I was experiencing was not solely my fault.

Bob got back to me after a day or two and gave me a name and number of a physician. Dr. Edward St. Mary was a mild-mannered man who was insightful and open to things other than football-related medical concerns. He contacted someone who gave him the name of a psychiatrist in downtown Miami, who I saw him for a couple of sessions.

Dr. St. Mary stayed in touch with me. He made a few calls, and when I got back home in California after the season he put me in touch with Dr. David Daniels, a clinical psychiatrist at Stanford. With the encouragement of Dr. St. Mary, I had several visits with Dr. Daniels. As usual, I did most of the talking, and, at the end of my first visit, I asked him what he thought. He made several observations, but he said one thing that stuck with me. He said, "If you are as conscientious as you seem here today, then there's nothing wrong with you."

I said thank you and left. It was what I needed to hear at the time, because I didn't think anything was wrong with me. I would continue to see him, but only sporadically. I wasn't ready yet to look inside for answers.

In my first meeting with Coach Shula in 1978 before ever playing a game for the Dolphins, I had said to him that I was there to do whatever I could to help the team win. If we got to a point where he needed to bench me and play someone else, I would accept this without hesitation. In all my pro career, I never wavered in that commitment. However, as in my last year in San Francisco, I was having serious doubts about whether my team was as committed to me as I was to them.

(*top*)
Breaking the tape for the Kashmere High School track team. Author's collection.

HIGH-SCHOOL ALL-STAR Delvin Williams of Kashmere High School takes time out from practice as Cong. George Bush of Houston presents him with a letter of commendation from Bud Wilkinson, head of the nation's physical fitness program. Williams was a participant in the 38th Annual Texas High School Coaches' Association All-Star Football Game at the Astrodome.

(*bottom*)
Receiving my certificate of commendation for the President's Fitness Program from Congressman George H. W. Bush in 1970 at the Universality of Houston. I was participating in the Texas High School Coaches Association All-Star Game at the time. Courtesy *Houston Forward Times*.

(*top*)
My grandmother, Pearlie
Young.
Author's collection.

(*bottom*)
My mother,
Dorothy Jean Williams.
Author's collection.

(top left)
Winning a football scholarship
at Kansas University was a major
step toward a different life. I
struggled academically at first,
but I graduated in four years with
a degree in physical education.
Courtesy Kansas University
Athletics.

(top right)
I guess the referees didn't see
the defender grab my facemask.
Courtesy Kansas University
Athletics.

(bottom)
I also ran track at Kansas but only
because I believed it helped me
improve my speed for football.
Courtesy Kansas University
Athletics.

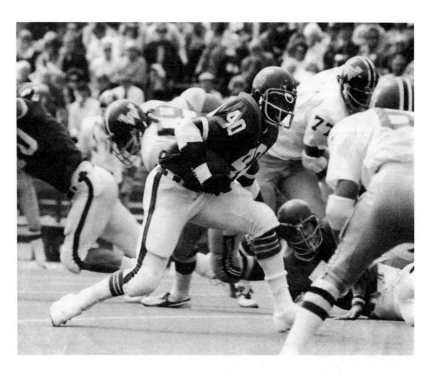

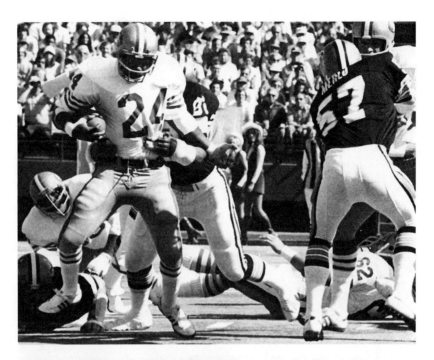

(*opposite top*)
Looking for a hole in the
Washington State defensive line.
Courtesy Kansas University
Athletics.

(*opposite bottom*)
Brought down by Tennessee
defenders. Courtesy Kansas
University Athletics.

(*top*)
Welcome to the NFL. Trying to
break free from the grasp of a Saints
defender. Courtesy Frank Rippon.

(*bottom*)
If I could make it around the
end, I had a pretty good chance
to gain some yardage. Courtesy
Frank Rippon.

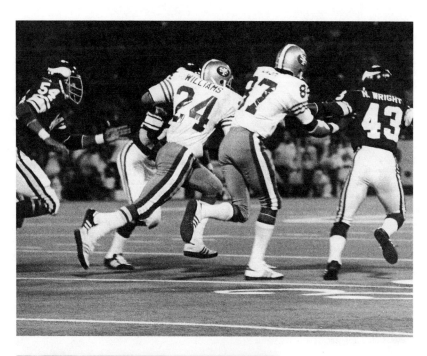

(top)
Through the gap
and into the Vikings
backfield. Courtesy
Frank Rippon.

(bottom)
Taking a handoff from
the great Norm Snead,
a sixteen-year NFL
veteran. Courtesy
Frank Rippon.

(top)
Trying to get past
Phil Villapiano of
the Raiders. Phil was
on the 1976 Raiders
team that beat the
Vikings in the Super
Bowl, 32–14. Courtesy
Frank Rippon.

(botom)
As a running back,
you've got to find that
hole in the line, and
it can close pretty
quickly. Courtesy
Frank Rippon.

Ref down! People sometimes forget that the officials are on the same field as the players, and they aren't wearing pads. Courtesy Frank Rippon.

Running backs can't do anything without good blocking. This block by my teammate Wilbur Jackson led to a touchdown. Courtesy Frank Rippon.

(*top*)
Wearing the Dolphins
uniform, trying to make
the cut upfield under
the lights for *Monday
Night Football*. Courtesy
Gary Levine.

(*bottom*)
If you were a running
back, you didn't want the
Jets' Ed Taylor looking
at you like this. Ed and
I were roommates my last
year in Miami. Courtesy
Gary Levine.

Game against the Dallas Cowboys in Miami. We won 23-16 without looking, I think. I was leading the league in rushing and had 26 yards that day.

We played the Bills that day in Buffalo, game #11. I had 144 yards rushing and 2 touchdowns to become the first player to rush for one thousand yards in 1978.

With Nancy Reagan and Joe Montana at a Pros for Kids banquet.
Courtesy Pros for Kids.

With my
grandchildren,
Anjeniqua and
Je'Marcus, at
Je'Marcus's high
school graduation.
Author's collection.

(*top*)
With Rodney Hampton at the Houston Independent School District Athletic Hall of Honor celebration in 2021. Rodney, a fellow Kashmere alumnus, was an offensive force for the New York Giants, 1990–97. He was a two-time Pro Bowler and helped the Giants win the Super Bowl in 1990. Courtesy Houston Independent School District.

(*bottom*)
With Andre' Walker, director of athletics, at the Houston Independent School District Hall of Honor ceremony. Courtesy Houston Independent School District.

17

The winds of change were beginning to blow in Miami. When the 1980 season rolled around, the Dolphins team that had dominated the NFL in the early 1970s had gone from showing its age to showing its lack of experience.

Bob Kuechenberg and Ed Newman were the only offensive linemen left who had been starters more than two years. The center, Mark Dennard, was in his second year and had big shoes to fill as a starter since Jim Langer, a Minnesota native, our consensus All-Pro and future Hall of Fame center, had been traded to his home-state Vikings. The left tackle, Jon Giesler, in his second year, was out at the start of the season with a shoulder separation. Starting tight end Ronnie Lee was in his second year, and Eric Laakso, starting for the first time at right tackle in his third year, replaced Mike Current, who had retired after thirteen seasons.

Larry Csonka, five years older than me, had retired after eleven NFL seasons and one WFL season. Steve Howell, a second-year convert from tight end, would start at fullback. I was hoping to return to my 1978 form by being the premier back without having to split carries in the upcoming season. In the newspapers, I was quoted as saying, "It's hard for people to realize I can't have a good year carrying the ball 10 or 11 times a game as opposed to 20 to 22 times a game." But every halfback still needs a blocking fullback and five offensive linemen to push back the defensive line and open holes. In both areas, we now lacked veterans.

Because of injuries, we went from Griese to Strock to David Woodley as the starting quarterback. Starting tight end Andre Tillman broke his femur, never played again. Bruce Hardy and Ronnie Lee were alternating at tight end, and Nat Moore was the only wide receiver and starter from my first year. Duriel Harris had some injuries and was alternating with Jimmy Cefalo.

Our lineups were not consistent, and after nine games we were 4–5. I had been a starter since midseason in San Francisco during my second year there, and any games I missed were because of injuries. I had been the only starting running back for the three years I'd been in Miami. From when I arrived in 1978 until the end of the 1980 season, I would start with seven different fullbacks. With the success I'd had in our offense the previous two years, defenses were now concentrating on me.

There had been talk I wasn't going to be the starting halfback. At the end of one practice during the 1980 season, Coach Shula asked me to come to his office. He told me that they were going to start Tony Nathan at halfback for a change of pace but to be ready to play, because we would be rotated in and out. I did not question his decision, and the meeting may have taken only one or two minutes. My perception was that Coach Shula thought I wasn't producing and that the running game had suffered because of my being in the game. To a certain extent that was correct, but that was not the whole story.

How I saw things was a little different. We were going through a rebuilding stage, but this was never stated by the coaching staff. Knowing what I know about Don Shula, he would never have said that we were rebuilding. He wanted to win now, today, and wouldn't accept excuses, one of the reasons he had great success as a coach.

Against the Rams in Anaheim Stadium, Tony Nathan started at halfback and caught a touchdown pass from David Woodley for a 7–0 lead. As a backup but rotating with him, I had more carries, twelve to his eight, and more yards, 151 to his 57, including a sixty-five-yard run I made. Tony did catch seven passes to my one. We won 35–14 to even our record to 5–5. What I took from that experience and is confirmed by today's players is how important it is to get rest or be fresh.

What happened in that game was not a fluke, because teams prepare for certain players, and the Rams knew I wasn't starting. They didn't know how much I would play, so I wasn't the target. Furthermore, teams that are having success running the ball today, like the San Francisco 49ers, alternate their backs. The 1970s was a halfback-fullback era, before the Bill Walsh West Coast offensive set. It would be very hard for Tony or any back in the NFL, then or now, to carry the weight of running, pass receiving, and blocking a third of the plays or more in a game. That was a problem, particularly in Miami, because you couldn't say you wanted or needed to rest a play or two.

Next game we played the 49ers in Miami, with Tony starting again, as he did for the rest of the season. I had fourteen carries to Tony's two as we won 17–13. Joe Montana, then a backup to Steve DeBerg at quarterback for the Niners, got in the game for four passes. (The next year, 1981, he would lead the team to the Super Bowl.)

Against the Chargers the following week, I scored a touchdown but had only nineteen yards on seventeen carries, and we lost in overtime. The next week in Pittsburgh I had just thirty-one yards on nine carries, and again we lost, dropping to 6–7.

Increasing Pressure

I was sitting next to running back Terry Robiskie in a meeting when I felt I was unjustly being targeted for something in the game film we were watching. Coach Shula, without looking, asked if I was asleep or awake. After the meeting, I said that I was done with this and wasn't going to deal with it anymore. I got up and walked down the hallway toward Coach Shula's office, when someone grabbed my arm. I looked around, and it was Terry. He stopped me and said, "Delvin, don't do it!" He went on to say, "You have three more weeks, you can do this standing on your head." We exchanged a few words, I gave it some thought, and I decided he was right.

We beat New England at home in overtime and then Baltimore away. But I gained only twenty-four yards against the Patriots and twenty-one yards against the Colts, each game with fewer than ten carries and no touchdowns. Woody Bennett, our big fullback, had become the lead carrier in our revised rushing attack but was out for our last game.

The last game of the 1980 season was against the New York Jets at home. We were 8–7 and out of the playoffs. Although I didn't start, the lumps and bruises were still there. As usual, I had been engaged in practice all week and hadn't been aloof or uninterested. This would be the last game of the season and probably my last in Miami. I had continued to take muscle relaxers that had been given to me for pain. I don't recall what I did, but I was at home as usual all evening Friday and went to bed about midnight or 1:00 a.m. I usually set my clock but didn't feel the need to this time. I woke up on Saturday morning, our last practice day before Sunday's game, and rolled over to look at the clock. By the time I would have gotten dressed to go to practice and suited up, practice would have been over. The day before a game, practice is an hour or ninety minutes. I just didn't go at all.

I have always been a night person. That's when I can mentally settle down, slow down, and be quiet. It wasn't anything about being up half the night or on alcohol or drug binge. I didn't set the alarm clock and had overslept. If anything, I had taken too many muscle relaxers. It was that simple. Soma, Flexeril, and Darvon were go to medicines for pain. Little did I know, taking them was like throwing gasoline on a burning fire.

I don't recall anyone in the three years I was in Miami who had missed a practice. At first I was uncomfortable and didn't know what to do or how the players and coaches were going to react to my absence. In fact, it was my first time missing a scheduled practice ever. I felt bad, and in my mind, I wanted to make it up on the field. Coach Shula told me over the phone not to come to the team's hotel the night before the game. I had to be there for the game, however, and he wasn't going to play me. I apologized to him for missing the practice, but in response the only thing I could say was "okay."

Defensive backs Ed Taylor and Don Bessillieu and their wives picked me up the morning of the game. Don had been given instructions to do so, and I must have said one or two words all the way to the stadium. When I walked into the locker room on Sunday morning, you could hear a rat walk on cotton. All eyes were on me. As I sat down and was getting ready to change into my uniform, Coach Shula called me into the coach's dressing room, and it was just the two of us.

He asked me if I was using drugs, and I told him yes—the truth—and said it was because I was bored and depressed, that I didn't like being in Miami and didn't think it was good for me to be there.

He said, "You need to go back to California and get yourself squared away" or something to that effect. I said, "I know what I need to do. Go back and see my therapist and continue to get myself together." With that, I turned around, walked out of the office, got dressed in my pads and uniform, and never touched the field that afternoon. After the Jets game, I think I was the first one out of the locker room. Within twenty-four

I later would come to understand that when a team is winning, it's all about "us," but when a team is losing, someone must take the blame.

hours, I was back home where I wanted to be. Gary Fronrath, the Chevrolet dealer, had given me a Corvette to use during the three years I was there. I left the car in the parking lot of my apartment complex. My only regret that day was not returning the car to his dealership.

We finished the 1980 season with a .500 record, 8–8. The press during the latter part of the season made it appeared that it was my fault we hadn't done better, or at least that's how I perceived it.

I must have seemed too much of an individual to the Dolphins in what had been the ultimate coordination of teamwork. While I was a team player, and my football persona was about the team, after my contract problems it became clear that they did not care about me, let alone individualism. The only thing they had tolerance for was winning. Though I understand the whole concept, it still affected me, as it would have affected anyone.

Even the press could see the changes our offense had gone through. One paper was quoted as saying, "What Williams lacks ... is a good straight man—an Ed McMahon to his Johnny Carson, a reliable sidekick who will make noise when needed and retreat off-camera when he's not."

My stats for 1980, 679 yards on 187 carries, leading the team, were almost what they had been in 1979, 703 yards on 184 carries. I had 1,258 yards on 272 carries in 1978, without Csonka at fullback that year but with a veteran offensive line and quarterback starting almost every game, and we made the playoffs with eleven wins. With Larry in 1979, we had ten wins and also made the playoffs. What a difference two fewer wins in 1980 made—no winning season and no playoffs.

Back in California

Perhaps my future in football had come to an end, because for sure I was prepared to quit playing football before I'd go back to play for

Miami. After not playing in that last 1980 game against the Jets, I left for California the next morning. I could not wait to get back home, because it was a safe and comfortable place for me to be.

I was glad to be in Los Altos, and I followed my normal routine in the off-season. I was sleeping until I was ready to get up for the first two or three weeks, and by mid-January I started watching my soap operas. However, during that time I began to think about my future. When I had left Miami, it was clear to me I would never play there again. I did not want to go back, and maybe they didn't want me back. I kicked that around with Greg Lustig, my agent at the time. He tried to convince me otherwise.

I was my own worst critic. You can never be as objective as you think you are, because you're talking about what you know about yourself that no one else knows. My first day in Miami and meeting with Coach Shula, I set a standard to always be open with him. My position was that if he asked me anything, I would answer him as honestly as I could. That was the relationship I had when Monte and I had a great relationship. Coach Shula was Monte's mentor, so why wouldn't I have the same with him?

Any time Coach Shula and I ever talked, there was never arguing or yelling. It was always a discussion, and I appreciated that about him. As far as I know, he was a man of integrity about our meetings and conversation. I never heard anything that we talked about from anyone in the press or otherwise. Because of that, I will do the same and not discuss any of our private conversations.

What started to resonate with me and kept recurring was my frustration and anger stemming from being traded away from the 49ers and not being paid by them what I thought they owed me. After years, I had still been feeling rejection by the 49ers that I hadn't reconciled, this in

Where do you go to express the feelings you're holding on to? You get along and coexist. Pro football players find themselves in a culture that wasn't designed for that level of human development.

addition to my experiences with playing hurt and getting a new contract in Miami that fell short of my ideal. Part of the frustration came from the inability to process the emotions and have things be all right. I didn't realize I had been compartmentalizing those feelings, that they were being repressed, because that's what I had to do. With the demands on a professional football player to produce and win, you don't have time to address your personal concerns.

Before the 1981 season, I had reporters calling me and wanting to know my intentions. There was all kinds of innuendo in the air. Some said I had narcolepsy and others said a drug problem. In truth, it was somewhere in between although we do not know as much about ourselves as we think. They had talked to Greg Lustig, who made it very clear he didn't know what was wrong and that I would fall asleep on the telephone talking to him.

It was publicized that I did not want to return to Miami, and so in March 1981 I decided to send a letter to Coach Shula removing any question about my intentions. Members of the press characterized my letter as an ultimatum, but it was not. Coach Shula responded to my letter in a professional way.

There are people I probably lashed out at who didn't deserve it and some who did. However, I accept all responsibility for whatever happened with me while I was in Miami, good or bad.

Weighing the Options

In March 1981, it had been three months since the end of the 1980 season. Since being back in the Bay Area, I had thought continually about my future in football as I would turn thirty in April. My health and attitude were excellent following a period of great concern. With this feeling of resurgence in my life, my desire and motivation to play became stronger than ever.

I feel there must be undivided trust between a coach and his players. I feel this is absolutely essential, but I did not feel that the trust shown toward me by the Miami organization was or could ever be sufficient for me to play for the Dolphins again. It was my firm conviction that a trade was the best possible solution for all concerned. That's what I wrote to Coach Shula.

In the letter, I also let him know that I did not see any reason for me to report to a preseason minicamp or summer training camp. At the same time, I let Coach Shula know that I had the utmost respect for him and had learned a great deal from him.

In late August, however, I let the Dolphins know that I had changed my mind and would come to training camp. Shula told the press that they had been unable to work out a trade and were putting me on waivers. My contract was $275,000 for any team to pick me up, which worked against me being traded.

I worked out for the 49ers. Sam Wyche, a former NFL quarterback and now quarterback coach for the 49ers, and Billie Matthews, my old high school coach and now running backs coach for the Niners, oversaw the workout. Sam and Billie had both joined the 49ers as assistant coaches in 1979. After I was done, I went in the locker room, showered, and got dressed. I then waited in the locker room for them or somebody to give me feedback.

After waiting a reasonable amount of time, I left. Nobody, not even Billie, came down to tell me how I did. I had followed Billie from Kashmere High to the University of Kansas. Billie had meanwhile left KU with head coach Pepper Rodgers for UCLA before my sophomore year. After that day of being left in the dark, I decided that I did not want to coach, either in college or professionally. I couldn't ask a player to put himself on the line for me and then shut him out.

In September 1981, I signed a one-year contract with the Packers. The starting halfback, Eddie Lee Ivory, drafted in 1979 out of Georgia Tech, had hurt his left knee after four carries in the opener against the Chicago Bears. He previously had torn the ACL in his left knee in his rookie season opener as well, also on the road against the Bears. I joined the team the same day as John Jefferson. I was surprised to see him there, unaware of his trade from the San Diego Chargers. Apparently, he had been holding out.

After meeting with the press, we each were given a playbook. I was told to learn some specific plays for Sunday's game against the Minnesota Vikings in Milwaukee County Stadium, where the Packers alternated home games with Lambeau Field in Green Bay. The next two days of practice were mainly mental work, learning the plays and watching the offense run.

Eager to play, I spent a lot of time with my playbook and was prepared to go in for what I figured would be at least a few downs. After dinner and the evening pregame meeting I went to my room, went over my playbook, and fell asleep.

Terrible News

In a deep sleep, I heard the phone ring and thought it was my wakeup call for the team bus ride to Milwaukee. As I reached to answer it, I checked the time—it was 5:30 a.m. My first thought was that the hotel had screwed up the time for my wakeup call. But my cousin Cecil was on the line, congratulating me on signing with the Packers. But why was he calling me so early? Thanking him, I asked, "But how did you know where we were staying, let alone get through to my room?"

He said, "Sonny, I have some bad news for you. Your mother had a heart attack and died last night." I immediately sat up in the bed and asked him what happened. Stunned, I had all kinds of questions to ask him but realized that the answers would not change anything. She was gone.

When I hung up the phone, I brought my hands to my face and started crying. I stood up and started pacing the room. The athlete mentality slipped in, thinking I had a game to play, but how could I? There was no question that I was going home.

I called Coach Starr. Before I could finish my first sentence, he said, "I am sorry to hear about your mother. You do whatever you need to do." The hotel had to get his permission to put the call through, so he knew. He said someone would be downstairs waiting to help me get situated. I thanked him for his help and hung up the phone, then threw my clothes in a bag, cleaned up, and went downstairs to the lobby.

I cannot tell you the names of those who helped me or even recall their faces. All I know is from the time I reached the lobby to landing in Houston, I never waited in line or purchased a ticket. Coach Starr and the Green Bay Packers office handled all the travel arrangements. It was a relief that I didn't have to think of anything else. I'll never forget what it felt like to get the help I needed at the right time without having to ask for it.

A month before she died, my mother had visited me in the San Francisco Bay Area, where I had purchased a home when I was with the 49ers. The Miami Dolphins had released me, and I was hoping to sign with another team while continuing to work out and stay in shape without being in a team's training camp. We ate Chinese food for dinner and visited friends, and I showed her around the area. We laughed about some things and disagreed about others. After five days, she wanted to visit Lake Tahoe, but Green Bay called, offering me a tryout. I had to rush and get ready to leave. Though she was enjoying the visit, my mother was also eager to get back to Houston, because she did not enjoy being gone long from home. When I took her to the airport and said good-bye, little did I know it would be the last time I would see her alive.

After a couple days in Houston mourning and visiting with relatives, we buried her on a Wednesday afternoon. When I flew out of Houston that evening, I was still a Green Bay Packer. My family and friends knew me as an employed NFL running back, ready to start a new season with my third team, having relocated from Miami, with its two-time Super Bowl–winning Dolphins, to Green Bay, known as Titletown for its Vince Lombardi championship years. I had a future to take my mind off my mother's death.

I flew back to Green Bay that night to make it to Thursday practice the next day. Back with the team, I received the usual condolences from the players and coaches, which I appreciated, but all of this still kept her death a distraction for me. We were going to play the Giants in New York on Sunday. I did not think that I would play that weekend, but I prepared myself as best I could. The Packers won, making their record 2–3.

Our next game was at Lambeau against the Buccaneers, and that was my focus. I was upbeat and looking forward to my first full week of practice. Two of my best friends from the Dolphins, defensive backs Neal Colzie and Norris Thomas, had been traded to Tampa Bay the year before. I was looking forward to seeing them. With a full week of practice, I figured I had a good chance of playing against them too.

Boy, was I wrong.

18

We all have a tendency to assume things will always continue as they are now. That certainly was my thought as I returned to Green Bay from Houston. Although I was new to the Packers and had not yet played, I felt somewhat detached from my teammates but had a good week of practice. It was early October and already starting to get cold in Wisconsin.

During practice, I could feel myself stiffening up between sets. Not being with the starters meant that you often stood around a lot. On the Saturday morning practice before the next day's game, I was told that Coach Starr wanted to see me and to bring my playbook. Everybody in professional football knows that when you're told to bring your playbook, that means the Turk is waiting. I had seen this before many times. "Going to see the Turk" means that you're going to be cut from the team. The term "Turk" to football players is meant to portray an anonymous executioner. We often refer to the aftermath of a meeting with the Turk by saying "There was blood everywhere."

I had been around the game long enough to know that someday I would meet the Turk, but I didn't think it would be now, just before my first opportunity to play with the team. I wasn't ready. No one ever is. As I walked into Coach Starr's office, I was trying to deal with the impending reality that it was all over. Bart Starr had given me an opportunity when no one else had. I liked him personally as well and could see the effect that being the Turk had on him. I wanted to make it easier on him, as well as save some face, and told him that I had been around the game long enough to know that someday this would happen. I thanked him and his wife for the support they gave me in my time of grief and wished him good luck.

At age twenty-nine, before unsuccessfully trying to make the Packers roster, I had left the Dolphins in 1980 with a career 5,598 rushing yards, then the seventeenth-most yards among all *retired* running backs (many still active players already had accumulated more yards). You get only one shot as an NFL running back, and it's over before you know it.

It was Sunday, October 11, 1981. As usual, the bedroom was pitch dark from the blackout curtains. I rolled over and searched for the remote control. Every off-season, I would take the month of January off to recuperate from the previous season's injuries, which included surgery in three of my eight years of professional football. While I healed, I would watch soap operas from 11:00 a.m. to 3:00 p.m. This morning, I was still drowsy when I found the remote and turned on a professional football game, not a soap opera. Now I was fully awake. I was in bed on a Sunday, and it was not because I was going to play on Monday night. Instead, I was there because I was no longer employed by any NFL team, two of which were now playing on TV.

Less than twenty-four hours before, I had been released from the Green Bay Packers. It was the first time in my eight years of playing professional football that I was home watching a football game on a Sunday like any other fan. I recall criticizing one of the running backs, because I thought I was better. Three years earlier, I had been first-team All-Pro. With Green Bay for only three weeks, I never really had a chance to learn the system, had not even had an opportunity to prove myself and contribute. I did not want to go outside for fear my neighbors would see me and ask why I was home. I was not ready to call friends. I did not want to discuss it. I was embarrassed.

Before I was drafted by the NFL at age twenty-two, I had never had a checkbook in my life. I didn't need one. The only tax question that had ever concerned me was how much of a refund I would get from my summer job. I'd had to adjust to the adult world. But now, at age thirty, my line of work was over. I would have to adjust to being in an environment where few understood the many underlying issues related to being a former professional football player.

I would have to deal full-time now with advice from investment counselors, attorneys, accountants, doctors, friends, and family, and most of them wouldn't be able to help me. In the past, I always had tackled challenges with hard work. That was how I had gotten from my

Houston neighborhood through the University of Kansas and into the NFL. But I soon came to realize that I couldn't manage my disengagement from football with hard work alone. In fact, I learned that I never could fully disengage from football. Those eight years as a pro would always be with me, and the transition required an advanced set of skills. Making the transition from being a pro athlete to a regular person was going to be my biggest challenge of all. At the time, I had no idea what lay ahead of me.

I watched my first NFL game in retirement off and on that day, not really interested, although I continued my critique of the running backs. After a point, I laughed and told myself I was being ridiculous. The backs had no awareness of my sitting at home watching them and certainly had nothing to do with my having been released. At some point, their day of being cut would also come.

Connecting the Dots

I remember my first year in the league, seeing the retired veterans around camp and after games. I recalled the look in their faces. It all was starting to make sense now. Despite the smiles, their expressions said "Our time has come and gone, but you will be here too someday." All current players, rookies and vets, respected those guys. As NFL veteran R. C. Owens would say, "They were the guys that put the furniture in the house." There was a distance between our realities that words could not express. They played before TV took over and when players, even the best, needed second jobs. Travel in those days was haphazard, and fields turned to soggy messes in the winter. But they had been on the field before cheering spectators; they'd had their moments in the sun. Their faces revealed that those days were now gone.

I saw that look, the one that said, "It's not going to last forever, enjoy it while you can." Mentally, they couldn't explain where they were, even if they had wanted to. As to post-competition psychological issues, John Madden stated it simply: "You have nothing to get ready for." To admit to dealing with emotional concerns about disengagement from football was blasphemy.

The televised game dragged on. I could tell it was going to be a long season of game- watching for me, all of it mental and all of it passive.

There was a disconnect between my mental and physical states, because I had been conditioned to play. I tried to identify where to put the energy and what I was experiencing. In those early weeks, I didn't go outside much, leaving the house only when I had to go to the store. Nobody knew I had been cut, nor did I want anyone to know. Now I can see that I was drifting in and out of melancholy and not owning it. I knew it was over, but I had yet to accept that I was done with football. I knew in my heart I could still play. I had seen guys trying to give it one more shot. It happens over and over again. When it becomes obvious, even you know, and you still don't believe it. The team bus had left, and I wasn't on it!

I followed the 49ers all the way to the Super Bowl during that 1981 season. The 49ers before 1981 were, well, pretty much eclipsed. Freddie Solomon, who had been acquired for me in 1978, scored the game's first touchdown. Every time his name was mentioned, it reminded me of how Joe Thomas purged me from the team in his attempt to embellish his own reputation by implanting O. J. on the team. Billie Matthews was O. J.'s position coach in 1979, O. J.'s final season as a pro.

As it was, I had no connection with Bill Walsh, and knew only a few of the current group of players. Guys I knew well while playing with them as a 49er or against them in my last year as a Dolphin included tackle Keith Fahnhorst and linebacker Willie Harper, who, having been born in 1950, was the only Niner in 1981 older than me. I was thirty, and knew I could still play. In my heart, I was still a 49er and it was painful to see them celebrate winning the Super Bowl in January 1982 without me being on the team.

I asked former trainer Chuck Krpata and Tommy Hart what they thought about the team's winning without them, and they felt the same way. On top of it all, Billie Matthews got a Super Bowl ring. I don't usually begrudge people something they've earned, and he certainly could coach in his own right. But I felt that twice he had frozen me out. Not qualifying for a scholarship as a freshman at Kansas was one of the lowest points in my life. Knowing that he got a Super Bowl ring was a dagger in my chest.

On My Own

All players know that even established football careers are going to end by around the age of thirty or possibly a few years longer if you're lucky. Everybody had talked about making sure you save something, putting some money away for that rainy day when you're out and have to start looking for your next income source. But no one ever told you how to save, much less invest.

I assumed that the NFL office or at least the players' association would have a process for retiring from a football career and entering another. Then one day it hit me that they have no vested interest in looking after retired players. More than 120 veterans are shown the exit each year, with very few voluntarily retiring. NFL is sometimes said to stand for "not for long." This can be said for careers as well as how long you are missed after a younger player takes your place. With the college system in place, lots of younger—and cheaper—players are always available.

Tommy Hart, seven years older than me, also had been traded away by the 49ers in 1978. He played two years for the Bears and finished with New Orleans. I called Tommy and asked how he felt being retired and now having to manage his money. He agreed with me that the league had nothing available that could help us. The more I thought about it, the angrier I became. I just did not want to believe that we would be left on our own, which felt like being put out on a limb and with no way to get back.

From high school, we admittedly are coddled with coaching all throughout our careers and then are paid based on a specialized skill sets that are not marketable anywhere else. We're told we are players playing for a championship. Nobody reminds us that we're entertainers. We can't perform into our seventies like the Stones and Tina Turner, and we don't have revival tours as do rock-and-rollers from the sixties. Some guys get to become sportscasters and a few, very few, get to act. Nowadays, those who had relatively long careers and don't go bankrupt perhaps can live off their savings and investments. But for the vast majority, especially back then, we hit the pavement on our own. Even with today's salaries, it's been reported that most NFL players go broke within five years of retirement.

Besides a financial transition, there also is an emotional transition when leaving professional football. Why not discuss it and prepare for it? For that matter, why not encourage getting in mental shape as a part of training to play the game at a high level just as we worked hard to get in the best physical shape we could? The mental aspect of football only came up in game preparation. We players buried the dark side of inevitably leaving football and didn't talk about it.

Like any player, I felt I could still play and be productive. However, I did not want to be one of those guys trying to hang on, a running back struggling with diminishing skills, watching holes close before I could get there. At least I had money in the bank to live off for a while. What I was feeling and experiencing emotionally wasn't about money, and I didn't think I had lost anything. I felt abandoned. Sure, now I can see that I was out of touch, and that's part of what happens. It ended like it seemingly began, overnight. The

Even after being cut, you think you still are part of the NFL family. In reality, you are a football orphan, and the orphanage has closed its doors behind you.

difference is that when we were beginning, we had an idea about what to expect, but when it's over, we didn't see it coming. And the path through transition is not short and easy. There is no shortcut.

My Mother's Shadow

My thoughts in retirement were still in part about my mother after her death. I remembered how she would not sign the consent form for me to play football in high school because she was afraid something might happen to me. Her sister, my Aunt Mary, forged her name for me. Once she knew I was playing football, my mother could have interfered, but she didn't. In retirement, I still questioned whether she had sanctioned me getting Kathy pregnant and whether she did not welcome my choosing my own future. Being successful as a pro player combined with living far from Texas had broken her control over me.

At the funeral I had felt an odd sense of relief. Most of my peers grew up in single-parent families with mothers, not fathers, as head of the household. Consequently, I felt a strong sense of responsibility from an early age. You were expected to help out and contribute financially, which usually meant taking on responsibility, and for some a loss of childhood.

Being too young to fully understand the adult world, I remembered that I had sensed when things were not well with her. As a kid, there was little I could do except try to cheer her up. As an adult, I had a better understanding and a deeper concern. But now that she was dead, none of that mattered any more. I couldn't phone her in Houston and could never visit her again.

Back at McDade Elementary School, I had peered through the chain-link fence separating our open field from the football field of Kashmere High, watching those older boys in practice uniforms, thinking how special they were and wondering what it must take to be one of them some day.

Now I felt that I was on the other side of the fence—the football side—looking at the outside world, wondering where I stood in the scheme of things. Peel away the football background and I was a thirty-year-old college graduate with absolutely no training in business. I had graduated from KU, but the professional skills I had developed were taking a handoff, cutting off a block, catching a swing pass, blocking a linebacker, and so on. My post-graduate studies were football playbooks. All the things I had mastered in my career were now obsolete for the business world. I had given all of my physical and emotional energy to football. After all the years spent studying playbooks and film footage, the hard work, the sweat and strain that you put in to become a specialist, your profession is taken away from you. What personal resources did I have left?

We always prepared mentally for our games and dealt with pain and injuries individually, but we never took an active part in the overall preparation. That was left up to the coaches. Intellectually, we understood the organization behind practices, game plans, and playbooks. We got the importance of having a practice time schedule and of managing a game in the span of sixty minutes. We saw that communication and leadership were critical to succeeding. All of that we'd been ingesting since high school football.

We also learned the value of being on a team, and perhaps we succeeded because we valued the team and our teammates. Football players at that level feel that to matter, to count in the lives of others, you must be part of a team. My best friends in life are past teammates. Each season we all strove together to accomplish the same thing. The goals were clear: win the game, win the division, win the championship. The results also were clear and immediate. Either you outscored the other team, or you didn't.

At the end of the season, either you made the playoffs, or you didn't. For the other six months out of the year, life and decisions weren't always so well-defined. Should I buy this condo or not? What price should I offer? What's a good investment?

In retirement you quickly understand that your life after football is longer than your life in football.

In 1982 the party was on at my house. The difference between retirement and off-season was that the party never had to stop. I had no off-season training regimen and no push to get my affairs in order before I left for another season in Miami. Everyone knew where I was and that my house was open: *mi casa es su casa*. But before too long, I noticed that not only was my booze being drunk and my drugs being used but also other stuff was disappearing from my house. People I had not invited were showing up at my house. Some of them I had met in unsavory circumstances and were not in the same social circles as me. Finally, overwhelmed by the blaring music, unfamiliar voices, loud talk, thick cigarette smoke and too many partiers, I had to leave my own house.

I began to ask myself. "Why am I sponsoring everything?" Over the course of a few weeks, I began to fortify my house by locking the front gate and all exterior doors, plus closing the curtains. I began isolating myself, doing the same thing I had done in Miami where I had felt detached from where I wanted to be, but this time I was home. I had to escape from my escape, and I realized that drugs never were going to provide the answers I needed. I could not continue just filling time.

Professional Assistance

I had started seeing Dr. David Daniels more often. Of slight build, he is a soft-spoken professional who cares about the human condition. He encouraged me to seek and be receptive to internal answers for my external problems, allowing me to see how my life had been driven by outside forces. While doing my personal work, feelings of anger and resentment started to come up about the game of football and how I was being treated. With both the 49ers and Dolphins, I had been told I was part of a family. My exits from each team had felt like being kicked out of a family and left an orphan. Organized football had been my love, but I was not being loved by it in return.

We went about building a tool kit for dealing with personal issues, with the understanding that it was my responsibility to take care of myself. I had excused cocaine as a means of allowing me to exclude all distractions so I could play week after week (although never while on it). With only one day to enjoy your victory (or depression if we lost), I had used it afterwards in an attempt to socially recreate the game-day high. Now it had to be about me and not the team, but I didn't know me. Letting go of the success took me to a place of emptiness without football. I realized that I longed for positive reinforcement beyond football. That was the start of putting my life back together without drugs.

I was thirty-one years old with a body that had been punished for fifteen years.

Professional athletes leave the world most others know to isolate themselves in months of training and then play before thousands in attendance, with millions more watching on television, with intense scrutiny in newspapers, on TV, and on radio sports shows. In doing so, they lose sight of personal needs. Metaphorically speaking, we put ourselves out on a limb without a plan of how we would get back to everyday life. Even if we looked for something else, we didn't look very far. We were limited to six months, making it hard to get hired or to be training for some other job. Furthermore, we had to stay in shape, and if you had surgery, whatever you planned, kiss that good-bye. Conventional thinking was that if you thought about yourself, you couldn't think about the team, and you weren't committed to the team. You had to be all in.

For the first time in a really long time, I had to put the team aside—I was not on a team anymore—and seriously think about myself. A chance meeting was about to give me a new direction and sense of purpose.

19

I often hear it said that the key to a successful retirement is to retire *to* something, not *from* something. Of course, that usually is said in reference to someone in their sixties, not their late twenties or early thirties.

I was going to need something to keep me busy and fill the void. One day I bumped into Marlys Powell, who was my Los Altos Hills neighbor and also an elementary school teacher. Casually, she asked me how I was doing. What do you say, other than put on a good face and tell her that all is well? Catching me totally by surprise, she asked me if I would be willing to speak to her class. Wanting to do something constructive at that point and having nothing else going, I said yes before I knew it. However, what would I tell them? Just retired, I felt still close enough to the game to be of current value to kids, at least in my mind, with whatever I had to offer. I decided to do it but had to ask Marlys what I should talk about. Her response was "Your experience." That stopped me in my tracks, because it forced me to dwell on my entire life in sports.

I was nervous all the way to the school, not wanting to mess this up. I had spoken to booster clubs, but they were there solely as fans, mostly to see you and get a little insight into the season. These were impressionable young minds, and I hoped to give them a meaningful message of some kind, although I wasn't sure what it would be. When I arrived in classroom, I looked around at all these young faces. They were excited and shocked to witness a real-life professional football player in their classroom.

It really didn't matter that I was a former player. Best of all, I had been a 49er, the team that had just won the Super Bowl. Right before

Marlys introduced me, what I was going to talk about came to me. I began telling them about having goals and dreams and that although some can come true, eventually they all come to an end. I used the example of having a real dream, thinking it's actually happening and then waking up.

I told them that is what happened to me. A few days later, Marlys stopped by to tell me what a wonderful job I had done. She encouraged me to do it more, because I was good at it. I brushed it off thinking, how can that be? I had just told those kids about my being out of football, which to me meant that I had failed to keep my dream alive. Had I gone out on my terms, I might have felt differently. But going to see the Turk and being cut meant that I was not worth it to them. Not succeeding in my workout with the 49ers didn't help either. To reach that level it takes a lot of hard work. With all the success I had, I still felt like a failure. The thing we couldn't grasp as starry-eyed kids.

After some more thought, I wondered if what Marlys had said was true, that maybe I should try more speaking to groups about my experiences. Expressing my thoughts and feelings was an outlet for me, though most of the time I expressed anger, because I kept things in until they boiled over. I had no idea whether my thoughts were right or wrong most of the time. What was the appropriate way to express a deeper thought without being pigeonholed as just another athlete? Fighting through the stigma of being just a jock would be a challenge. People other than my friends knew me only as No. 24, if they even knew that. What I used to do was rapidly fading from memory as new players took over the sports headlines. I had to convince the outside world that I could do something else.

Dr. Daniels helped me be open and receptive and aware of my own needs, preparing me to make better choices and also become more consciously aware of my environment. He embodied the humanistic piece that had been missing in my life. Pointing out what was going on with me, he was supportive, firm when he needed to be but never inflexible, and never told me what I should do even though there were times I wanted him to. He became my support system and resource, nurturing me and guiding me to a spiritual path that I have been on ever since. However, at the time, my personal work was just beginning.

Self-Evaluation

When I decided that I wanted something to do with the rest of my life, which at age thirty-one I expected to be a long time, I considered a wide range of possibilities, but it came down to what I knew and what talents I had. I felt I knew the ins and outs of football, and basically I knew that something was missing for players.

As far as my talents went, I knew I could digest a game plan and also that I mixed well with people. Putting that together, I felt I could be a factor in an organization that could assist professional athletes with non-sports-related issues, such as finance, emotional counseling, and retirement. I knew about being a professional athlete, and I knew what was missing for us—or at least what had been missing for me. I had lived it. From inner-city kid to high school All-American, from teenage fatherhood and academic ineligibility to bankruptcy. If I had gotten married, I probably would have been divorced.

There was nothing guiding you in regard to the outside world. When you were playing, you didn't pay much attention to it, but once you were done, you were entirely on your own.

I realized that speaking to groups could be an emotional outlet for me and an opportunity in which I wouldn't be complaining or acting disgruntled. I enjoyed talking about playing football and what it was like to be out of the game. Fred Marcussen, my accountant at the time, got me speaking to every major Rotary and Elks club meeting from San Francisco to San Jose. During these interactions, I was able to meet people in business and learn more about what they did.

After I had spoken to audiences at so many organizations and schools, one day Fred asked me, "Why don't you start a nonprofit organization?" When I replied that I didn't have the slightest knowledge about nonprofits, he said not to worry. Fred became my conscience for the NSCM/Pros for Kids movement. We talked about what it would take to get up and running. Things were coming together faster than I expected. I was becoming increasingly excited about the possibilities of providing something to help players transition into retirement. To my knowledge, neither the NFL nor the players' association had ever addressed how to guide an ex-player going on his own.

I previously had similar discussions with Larry Schreiber, a former 49er fullback and friend. From Kentucky, Larry had attended Tennessee Tech and had been the starting 49er fullback when Wilbur and I were splitting time at halfback in 1974 and 1975. We scheduled a meeting at Larry's house in Woodside with experts in strategic planning and organizational design. Our mission became to reach players before they left the game, and to do that we would need an organization. Larry and I agreed to be cofounders of a professional football player support organization that we named National Sports Career Management (NSCM). I was named president, and Larry became vice president.

At the time, through Claudette Inge, whom I was dating, I met a good friend of hers, Rita Gonzalez, and her partner Byron Kunisawa. Occasionally, we would get together for dinner and attend jazz nightclubs in San Francisco. During our evenings out, I shared my thoughts about the void in the lives of retired professional football players. Among other career talents, Byron was an expert in designing multicultural systems. The more I talked about how it felt to be cut loose without any guidance, the clearer a vision became as to what was needed. Each conversation I had with Byron brought up more questions than answers.

Byron brought two colleagues, Jon Sagen and Terry Adelman, to one daylong meeting. Both were experts in strategic planning and organizational designs. By the end of the meeting they had extracted everything we had ever thought about athletes and professional organizations.

While this was moving fast, I still had to get my head around being the coleader of this business. Previously, I had always been part of an eleven-man unit, doing my part with whatever play was called. Now I was a businessman for real, with only my life and football experiences to rely on.

I realized that this was going to be a change for me, and change is the one thing that most retired players find hard to do. Though I had relished accomplishing individual goals during the season, I also had learned to sacrifice individuality for the team. Along with trying to win each game, being on a team also meant a hard-work ethic, brotherhood, and camaraderie, win or lose. Many players can't get past nostalgia for their days in the NFL and that feeling of being on the field with time standing still. Though the experience of being a professional football player would always be with me, I knew it was time to move on.

Outside the Norm

When pro football players say "It's a game," owners say "It's a business." When players say "It's a business," owners say "It's a game." Professional football is an industry. It always has been, but we players weren't sophisticated enough to see it that way. Those running professional teams didn't deal with emotions, but the game of football is very emotional. Believe it or not, sometimes we need more than money to go out there and put ourselves through what we do. Most of the time, we do it for something or someone else—coach, parents, or kids—because, in a normal state of mind, you wouldn't do that to yourself: my God, playing with broken ribs, dislocated joints, a strained neck, and multiple injuries to other body parts. These are some of the things players go through and the NSCM was intended to address.

On October 15, 1982, I sent letters about our endeavor to NFL commissioner Pete Rozelle; Dick Anderson, former Dolphin player who was a Florida state senator from 1978 to 1982; Ed Garvey of the players' association; Lamar Hunt, president of the AFC; George Halas, president of the NFC; John Underwood of *Sports Illustrated*; and Tad Taube of the Oakland Invaders USFL football team. Along with the letter, I outlined what the NSCM intended to offer in the way of substance-abuse prevention and education. as well as psychological, social, educational, and financial assistance—all the things that I had needed but not had as a player.

The USFL, formally founded in May 1982, was the only organization to follow up on our proposal. We offered a smorgasbord of items worth $450,000. From that, the league chose to direct $100,000 (not enough, but it was a start) toward a recreational drug prevention educational program (at the time it was the first prevention program of its kind for professional sports). The success of the is getting in For each of the USFL's eight teams, we dispatched teams of three persons to each training camp. We hired contractors to conduct the sessions and trained them as well. I put my other interest, the antidrug program called Pros for Kids, on hold.

Our NSCM group continued to assess what we needed to do to succeed with professional athletes. In January 1984, Harry Edwards, a professor of sports psychology at the University of California, Berkeley, was interviewed about what we were trying to do. Edwards said that NFL players' problems begin at the junior high level, when kids are encouraged to be one-dimensional athletes. When they are one day cut and their pro careers end, they are then "sentenced to their own wastelands."

That resonated with me, and I turned my thoughts more toward youth. During the summer of 1983, I had spoken at youth camps as well as with parents and community leaders. In 1984 I continued speaking wherever I could. The USFL didn't continue with their commitment, and the NSCM had no other takers. However, our antidrug message had been fine-tuned and was in shape to be incorporated into a high school program.

Having learned from the NSCM experience, I was ready to proceed with Pros for Kids, a substance abuse prevention and education program for youth. The concept was to use professional and amateur athletes as role models to encourage and support the development of a game plan for a successful life, while helping prevent substance abuse. Our programs ranged from summer camps to group presentations at schools.

In the early 1980s, substance abuse was on the rise in society as a whole. I was the both the public face and spiritual leader of Pros for Kids. My own drug addiction had been admitted privately and publicly and put behind me. However, I was beginning to understand that I needed to be active in an all-consuming way, similar to an addiction but positive and constructive. I became a Pros for Kids zealot, now with an outlet to talk about my addiction and the issues that led to my making that choice.

Needing someone to run the day-to-day operations of Pros for Kids, I was introduced to Orle Jackson, a longtime friend of Byron. Orle was an educator who had run unsuccessfully for superintendent of schools in Alameda County. If elected, he might not have had a long tenure as superintendent, because he was a nonconformist, which made him perfect for our organization. We were awarded every proposal he wrote for the organization, gaining us both contracts and grants, and could not have survived without him.

In 1983 Pros for Kids was getting coverage from local and some national media. We were building a team that was depending on me, which gave me a purpose as well as responsibility. Although it had not been my intention in starting Pros for Kids, I was back in the spotlight and, after years of creating headlines favorable and unfavorable, it felt familiar. Best of all, perhaps, I did not have to deal with battling professional football's underbelly.

I went to Anna Eshoo, when she was a supervisor in San Mateo County, to talk about Pros for Kids when we first started. She said there wasn't much she could do, given the county's limitations, but suggested that I see Assemblyman Art Agnos. He and California state senator John Seymour from Anaheim cowrote a bill to create funds for programs such as Pros for Kids.

The basic message of Pros for Kids was that using drugs can stop you cold. We were committed to keeping young people from learning the hard way by using sports stars to reinforce that message. We paired athletes with business professionals, using men and women from diverse sports and professions. Needing athletes to deliver the message, we began to get more of them buying into our program and wanting to speak to kids. As it did for me, participating in Pros for Kids filled the athletes' void as much as it was an eye-opener for the young people.

Constant Fund-Raising

The difficult part about all of this for me was fund-raising. It was a constant battle to raise money, and we were always looking for new and innovative ways to do so. A former teammate with the 49ers, Tim Anderson, and his college roommate Jack Tatum, both Ohio State All-Americans, got involved. They asked Woody Hayes, the former Ohio State football coach, to be the keynote speaker at the first annual Pros for Kids fund-raising dinner. Without hesitation he said yes. At the dinner with 250 in attendance, Woody talked about parent-and-child relationships. He said it was important to be with your kids while they were studying and to always be present for them. He went on for forty-five minutes and received a standing ovation when he was done.

But Pros for Kids seemed to be fighting an uphill battle. Corporations seemed to think it was just another antidrug nonprofit with nothing new to offer. I had taken $25,000 of my own savings to keep it afloat. A fund-raising jazz concert we had scheduled at the Circle Star Theatre in San Carlos was canceled because of a lack of tickets sales.

In September 1984, Orle walked into my office and sat down. He started talking to me about something, but all I could hear was "We should invite Mrs. Reagan to be our guest speaker at the next dinner."

I looked at him and said, "No, she won't come for our program."

He said, "Why not? She supports the 'Just Say No' program in Oakland."

Orle was confidant and said, "Let's send a letter and invite her. At worst, she'll say no."

The more we talked about it, the more it didn't seem so far-fetched, although it was a long shot. I was concerned about the content of the letter. After all, she was the wife of the president of the United States.

I talked with Ken Barun, director of project and policy in the Office of the First Lady, a couple of times between January and May 1985. During one of our conversations, he took me by surprise when he said he remembered me when I was in high school. He was in Houston at the time, where he received a bachelor of science degree in sociology from the University of Houston. During our conversations, he asked questions about the event and how I envisioned it going. In our conversations, I was trying to stay realistic but hopeful that Mrs. Reagan might accept.

Eventually I received the phone call with the news. When our receptionist, Jennifer, told me who the call was from, my first thought was that Mrs. Reagan had declined. I picked up the phone and said, "Ken, how are you?" He said, "We have a date."

The old saying is to be careful what you ask for because you just might get it. It slowly sank in: the First Lady of the United States was going to be the guest speaker at Pros for Kids annual fund-raising dinner.

It would be hard to think of two people with less in common than Nancy Reagan of Hollywood and Washington, DC, and Delvin Williams from Houston's Fifth Ward. Yet we were to develop something much closer to friendship than simply a business relationship.

Mrs. Reagan had launched her Just Say No drug awareness campaign in 1982, about the same time I started thinking about Pros for Kids. Asked by a schoolgirl what to do when offered drugs, she had responded, "Just say no." The phrase proliferated in the popular culture of the 1980s and eventually was adopted in the name of organizations and school antidrug programs. It was her primary project at the time. Critics, including me, argued that the Just Say No program did not go far enough and labeled it as simplistic.

I had lived with and seen the effects of drug and alcohol addiction when I first heard of Just Say No. At first glance, I felt it wasn't enough, because the problem stemmed from deeper issues that just couldn't be overcome by simply refusing substances. Those of us caught at the intersection of several personal issues have trouble identifying the causes of drug abuse. Others just do not want to deal with the reality of being off substances. I felt it couldn't be that simple: You can't quit by just not wanting to do it anymore! Deep inside, you want that time to come, and you don't know when or if it ever will. You hope that you can outlast the bad until you come to that point of knowing that quitting is best for you.

Those with addictions usually are unaware of the problems leading to drug use until it's too late. Understanding why we turn to drugs is the first step in solving the problem. Knowing what drugs can do to us is the next important step to understanding a reason not to get involved with them. Just Say No organizations educating young children and teenagers about the effects of drugs also addressed how to ward off peer pressure to use them. But simply "just say no"? Even with our criticism, however, we were better off having Mrs. Reagan involved, because a laser beam of attention was brought to the problem when she stepped in.

I still hear Grandmother Pearlie's voice ringing in my ears: "Don't put your hands on nothing that don't belong to you, respect your elders, and don't forget to say your prayers." All my life it seemed as though she had been watching me to make sure I followed her instructions. In that moment, it felt like a by-product of heeding her words. But I don't blame anyone for not learning lessons that they weren't taught. After all, how could they know beyond their day-to-day world?

You were supposed to conform without questioning parents' way of doing things. The confusing, prevailing mentality was "do as I say and not as I do." You were punished verbally and physically if you didn't. You inevitably reverted to the way you had learned how to do things, even though you might think doing the opposite was correct according to what you believed inside. But going your own way meant you were a rebel, part of the counterculture. Unlike my childhood best friend, Evans Ross, and cousins who died tragically, I avoided the traps and pitfalls that lay before me by the grace of my grandparents, using the tools they passed on to me as a child.

What I was going to experience with the First Lady was something I had never dreamed. Had somebody fantasized about it during those days growing up in the Fifth Ward, such a notion would've been squashed immediately. It would have been seen as too foolish to even think that something like that would ever happen. As with most things of importance in my life, I had to learn on the fly.

When Ken Barun said she was coming, I asked, "Are you kidding me?" But the detailed information he then relayed was all the confirmation I needed. In a daze, I missed some of what he was telling me, because my head was swimming, thinking about what we had to do. Ken said I would receive a letter from the First Lady's staff confirming her attendance at the November 26, 1985, Pros For Kids dinner. He was clear that our organization had responsibility for the dinner and that Mrs. Reagan would only speak to the dinner guests. In addition, she would not raise money or call anyone on our behalf.

We were on our own, but we had the backing to make it happen. I had convinced Mrs. Reagan through her staff that we could make this a wonderful event and that the children would be the beneficiaries.

I called Bruce Bosley, an ex-49er from the 1960s who now was president of the NFL Alumni Association to tell him we had confirmation that Mrs. Reagan was coming. We next called the Pros for Kids chairman, Jim McMasters, a real estate developer, and the rest of the directors. After we calmed down from this unbelievable moment of excitement, the reality set in. I thought, *How do you host a dinner with the First Lady as the primary guest?* The magnitude of this was daunting, and I knew we had our work cut out for us.

Myriad Details

I sat in my office most of that first day thinking about what this meant, including the politics of it. Pros for Kids had been nonpolitical. After receiving our tax-exempt status as a nonprofit organization, I had changed my voter registration from Democrat to independent. As the head of Pros for Kids, I wanted to be neutral with the political system.

That was natural for me because I pride myself in getting along with anyone. I grew up a Democrat (and will probably die a Democrat), though my family was mostly oblivious to national politics as I grew up. There were no Republicans around, not to mention no Republican Party to speak of. As far as we were concerned, where Republicans controlled the purse strings, the after-school activities programs and equipment money dried up. Where Democrats were back in office, the programs activities and equipment returned. That's what I knew about politics besides understanding at an early age that Presidents Kennedy and Johnson were Democrats. My political baggage, what little there was, was that of my family. Now at age thirty-five, I was going to meet the most powerful woman in the world, as far as I was concerned, who was the wife of the president of the United States, a Republican.

We began to build a dinner committee headed by Bosley, who had headed the local NFL Alumni Association chapter out of Redwood City before he became president of the association. He also had participated in several charities and civic events, besides running his own remodeling business. Drafted from the University of West Virginia by the 49ers, he had been selected as a Pro Bowl offensive lineman four times before retiring after the 1969 season following one year with Atlanta.

Bruce let us know that we needed to broaden the committee beyond the Pros for Kids board, which meant including more members of the Republican Party, which was fine with me. Otherwise, it would be an affront to Mrs. Reagan. Getting the different committee members together and focused was a political task in itself. However, signing up the athletes to attend wasn't a problem at all.

Frank Gifford, former New York Giant and *Monday Night Football* broadcaster, agreed to act as master of ceremonies. We had received confirmations from 49ers Joe Montana, Keena Turner, Ronnie Lott, and Dwight Clark, plus ex-49ers Y. A. Tittle and R. C. Owens, among others. Former tennis star and San Francisco native Rosie Casals and LPGA rookie of the year Julie Inkster from Los Altos would attend. Baseball players would be present as well, including Bob Brenly, the Giants catcher, and Bret Saberhagen and George Brett of the 1985 World Series–winning Kansas City Royals. Both Royals baseball players were sponsored by Puma, which also supplied jogging suits and shoes for our sports camps.

Also volunteering were various A's players as well as several Northern California Olympians. The Gatlin Brothers agreed to provide the entertainment. Dinner was set at $125 a plate, and around a dozen corporate sponsors signed up, offering between $5,000 and $10,000 donations.

I was amazed at how far I had traveled in such a short period of time.

This was a new kind of team and a whole different kind of spotlight and pressure.

Unexpected Phone Call

One morning, I woke up to the telephone ringing. It was 5:00 a.m. Nobody ever calls me at that hour unless someone has died. Three years before, a call at five in the morning had informed me of the death of my mother, and I hadn't forgotten it and never will. Usually, I won't answer such an early call, but, with the upcoming event, this time I did. It was Kathy, my daughter's mother, on the line. She called me only when it was about Dositheia, our daughter. Still waking up, I thought I heard her say that she had put Dositheia on an airplane flying from Houston to San Francisco. Whoa, what's going on here?

She continued, telling me that it was my turn and that she was "tired of it" (the responsibility of parenting, I assumed). I tried to tell her that I had this dinner happening and that she should have called me earlier so we could have talked about what was going on and what we needed to do. Nope, she let me know that Dositheia was on the plane and that the plane was in the air en route to me.

I hadn't been involved in raising my daughter. I saw her only when I went home to Houston for holidays or if she was in trouble. Kathy had always insisted on involving me in every problem, and I was just as insistent in having her deal with our daughter's life. Dositheia, now sixteen years old, was caught in the middle, as she had been all of her life. She had to live out the anger that had been created, none of which was her fault and so difficult to explain to a child.

Even though Kathy had given me the time of arrival, I wondered if this was really happening. The dinner with Mrs. Reagan was two weeks away, and her advance team was to arrive in a little over a week. There still were plenty of loose ends that I barely had enough time to tie up. Now I had to get dressed and get to the airport.

I fiddled around, hoping Kathy was just pushing my buttons and that it was a false alarm just to let me know we both had responsibilities and I wasn't living up to mine. But if it were true, I was unprepared to handle my daughter living with me and everything that went with that, not the least of which would be enrolling her in school. Not that there ever had been a good time for me to have her with me in California, but this was the worst timing. The irony was that she could benefit from the dinner's antidrug message. Like her father, she had her share of substance problems, and like her father she was defiant.

Continuing to think about how to handle the situation, I drove to the airport, parked, and arrived at the gate thirty minutes early. When the plane arrived, I stood there waiting, and as the last of the passengers came out the passageway, sure enough, there she was. When we made eye contact, she started smiling, and so did I. We reached each other and hugged. I suggested getting breakfast before leaving.

As we talked through breakfast, I came to a decision in my mind. I reiterated what I had told her about the Oakland dinner and time constraints with it. Then I said to her, "I have to send you back home." When I said that, I could see the frustration, dejection, and feeling of rejection, the last biggest of all. What an empty feeling I had, having to do it, and how much worse it was for her on the receiving end. I had not been involved in her day-to-day life in Houston, and now I would not be involved here either. I apologized, hoping that she would understand and forgive me. It was the worst thing I have ever done to her. All I had to offer was that I would stay at the airport until I had put her on a flight back to Houston.

No matter how I talked about the importance of the upcoming dinner, it didn't make me feel any better. Two and a half hours later, I put her on a flight back to Houston. Running late for my next meeting, I then left the airport.

Some years later, we talked about that incident, and she told me that her mother had told her that I had sent for her! That blew me away, and I let her know that was a lie, but she had already figured it out by the surprise on my face and knowing her mother so well. Even so, I told her that it was probably the worst thing that I had ever done to her. Smiling, she agreed with my assessment and said, "Damn, at least you could have taken me to your house!" That was not a debatable issue at the time, and all I could do was agree with her.

Staying away from drugs was one of the issues she was struggling with, even then as a teenager. I believe that new scenery can help, but you have to want it and be willing to work at changing your way of life. I have sat down with her on several occasions to talk about developing a plan, but she never wanted to hear that. I often demonstrated that I would help her get off drugs, but I couldn't want it more than she did. First getting herself clean, getting into counseling, and trying to find a job were all necessary. Maybe that was asking a lot, but she wouldn't have had to do it alone. I was willing to do my share, but she needed to make a consistent effort and want to change her life.

That was what I had learned at age thirty-one. That day at the airport, my daughter was sixteen and had grown up in an environment that I had been able to leave behind due to my football scholarship to college. Sure, I had some unexpected challenges on the way, and I'd had to work hard to make it, but I had the benefit of a whole other perspective. Putting her on the plane for the sake of the Pros for Kids dinner with the First Lady as speaker was not my finest hour with my daughter.

Finalizing Plans

The dinner was to be held in the convention center in downtown Oakland. Although we did not have an office or presence in the Oakland area, Mrs. Reagan had been to the East Bay city on several occasions for her Just Say No program and was familiar with the surroundings. Before that evening I didn't know anything about advance teams but was told they would be arriving days ahead of the scheduled dinner. Their job, I learned, was to check out the route and make sure everything was organized and coordinated, to ensure the safety of the First Lady, plus see that we were doing what we said we would do.

Waiting with our committee in one of the convention center conference rooms, I saw three or four cars pull up outside and a couple dozen white males dressed in suits get out, including Ken Barun, Marty Coyne, and David Rabin, three members of her advance team whom I already had gotten to know. Out of the fifteen to twenty people in the room, eight were from the advance team. Ken was my contact person. After introductions and pleasantries were exchanged between the team and the committee, we got down to business.

I sat randomly at mid-table before I heard Ken say, "Delvin, come and sit up here" as he pointed next to himself. He told our committee, "It's a Pros for Kids event, and Mrs. Reagan will be here as Delvin's guest." Then he clarified some things and answered questions. There had been bickering beyond my control between the alumni and some of the committee members. Ken let everybody know that the advance team was in charge of Mrs. Reagan and what the committee members' roles were going to be. As he took over, all of the tension over resolving such issues left my body.

We had several walk-throughs of the route the First Lady was going to take. After a couple of days, the advance team comfortably settled down, and team members were even able to laugh and kid a bit. At times,

I had to remind myself that I was working with the Secret Service. Where I grew up, you avoided the police as best you could, but here I was with one of our nation's most elite police team. Protecting the president and First Lady was their job. They were really great guys with a very intense job in which mistakes are not allowed.

The 49ers, who were defending Super Bowl champions, were playing Seattle at Candlestick in a *Monday Night Football* game. Bruce got the advance team sideline passes as well as NFL alumni T-shirts. The 49ers won 17–6, with Freddie Solomon and Dwight Clark both catching touchdown passes from Joe Montana. Looking back, it was a vintage game, but I had much more than football on my plate.

Dinner the following night was a sellout, with twelve hundred people in attendance and a celebrity athlete at each table. The Gatlin Brothers and Frank Gifford arrived along with the owner of Puma. We all were running around getting last-minute things done. Finally, I took a last walk through the convention center. The show was under way, and I figured certain things would just have to work out, whether I knew about them or not. The volunteers were there setting up the tables and decorating them with blue and yellow napkins, the theme colors of Pros for Kids. Others dealt with any problems signing people in and getting them seated. The police and Secret Service were sweeping the facility with dogs, even on the rafters. Soon people were starting to enter the venue. I waved at some people and avoided others who would have wanted to talk, taking my time away from what I needed to focus on.

"The Eagle Has Landed"

While we were in the reception room, Ken and I were talking when one of the Secret Service members said to him, "The Eagle has landed. She will be arriving in twenty minutes." I thought that would be a fast trip from the Oakland Airport but then realized maybe not, with police escorts and not having to stop. Walking around and talking to different people, I was getting nervous, thinking about what I should say and how to hold a conversation with Mrs. Reagan. Before I knew it, Ken said, "We have about two minutes before she arrives. Come with me."

Ken and I walked out of the private reception around a corner and through a door into the bowels of the convention center to a side entrance. He opened the side door to check on her arrival. I could see the snipers on rooftops and police officers with dogs patrolling the blocked-off streets. Within thirty seconds of closing the door, he was informed that she had arrived. When he next opened the door, her motorcade was pulling up, led by police officers on motorcycles and followed by three limousines. The second limousine stopped at the door where we were standing. Secret Service staff ran from both limousines to the one in the middle.

Gathering about the car, they looked around and opened the door. As the door opened, they formed a protective walkway. As an agent grabbed her hand to assist her, she stepped out of the car. Standing inside the building and filled with anxiety, I watched this take place. In a black dress and wearing a pearl necklace, she walked in with such ease and grace. Diminutive in stature but having a strong presence and a slight smile, she reached out to me.

With both hands I took her hand and said, "Welcome to Oakland, Mrs. Reagan, and thank you for agreeing to be Pros for Kids guest speaker tonight." She replied simply, "Thank you for inviting me." I shared with her that twelve hundred people were due to attend the dinner and that our organization hoped to net $125,000, a huge amount for us that was largely due to her attendance.

Led by the Secret Service members and her staff, we walked back into the private reception where everybody was in line waiting for us. All of this had been predetermined, timed and rehearsed. She entered the room ahead of me to her position behind the ropes. I stood between Mrs. Reagan and the procession of guests that I would introduce to her. Having done this on many occasions, she was as cool and calm as anyone could be. On the outside I was calm, but on the inside I was nervous as all get out. When Chuck Krpata, one of our board members, stepped forward with his wife Brenda, I couldn't remember her name. That was an embarrassing situation, and in a fun way she has never let me forget it.

At this type of dinner, it is typical to have a private reception to thank those who support such causes by allowing them to meet the dignitaries. Those who had supported Pros for Kids were to have an opportunity to meet the First Lady. Our limit was 126 people. Among our board of directors, corporate sponsors, and athletes, it was hard to hold it to this number, but it was limited to the amount of time Mrs. Reagan had. A line was formed for those to be received by the First Lady and myself. So many folks who wanted to be and should have been included weren't able to participate, but just before the reception began, we were able to allow a couple dozen more guests to join.

After we finished the receiving line, time was left for Mrs. Reagan to listen to board members talk about the program and the good things we were doing. I think she was impressed. Soon it was time for her entrance, which meant I would escort her out to her seat. Before the introduction to the crowd by Frank Gifford, we were standing there looking at each other. I said, as if she didn't know, "All of those people are here to see you." She looked at the crowd and then at me with a slight smile as though she were surprised at the attention.

About that time "Hail to the Chief" began to play. When Frank spoke into the microphone, "First Lady Nancy Reagan, escorted by Delvin Williams," all twelve hundred people stood up with spotlights shining as she walked out, waving to the people as I escorted Mrs. Reagan to her seat.

The program, which was precisely scripted, went as expected. The 49er tackle Bubba Paris gave the invocation, and the Gatlin Brothers entertained through the dinner. During the meal, many people tried to get pictures of Mrs. Reagan by gathering around us while we ate. The Secret Service agent asked me if I would help them try to keep people away. He said, "This is your event, and she's your guest. It's our job to protect her. If you could help keep some of the people away, I would appreciate it."

While I was insisting on some of the people moving back, I felt an open hand patting my left arm. As I looked around at the guests, sitting on my left and smiling in a motherly way, Mrs. Reagan said, "Eat your dinner. It's Okay." Her words let me know she was comfortable and enjoying herself. I said, "Yes, ma'am." I appreciated that she let me know she was having a good time. As much as we could in this type of situation, we bonded.

A group of kids from the Just Say No club in Oakland performed songs for her. I spoke briefly, and then George Brett made a special presentation. He gave her a jogging suit that read "First Lady" with a number 1 and a second suit reading "President" with a number 2. Of course, the audience started laughing and clapping. We stepped back, and she said a few words. During her speech, she was talking about a young kid who was addicted to drugs, and she began to cry. Standing behind her and out of the spotlight, I walked up and gave her my handkerchief. She acknowledged it and finished her speech.

I walked off the podium ahead of her so I could assist her coming down the stairs. I stepped out of the spotlight as she left the room, waving to the crowd. We returned to the holding area where the Secret Service gathered around, ready to move out. I thanked her again for coming and told her how much it meant to Pros for Kids and to me personally. She thanked me once more for inviting her. As they whisked away, she said to keep her informed. Once again, I said "yes, ma'am" and exhaled.

> *It felt like a dream, beyond any reality I had ever known.*

To our organization, it meant so much having her there, in essence legitimizing Pros for Kids. We had something greater to live up to. The bar had been raised. Our work had just begun. But we now had the funds to get more programs in motion. A celebrity golf tournament was planned for the following summer as well as another fund-raising dinner plus an annual recognition dinner held in the spring.

Building on Experience

My own background of substance abuse was a two-edged sword. It gave me the experience to speak about drugs, which to others looked like credibility. To demonstrate the damage drugs do, I could go with the story that cocaine use primarily prematurely ended my playing career. But I didn't feel that actually was the case in my situation. So much more was involved with my feeling isolated in Miami for a number of reasons.

When you hear eighty thousand fans roar as you score the winning touchdown and teammates jump on you and give you high fives on the sidelines, that's immediate gratification. It's hard to turn off that adrenaline. Not being able to unwind very well could be one reason a player might turn to drug use. That's not to say that cocaine isn't harmful, because it is. It can be even more disastrous for retired players, consuming precious savings. It also can lead to excessive carousing, which presents its own set of problems when playing but once out of the rigorous structure required by professional football for at least six months out of the year, there can be no end to it.

The antidrug campaign gave me a forum to express myself. Besides the "don't use drugs" message, my theme also was about detours in life. I wanted kids to quit drugs but not quit in life. There are lots of choices to be made, with drugs being one of them. My turning point was when I lost my scholarship. In my talks, I let kids know I was the one who had gotten the poor high school grades. Because of that, I had to pay a higher price to stay in college, which I did. Education is the long-term answer, but it's a slow process, with the devoted classroom teacher never getting enough credit.

None of us thought that successfully organizing Pros for Kids was going to be easy. Life consists of slow, gradual changes, and pro football is a series of violent moments of quick change ending with one extreme or another, either winning or losing. The process starts from the time a team gets the game plan on Monday as the players focus on Sunday's game, so they will take the field both physically and mentally prepared. The efforts they put in pay off in immediate results on game day. After a few hours, the game is over, and players know whether their hard work paid off or not. In contrast, it wasn't clear to me as a freshman at Kansas that I would graduate four years later. Likewise, we had spent many months and trying to implement NSCM and then Pros for Kids, without knowing if either of the programs would succeed and without any way to measure results as we went.

Two weeks after the 1985 dinner, our Pros for Kids board had not yet come down from the excitement of having Mrs. Reagan as our guest speaker. The congratulatory letters and phone calls still were coming in. Inspired by the successful dinner, we hoped to raise enough money to keep the program going, pay those like myself management salaries, and pay our debts. Although we were a nonprofit organization, we still had to run it like a business, which I was learning daily how to do.

I was never good with numbers, nor had I been in a leadership role, because I was always a team player. Larry Schreiber, as vice president, was not involved in the day-to-day activities with Pros for Kids. In my leadership role as president, I was the one pushing our agenda. Keeping Pros for Kids going was a struggle during the first three years. Scheduled to earn nearly $38,000 annually, I hadn't ever taken my management salary. Getting corporate sponsorships, grants, and contributions had been all-consuming and difficult to achieve. I found that raising money for a nonprofit organization would be one of the hardest things I've ever had to do. I wasn't used to asking for anything, particularly money from someone else. Nonetheless, I had to do it, and the dinner helped open some doors.

As it got close to Christmas 1985, I made plans to travel to Houston for holidays. This meant going back to the projects of Fifth Ward after having as my dinner guest the First Lady of the United States. Still in a daze over the November event, I thought about it for quite a while. It wasn't every day a kid from my neighborhood would have such a special opportunity.

How could I explain the impact on me and what I was trying to accomplish that my friends and family would understand?

I would find out back home in the Fifth Ward.

I traveled to Houston whenever I could during holidays to see family and friends. Although I hadn't lived there since I left for college, the town was always with me. There were guys there who had come before me with similar opportunities toward a pro sports career but hadn't made it. When you leave the neighborhood, you must grow beyond the persona that you developed there.

In order to make it, I had to grasp that growth was the difference between moving on or holding on. When I left home, I wasn't sure of who I was beyond football. By not giving up, I was growing, albeit not sure who I was becoming. Leaving a segregated environment behind wasn't a cure for racism. However, I was proud of where I came from and wasn't afraid to let my roots drive my response to things I disagreed with. But I was always open to new learning, which meant changing as well as growing. Fifth Ward was a grounding force that helped me move forward.

Living in Fifth Ward, personal change wasn't supposed to occur to someone like me, the oldest in a single-parent welfare family. Someone

My life was different now, and my experiences were pulling me away from a myopic view of the future. Those who never leave the neighborhood can't ever see beyond Fifth Ward.

like me wasn't meant to get out of this neighborhood. Growing up there, I had to learn the ways of the streets and how to survive in the environment. It was now December 1986, and I had not lived in Houston since August 1970, almost half my life. I was on the fence between growth and resistance.

I was standing on the corner of Lyons and Gregg, where we once congregated before classes started at E. O. Smith Junior High School. After reminiscing for about an hour or so with some of the guys, I decided to check in with Pros for Kids back in the Bay Area. At a nearby phone booth, I called the office collect. Taupo, our receptionist, answered the phone, and, as always, I kidded with her for a few minutes before asking her what was going on.

Before I could as, she said, "Delvin, you have a letter, and the return address is the White House."

Shocked, I asked her more about it, and she replied, "It's the size of an invitation. Do you want me to open it?"

"Yes, please!"

I did not have the slightest idea of what it could be, other than a thank-you card of some kind. Because I already had received a thank-you letter from Mrs. Reagan, I wondered what it could be.

Opening the envelope, Taupo read, "The President and Mrs. Reagan request the pleasure of your presence for a state dinner at the White House honoring His Excellency, León Febres Cordero, President of Ecuador."

I had her read it again just to make sure it was an invitation to the White House for dinner. I could not believe it! She read me the brief details, which included a welcome ceremony in the Rose Garden and the dinner date of Tuesday, January 14, 1986. I said to myself, "Wow," which was all I could think. Hanging up in the phone booth, I walked back to tell the few of the fellows where I had been. Of course, they thought I was kidding. When they realized I was serious, they questioned if it was real, but, once convinced it was, they were happy for me.

Upping the Ante

Having Mrs. Reagan attend the Pros for Kids dinner was one thing, as it tied in to her Just Say No campaign. However, this invitation was voluntary on her part and personal. It was one of those moments in life when there is no reference point on how you should respond or react. To Johnny Ray Peacock standing next to me, I said, with Fifth Ward bravado, "Who else do you know can stand on the corner of Lyons Avenue and Gregg Street one day, and in a matter of days, have dinner at the White House?"

After hearing my White House news, Peacock looked at me, smiled briefly, and then burst out in laughter, first as if I was lying and then as if I wasn't, which would be even more far-fetched. I laughed right along with him. Laughter was his way of disarming a situation, and I was used to it, but something in my eyes must have let him know it just might be true. I reassured him it was, and, after he settled down, he got serious, asking for details. At the time, I did not have any to give him, because I had just gotten the news from my secretary, but I did remind him of the Pros for Kids dinner that Mrs. Reagan had attended. Because it was right before Christmas, I would have to cut my Houston visit short to go home and prepare to leave for Washington for the January 14 dinner.

Flying back to California from Houston, I kept thinking about the state dinner and how it represented the metaphor of crossing to the other side of the track. Pro football, for all its glory, wasn't glamorous. The Reagans, of course, had combined the mystique and power represented by both Hollywood and Washington. That way of life was something I was not familiar with and had seen only on television. For the moment, being briefly invited into it was something quite exciting, like flying into San Francisco for the first time and seeing the glittering lights of the homes in the Bay Area hills. The allure of it all was seductive. Sports had catapulted me into this position of connecting with the First Lady.

However, coming from Fifth Ward kept me grounded, and I understood that being included in the dinner didn't mean equality. The elders would always tell a youngster, "Don't get too big for your britches" and "Don't ever forget where you came from." But they forgot to add, "Keep pursuing your dreams."

I had not been invited for my reputation;
rather, it was for my character.

I arrived in Washington on Monday night, January 13, 1986, as I planned to attend the welcoming ceremony the following morning. The next day at 10:00 a.m., President Reagan welcomed the president of Ecuador and his wife to the United States of America. During the ceremony, I stood on the White House lawn to the left of the president, behind the ropes along with other invited guests, and observed the ceremony. It was another first-time experience and, as with most, I would never forget it. After the ceremonies, I was ushered inside the White House. I do not know in which room we were, but it was a greeting room for invited guests.

Inside, much to my surprise was Karen Matthews, the daughter of my high school football coach Billie Matthews and the youngest of his three children. I did not recognize her at first. Besides, who would have ever thought of running into someone you knew in, of all places, the White House? It so happened that she was married to someone on the Washington pro football team, a person whose name I no longer can remember. She introduced me to her husband, and we had a brief conversation. It was good seeing her.

I said good-bye to Karen as I was escorted to the First Lady's office. Having had conversations with most of the people in her office regarding the Pros for Kids dinner, I was pleased to put names with faces. Mrs. Reagan was in her office, and I spoke with her briefly, thanking her for inviting me as she was leaving for appointments. While sitting and chatting with some of the people I had spoken with before, I did not want to overstay my welcome. However, as I thought it must be time for me to go, they gave me a brief tour and an opportunity to see the Oval Office, which was smaller than it appears to be on television. After the tour, I took a taxi back to my hotel, where I took a nap.

Waking up and getting dressed, I could feel my tension rising and fretted over many details. Thankfully, my tuxedo arrived with the wrinkles removed, as I had requested before I left that morning. Just before leaving, I called my Aunt Delphine. As we talked about the upcoming moment, I stated my wish that both my mother and grandmother were alive. So did she, and as we hung up, we both said, "I love you." Leaving the hotel, I took a limousine taxi and felt like a real dignitary when I arrived at the gate. The guard checked my ID and let us through to the circular driveway that I had seen many times on television.

When I entered the White House, a guard directed me to stand in line behind a group of people. Thinking the line was for security reasons, much to my surprise, it was quite the contrary. Each individual or couple attending the dinner was introduced to the press. When my name was called and I walked across the room, though, I felt uncomfortable with the moment of attention. I still had a mind-set of always being humble and knowing that I am not bigger than my team.

Rubbing Elbows

The evening was the ultimate in formality, which I wasn't accustomed to. However, I soon settled in and absorbed the evening. I talked to Vice President George Bush during the reception. When the vice president was a congressional representative from Houston—the first Republican one—my picture was taken with him at the high school all-star game practice held at the University of Houston. I reminded him of that, and, of course, he did not remember but, as a seasoned politician, he did not miss a beat. While surveying the room, he saw someone he wanted to talk to. Before leaving, he mentioned that Jack Yates High School had won the previous year's (1985) Texas state football championship and said he needed to call the head coach and congratulate him. I was impressed because I didn't know that.

At Mrs. Reagan's table, I was seated next to Ann Getty. A layman as far as politics goes, I thought it was odd that Getty, a lifelong Democrat, and Mrs. Reagan were friends, sitting next to each other, smiling and having a conversation. At that time, Ann's husband, Gordon, was ranked as one of the richest men in America and was officially a Republican, living in pro-Democrat San Francisco. The message I got was that you could have different political views and still be friends, and it didn't hurt if one husband was a billionaire and the other the president. There were tables of eight, and, although I cannot remember everyone in attendance, I do recall Bob Schieffer from CBS News, and David Hasselhoff, then starring in the TV show *Knight Ryder*. The guests at our table were journalist Andrew Rosenthal, golfer Nancy Lopez, and ballerina Heather Watts.

While we were sitting, Mrs. Reagan introduced me to Ms. Getty. She then asked me to tell Ann and the other table guests what I did. That was unexpected, but I ad-libbed with a Pros for Kids overview, all the while conscious of not being long-winded as I have a tendency to do. Arriving at our table, the president introduced the honored guest and his wife. After a few words, President Reagan raised his glass and made a toast to the United States and the Republic of Ecuador. After dinner, we were entertained by soprano Jessye Norman. I am not an opera aficionado but recognized she had a beautiful voice.

Evening to Remember

It was a long night, but what a great experience. Afterward we were ushered to the front of the White House where a US military ensemble performed. The president and First Lady took the floor for the first dance. As the orchestra played, I took in the ambience to appreciate where I was standing, juxtaposed with where I was three weeks ago in Houston's Fifth Ward on the corner of Lyons and Gregg.

As the music stopped, the guests all seemed to move closer to the president and First Lady. The flashbulbs from the cameras were reminiscent of a Hollywood opening. Shaking hands and talking with friends, arm in arm, they started waving good night to their guests. Relieved that I hadn't screwed anything up, I stood there smiling, relishing the moment.

I waved and called, "Good night, Mrs. Reagan!" She saw me and called out "Delvin!" Reaching out to me through the crowd of people surrounding her, she pulled me to the president. With my hand and the president's arm, she brought us together. Although she did not say a word, it felt as though she personally introduced me to the president. I wasn't prepared for the moment, but I shook his hand, thanking them for inviting me to dinner. As they walked away, Mrs. Reagan said, "Keep me informed," and I said, "Yes, ma'am." By the gesture she made to embrace me, she solidified a friendship, and there was no question, we were still bonded. It left an indelible and vivid picture in my mind that I see every time I think about it, a time I will never forget.

Back to the Real World

Fund-raising remained an issue. Outside of our annual dinners, Orle Jackson suggested something that should have been obvious to us, which was that we invite Mrs. Reagan again for our Pros for Kids annual dinner.

Given our record of accomplishment from the 1985 dinner, he was even more enthusiastic about it. I thought we might be stretching it, because a year hadn't passed since the last dinner. I worried about asking her to basically repeat her message of last year's dinner. Instead, I suggested that we could honor her for her Just Say No drug prevention campaign. Orle reassured me that because Mrs. Reagan had invited me to a state dinner, she might be open to attending our event again. I agreed to pose the question to Ken Barun, my contact in her office. When I did, he said he would ask.

I began to tell him about the good feeling and goodwill of the people who attended the 1985 dinner, as well as the athletes. Everybody enjoyed themselves, and we probably could have a larger turnout. There were people wanted to come in 1985 but couldn't get in.

The First Lady agreed to come back as guest of honor at our third annual fund-raising dinner, this time in San Francisco at the Westin St. Francis Hotel. After our experience with her, we were confident that we would have just as much success in 1986, if not more. Governor George Deukmejian declared our dinner date of October 29, 1986, as Pros for Kids Day in the state, and he declared a Californians for a Drug-Free Youth Red Ribbon Week. Mayor Dianne Feinstein proclaimed it Pros for Kids Day in San Francisco. More than eight hundred Bay Area middle school students attended the Pros for Kids, Just Say No to Drugs, and Yes to Life rally at San Francisco's Union Square.

The evening, shared by more than thirteen hundred supporters, was standing room only, including prominent politicians, sports figures, educators, law enforcement personnel, and the nation's number one supporter of Pros for Kids, First Lady Nancy Reagan, making her second consecutive appearance at our event. This year we also honored her for her Just Say No program.

In the private reception, Joe Montana and Keena Turner presented Mrs. Reagan with two red 49er football jerseys. I presented Mrs. Reagan with a diamond and gold pin, handmade for the occasion by Ally Brunner, one of our big supporters, in honor of her continuing work and her support of Pros for Kids. Frank Gifford agreed again to serve as master of ceremonies. The evening's opening entertainment was provided by the Castileers singing group of Oakland's Castlemont High School. The grand ballroom was laden with athletes from the world of professional and amateur sports, including Olympians and current NFL, NBA, and MLB players, boxers, golfers, and tennis pros. Swimmers John Nabor and Diana Nyad addressed the audience on the importance of the evening and the meaningfulness of the First Lady's support.

After a performance by the internationally renowned magician Doug Henning, the First Lady spoke. She delivered an eloquent and emotional speech that brought tears to her eyes as she talked about the root causes of the youth drug problem. At the core of her message was the importance of kids having faith in themselves and in those they admire. She went further by addressing changing attitudes in television and the recording industry with their shift away from glamorization of drugs. She departed the dinner to another rousing standing ovation. We netted $300,000.

Search for Funding

We held our first Pros for Kids Celebrity Golf Tournament in the summer of 1986, as well as our Pros for Kids Summer Sports Camp. The Teen Alternative Program was doing well under Colette Winlock's direction at San Mateo County's Martin Luther King Center. We were busier than ever, as more programs and potential grants were available. But the NFL and the DEA had joined together to do more prevention work in high schools. Their partnership was to use athletes and drug enforcement agents to talk about the substance abuse problems on the preventative and the enforcement side. Commissioner Rozelle asked me to participate, and I did several presentations.

A three-year California State Department of Education grant provided $350,000 annually for our Pros for Kids On Track program. Endorsed by the California Teachers Association, On Track used celebrity athletes to address junior and high school students about drugs and choices. The demand for Pros for Kids school assemblies, the numbers of kids and families we reached through the On Track program, and word of mouth from schools and parents were indicators that we were making a difference in kids' lives. Our 1986 annual dinner, Mrs. Reagan's second with us, helped us to keep our momentum, but it would turn out to be our swan song.

I was the face of the organization and did what I could do best, which was not sitting behind a desk pushing a pencil all day. Instead, I was out meeting people, generating leads, and gathering contributions. The future seemed bright, and I thought that I didn't have to maintain a high profile anymore, but I would find out otherwise. The budget for fiscal year 1986–87 was $900,000 and probably would top $1 million the next year. Now more concerned than before about managing the money properly, as executive director I had to be a good administrator.

We won a bid for a county grant to open a drug treatment and counseling office in South San Francisco, which we called our San Mateo County Outpatient Drug Counseling office. That brought our total staff size to between thirty and thirty-five people.

The Pros for Kids grant though On Track in the state Department of Education was our major funding. I thought we had done a good job of fund-raising and delivering the program, and we'd showed that we had the support of athletes. The independent evaluators' report said we had some gaps, but they could be closed if we implemented their recommendations. I thought it was a good enough report that warranted continued funding. However, it wasn't about the report as much it was about the politics of Northern and Southern California, particularly the San Francisco Bay Area and Orange County.

Political Infighting

More than two years into our three-year grant, we started to hear rumblings that we weren't spending equal amounts of money on Southern California and Northern California. The original legislation had called for equal presence in both parts of the state. There were programs implemented in six high schools, three each in Southern and Northern California, but our office was in San Mateo in the northern part of the state. However, the feud wasn't about program in Southern California as much as it was about control of the funds.

When the Department of Education decided not to renew funding of the program after the final year, it was a right hook to my gut and left me with an empty feeling. The time, money, and goodwill put into developing On Track felt like a waste. The organization had hit a wall, and so had I. Till that point, my life had been renewed with Pros for Kids. I had put years into getting the program to work, and it was working. It had proved to me that athletes have tangible skills and that what they learned playing football can be transferred.

Ultimately, the program was not sustainable because we did not have a viable revenue model. Doing fund-raisers all the time would not keep us afloat. With Pros for Kids closing, losing my leadership role was reminiscent of getting released. This time I saw it coming, and I was better off in this transition than I was when I left the NFL. Nonetheless, it was another disengagement. The crushing feeling of having to start all over came back. After leaving football, I was smart enough to know I couldn't do it over.

One essential truth in life is that each of us must play the hand we are dealt. Because I'd had to deal with poverty, racism, substance abuse, and injuries, some people may think the deck was stacked against me. Instead, I refused to be a victim and found ways to turn perceived defeats into some of my greatest victories.

22

I was fortunate to play behind some excellent offensive lines that cleared the way for me as a running back. Sometimes, however, the protection broke down, leaving me desperately looking for a way to escape from the big linemen, like my friend Sherman White, who were bearing down on me.

That is often the way I feel as I look back on my early life. My genetic makeup, environment, and society all were strong influences on success and failure, and several poor choices on my part only made things worse. I know I am fortunate to have been able to reverse field and break free before these things destroyed me.

My family history is filled with use and abuse of substances. My grandmother and her brother; Aunt Mary; Aunt Delphine and her husband, Uncle Big Guy; my father—all were alcoholics. My cousins Robert and Richard were heroin addicts and died from overdoses. Wayne, my daughter Dositheia, and I are recovering cocaine addicts. It made sense for me to make that choice, particularly when I didn't know how to address the issue or the depth of it. No individual of sound mind would want that for themselves, but who was of sound mind?

In my case, the merging of hereditary (genetics) and environmental influences impacting the neurophysiological processes led to the development of ADHD and dyslexia. Severe obstructive sleep apnea was a structural problem affecting my ability to get enough sleep on a daily basis, and for a long time I was unaware of the impact on my behavior and personality development. That would not be revealed until I was an adult and the damage was done. But these challenges could be managed, time would prove, and I doubled my efforts to make the best of it. Even today people ask, "What makes you think you have ADHD?" If they only knew firsthand the effects of that lifelong impairment on multiple areas of my life—academic, social, and vocational, influencing career advancement, parenting, health, intimate relationships, and substance abuse. The work has been hard and more than you can ever know.

Not least among environmental influences for my family were the invisible boundaries of segregation and racism, which influenced an individual's tendency to involuntarily repeat certain self-defeating behaviors that retarded the maturation process. I woul not understand the impact of this until later in my life. We only now are understanding the profound psychological impact of racism. Anthony Ong, assistant professor of human development in Cornell's College of Human Ecology, says, "Chronic exposure to racial discrimination and an accumulation of daily negative events combine to place African Americans at greater risk for daily symptoms of depression, anxiety and negative moods. Individuals who are exposed to more daily stress end up having fewer resources to cope with them. What we found was that it is the daily discrimination and daily stress that are driving the psychological distress." There is not a day I leave my house that I do not remind myself that I am black. If I don't, somebody else will, and it may not be in the way I want to be reminded.

I grew up in an era when discrimination, for some, was an accepted way of life. Leaving the Deep South for Kansas and then the West Coast heightened my cultural and social awareness. Almost every open-minded adult paying attention to what goes on around them knows that discrimination exists. However, a lifetime of dealing with unspoken discrimination and overt racism removes the doubt and questioning that what you're feeling is real. Maybe now others will process it instead of dismissing your feelings. Thank you, Professor Ong.

Chain Reactions

In social interaction, one act is a stimulus for the behavior of another and vice versa, as A. S. Reber explains in his *Dictionary of Psychology*. Interactions with others are crucial to developing awareness and the capacity for high commitment. Reber believed that social interactions

> *Our paths at first appeared the same,*
> *but ours led to dead ends or endless detours.*

and relationships enable an individual to directly discover, uncover, encounter, and experience one's actual self. In our daily interactions, the feedback from others offers us opportunities to experience ourselves.

There wasn't that big of a difference between my family's wants, needs and desires and those of white families. Our nature was to seek the things whites expected but that we were missing. The only thing that separated humanity was color, but the imposition of race blocked our way.

For some people, environmental factors are overwhelming influences: Child abuse or any early childhood trauma. Alcohol- or other drug-abusing parents, friends, or relatives. Chaotic family relationships. Peer pressure. Extreme stress.

Easy access to alcohol (and a permissive societal view of drinking), unsafe living conditions, poor nutrition, and limited access to health care and drug recovery programs also are contributing factors, and all were evident in my community.

Sexual, physical, or emotional abuse at a young age are the most powerful environmental factors increasing susceptibility to alcohol or drug abuse. In one study of 275 women and 556 men receiving detoxification services, 20 percent of the men and 50 percent of the women said that they were subjected to physical or sexual abuse in childhood. Abuse also is a powerful factor in the development of behavioral addictions.

When I left Dr. David Daniels's office in the spring of 1981, my life would never be the
same. Things that I had wrestled with internally began to surface. In a way, I could see who I was rather than reacting the way I thought I was supposed to. I begin to observe myself. My ups and downs, frustrations, celebrations, and motivations all were part of nature's design in the development of my personality.

In coming to understand my personality, I learned about typology. There are many personality typology systems, but I embraced the narrative tradition of the Enneagram. In this system, I am identified as Type 3, the Performer. This type believes you must accomplish and succeed to be loved. Consequently, Performers are industrious, fast-paced, efficient, and goal-oriented. They also can be inattentive to feelings, as well as impatient and image-driven. Receiving this information was an awakening. My personality was congruent with football and why I was dialed into the game.

As I have grown older and had the opportunity to look back on my life, I now can understand the development of my personality through the influences of my family, as well as the social environment I grew up in and how problems were solved. Again, I learned that I am predisposed genetically and environmentally to certain influences on behavior.

As a football player, I was frequently injured, stressed, with no support, and in physical pain, and I experienced anxiety and depression that brought my history to the forefront. Some years later I discovered why I was hyperactive as a kid. I am dyslexic, with Attention Deficit Hyperactivity Disorder (ADHD) and Severe Obstructive Sleep Apnea (SOSA). I struggled with these issues for years, so just learning what was happening was a relief.

In my own head, I became a victim by failing the fourth grade and then had to find another way if I wanted to avoid continuing to fall behind. When I read something, I made a mental photograph of how the sentence was structured and how it flowed. I knew what nouns were but couldn't tell the difference among a verb, a consonant, and a phrase. There was no such thing as "dyslexia" in my day. I began to learn how things would sound. If I didn't know what a word meant, I would look it up in the dictionary. I started to piece together ways to make things work for me.

I still have a problem with verbs, which makes writing hard. I *feel* language more than I understand the structure. It is easier to say what I feel than to write what I think. Sometimes I express myself through behavior. It is important that someone be truthful and consistent with me. The trouble with is that there's no measurable way to affirm this until demonstrated otherwise. The other problem is that using behavior as expression makes ADHD more pronounced, but it wasn't even a diagnosis when I was growing up. Among ADHD, dyslexia, and sleep apnea, I didn't know which one was most overriding, but SOSA affected me daily.

At KU, I knew I had to stay ahead of any learning problems, because I didn't have the skills to play catch-up, and when it comes to academics, not much has changed. When issues arose, I sought help through social means, such as discussions with friends. I wasn't afraid to ask. I also tried to find ways to resolve a stressful situation without resorting to using drugs. I liked reaching out to the people I thought I could trust.

Seeking Understanding

At first, what I learned about these disorders generated anger and the questions that someone who felt victimized would ask. I wanted to point a finger at someone, but there was no one. Then I would turn inward, turn on myself, because I felt there was no one else to blame. I never saw any other ADHD or dyslexia in my family, but I didn't know what it looked like. A lot of times these can reveal themselves in emotional outbursts when alcohol or drugs are involved. No one else had the same exact experience I had, but others too have genetic and environmental factors in their lives that need examining, especially if they entail barriers to overcome.

A study has found that blacks may, in general, have poorer mental health as a result of two mechanisms. First, chronic exposure to racial discrimination leads to more experiences of daily discrimination. Second, it also results in an accumulation of daily negative events across various domains of life, from family and friends to health and finances.

Professor Ong reported that the combination of these mechanisms places blacks at greater risk of daily symptoms of depression, anxiety, and negative moods. The difficulties generated by these symptoms can range from moderate to extreme. The inability to effectively structure one's life, plan daily tasks, or think of consequences results in poor performance in school and work. In young adults, it may lead to poor driving records or histories of alcoholism or substance abuse. As problems accumulate, a negative self-view and vicious circle of failure are established.

My struggles with ADHD and other disorders are nowhere near what they were like during my years in the NFL. I would come to understand that I can be intense and fast-paced, and that I appear confident, outcome-oriented, and high-energy. But I may also be perceived as impatient and overriding of others' views. I am highly competitive and love winning, and I feel constant pressure to perform. From this expanded psychological perspective, people with these neurotic trends can be seen as teachers and as good friends who lead us honorably forward to our next phase of development.

As a child, I wasn't comfortable unless I was active, and relief came through doing something externally and free from judgment. My grandmother and some family members took BC and Stanback headache powders. It felt like I ran to Hing's market every other day. I'll argue that my grandmother was addicted to them. Talking didn't help, because nobody understood. At that time, we were not aware of the concept of being predisposed to such problems as addition. Most attributed addiction to moral weakness and made it personal. Someone would say, "You know, it runs in the family. His father was the same way: once he started, he could never stop drinking."

We are highly adaptable and excel at meeting the expectations of others. A danger for me is concentrating on external praise or material rewards instead of my own feelings and my personal needs and health. This is the flip side of a personality type. Performers (in the Enneagram typology) like to stay active and on the go, so we find it hard to stop or slow down. Security is in doing, so ideas of quantity and efficiency are appealing.

These various personality types are like teammates, but we need to be mindful of losing ourselves if we don't pay attention to our feelings. I learned that I would always feel discomfort in arguments or disagreements if I did not look inside. Football nurtured the fixation on doing. If there was one thing that you repressed and could not do as a football player, it was to feel and express the pressure of human emotions, especially if it wasn't for the team. That's how nature set it up and why the fall is so hard when it's over. In hindsight, I was harboring anger and frustration subconsciously regarding what I had given for the good of the team.

I was aware that the football industry cared only about bottom line, but I didn't understand or know that management was emotionally detached from the physical price we were paying. If for no other reason than the physical price I was paying, it was personal to me. You don't brush aside six surgeries in eight years. That's personal.

My life force is strong, especially when I am moving forward. As Type 3s, we usually don't slow down enough to experience the natural rhythms of the body. Researchers in the mid-1970s found that certain personalities are more susceptible to diseases and physiological changes than others, such as the "Type A" personality. Research Kenneth Pelletier wrote in 1977 that "a purely physical stressor can influence the higher thought centers, and a mentally or intellectually perceived stressor can generate neurological responses."

My task is to slow down and practice focusing my attention on what's happening inside. This is not a waste of time but opens up space to really know myself. For a long time, that inner self wasn't safe to access, and so there was part of me to which I hadn't yet been introduced.

Search for Solutions

Two years out of the NFL, I was thrust into the disability legal juggernaut full-time. By then I had just discovered information about dyslexia and ADHD. Furthermore, I was attempting to rectify my sleeping disorder. My latest SOSA test revealed the sleep disturbance of 74 episodes of apnea per hour, and my oxygen saturation was down to 62 percent. For a long time I had been doing what it took to survive and continue doing my job, unaware of what was happening. If it wasn't football-related, it was left up to individual pro football players to figure it out. For me, the answer turned out to be radical surgery, and it worked. In this category of bodily malfunction, there was a fix.

I had done some research on SOSA and learned that Stanford University doctors were the most noted in the field. Robert W. Riley and Nelson B. Powell, internationally renowned surgeons and sleep apnea experts, were in Palo Alto, which was right in my backyard. Powell and Riley developed methods and surgical procedures for SOSA in early 1983, at a time when few physicians at the time believed in the significance of the disorder.

At the time, few treatment options were available. I'd had two surgeries before seeing them, and both were unsuccessful. My first one, at Kaiser, removed my uvula, and the other one, which was more radical, attached Gore-Tex to my hyoid bone (the bone the tongue sits on) and attached it to my chin. I got an infection, and three days later they had to remove it. It was back to the drawing board, and I was hopeful with Powell and Riley. How can anyone hold down a job having the number of injuries and surgical procedures as I was experiencing?

In high school, I fell asleep in my English class. In front of me, Leon Strauss, one of my teammates, woke me up. Of course, I denied having been asleep. He said, "You're snoring," and, when I raised my head, everybody in the class was looking at me.

Randy Robinson, my roommate in college, frequently woke me up by hitting me with his pillow, telling me he could not sleep. At KU, I fell asleep looking the instructor right in the eye. In San Francisco, Wilbur Jackson was my roommate, and he did not complain, but I know he was frustrated. But I did not start giving it serious thought until the morning before a Dolphins game.

Larry Csonka and I were roommates for a couple of weeks. One Sunday morning when I woke up, Larry was sitting on his bed telling me I was snoring and that he could not sleep. "I didn't know if I should wake you up because I couldn't sleep, or because you were going to die in your sleep!"

The confluence of ADHD, dyslexia, sleep apnea, anxiety, depression, and environmental and genetic predisposition created a vicious cycle. It may be hard for nonathletes to grasp the concept that football is a trigger for substance abuse and can lead to addiction. It's true. Even without my specific conditions, football itself is a trigger for abuse. It starts the natural flow of adrenaline, a neurotransmitter, which is one of several natural stimulants that affects human beings, especially athletes. We often hear coaches and athletes refer to getting the adrenaline going. Building up to that crescendo for Sunday's game, week in and week out, is a drain on bodies.

Football was my escape, but there came a point when I had so much riding on a professional sports career that playing became an additional pressure. The fear of failure that I repressed ignited the fuel of my genetic engine. Little did I realize that my family history was working against me. I accepted stress as a rite of passage, because I was prepared to do whatever it took to succeed and win. Therefore, each ascending level of my football career brought me a step closer to going over the line into substance addiction. Had my playing abilities plummeted, the same result may have happened, but I was never going to let that happen.

ADHD and addiction are distinct disorders, but they both have dysregulation of one or more of the dopaminergic circuits. ADHD is associated with earlier onset of substance use, more severe addiction, and more difficulty in maintaining abstinence. Playing football has a potentially addictive impact on someone who is genetically predisposed, frequently injured, stressed with no support, in physical pain, and with anxiety and depression. I was following the path of "whatever it takes" to play football. While motivations are different from person to person when it comes to playing professional football, what I experienced isn't much different than the average player experiences today.

Football players have the same vulnerabilities as anyone. But they tend not to say that they are hurting. I believed that playing with injuries and playing with physical pain was necessary for success.

Facing Our Fears

Our façade is at war with our true nature about who we really are. This war between the two is about fear. I believe we pro football players all knew what this was and had accepted it, but we had to meet the challenge or we wouldn't have been there. Each individual had his own way of getting through it but never acknowledged it. We were defined by where we stood when the dust settled.

In college, you were sore after maybe one or two games, but in the NFL you were sore and stiff after every game. Going from college to the pros, the difference between pain and injury rose to a new level. In high school, we played with scrapes and bruises, but in the NFL it was dislocations, broken bones, compound fractures, and damaged organs.

Every professional player has awakened on a Sunday morning and thought, *I don't want to go to work today*—with the likes of cracked ribs, a knee that needs draining, and a sprained ankle. *But if I have to play*, they think, *I don't want to imagine how I'll feel when I get a direct hit in the ribs, helmet first*. Because thinking about it means you're not focused on what you have to do, and that can get you hurt again. There were times guys would have played for nothing. Count me as one of them. On a deep level it's a reckoning. There was a reckoning in growing up, a realization that the game could catapult you into the higher social order of the neighborhood. There was a reckoning in looking ahead to manhood, and there is a reckoning in seeing who we are among our peers—and where we are, our position within the tribe. Football filled a need, and I am willing to bet that if it were not for that reckoning, a lot of us would not have played. Why would you play despite being injured? It's about manhood.

> *What I learned early from my grandfather was: you don't feel; you just do it.*

On those days, what performance-enhancing drugs would do is remove the doubt. And, on this level, that's what players do. Would you play with a broken wrist? Why would you put yourself in danger without being in an altered state? That is one of the reasons why performance-enhancing drugs are used in professional football. If it wasn't painful, it wasn't an injury. I watched players in the locker room do what was necessary to play. Drugs were used to get you through another game, and peer pressure was nuanced and unspoken. Get through the game and reaffirm who you are.

At first, it seemed to be the veterans using drugs the most because of their accumulation of injuries. They took as Xylocaine, Lidocaine, performance-enhancing uppers, and other so-called legal substances that they were given. Without them, there wouldn't have been enough veterans to make up a decent team. It wasn't easy playing with extreme pain and broken body parts. This was your job and your way of life.

One day at a 49ers practice, someone got hurt on the field. The trainers ran out to look at him. After he had been lying at the line of scrimmage, the coaches moved the ball about fifteen yards farther up the field, past the spot where he was being attended to, to keep running plays. The message was to not dwell on it—practice had to continue, just as a game would go on. If you want to keep your position, you do whatever it takes to continue. We were not cheating; it was an innate instinct, survival.

It starts with the painkillers and the injections the team doctor gives you. I was fine with that and took what I needed to take every time. However, sometimes you face injuries that are beyond simple painkillers. It's organized violence that most people would not subject themselves to any in other areas of life. But there you are during the season, after surviving the intense team training camp, and now you've hurt your ankle, your knee, your neck, or maybe cracked some ribs. The team doctor gives you something to play, a cocktail of Xylocaine and Marcaine. That mix is not on the banned substance list, but does that make it all right?

Something like this gets injected into your ribs. It may help you heal faster. Is taking a drug to be able to play with cracked ribs performance-enhancing? You would rather play without a torn muscle, broken wrist, or chipped bone in your ankle. But that option is gone. You were going to play regardless.

Observing and repeating how things got done was how I learned to survive. Some may call it cheating, but I call it surviving and doing the things that got you there. To go from street drugs to training-room medicine was acceptable and seemed to be a natural progression. Hell, if I had to play hurt, where should I get medicine. Afterward, who should help me when I'm home and in pain?

Throughout history, there has existed a desire in most humans to experience other states of consciousness and escape the perceived limitations of their lives. Drugs have been one way to achieve this experience. Sometimes the urge is spiritual, sometimes emotional. In football, the urge is spurred by pain.

We make choices every day, and sometimes they're driven by things that we don't fully understand. In playing pro football, I think in part that it was things I didn't understand that were driving me. I'm not abdicating responsibility, because I made the choice. No one put a gun to my head to make me do anything. Furthermore, there's no one else to blame. In addition to pain and injuries, the confluence of dyslexia, ADHD, and severe obstructive sleep apnea complicated things without me knowing how much. No one had given me or even mentioned a map or a guide to the other side.

Adrenaline is the most widely recognized neurotransmitter related to sports. However, it is associated with Excessive Daytime Sleepiness (EDS), which is related to sleep apnea but is more than just being exhausted during the day. It's a different kind of tired. I could not explain why I would fall asleep. I felt something was wrong, but I didn't know what was causing me to be so fatigued, other than playing football in the Miami heat.

EDS, a real medical condition associated with Severe Obstructive Sleep Apnea, may leave you feeling drowsy or cause you to fall asleep when you shouldn't during the day. This can lead to problems with work, school, and even your relationships. It affected me in all of those areas. The Dolphins were fining me for sleeping in meetings, and I was enrolled in graduate school the first year, taking Darvon, Flexeril, and Soma for pain. I was trying to stay awake to do my job and live a normal life, but life was anything but normal. Fooling ourselves by trying to do so was like pouring gasoline on a fire.

Taking a Toll

Week in and week out, the routine and the injuries started to wear on me my first year with the 49ers. The weekly schedule:

- Monday after a Sunday game, we watched the game film and graded ourselves, and everybody on offense knew who screwed up.
- Tuesday we had off unless we needed treatment for an injury. We might exercise, take pain meds, stay home, rest or nap, make phone calls, and run errands.
- Wednesdays were practices for the offense, using the defense as opposition.
- Thursdays were for the defense, using the offense.
- Fridays were for special teams and special situations, such as two-minute drills, first-and-goal, and so on, unless we had a cross-country flight, and, if so, we did the Friday routine on Saturday.

The schedule varied if we were playing an away game. When I was with the 49ers, if we were playing LA, for example, we practiced at home on Saturday morning, flew into LA that afternoon, and checked into the hotel between seven and eight. Team snack was at 9:00 p.m. and 11:00 p.m. was curfew. Flying to the East Coast meant leaving on Friday, and it was same thing when I was with Miami and flying to the West Coast.

CHAPTER 22

Those trips meant Friday night check-ins to the hotels. This was the routine for all my pro football seasons, year after year.

Sunday, game day:

- 8:30–9:00 a.m., chapel service;
- 9:00–10 a.m., pregame meal;
- 10:30–11 a.m., first bus for the stadium;
- 1:00 p.m., kickoff;
- 4:30–5:00 p.m., end of game;
- 7:00 p.m., flight for home.

Afterward, if you've won the game, you're excited and motivated to have fun and let off some steam. If you lost, however, you're down, have a bad attitude, or are depressed. There is no in-between. Win or lose, what will you do after the game? If you're single, go home and watch television? You have the night after the game (if you didn't get hurt) and your off-day on Monday or Tuesday.

Darryl Inaba, PhD in pharmacology and director of Detox at the Haight-Ashbury Free Clinics, affirms what I noted above about the human urge to alter consciousness. This can be achieved through drugs, alcohol, sex, and even food. You name it. He explained to me the reason why cocaine and other substances can become addictive. Psychoactive drugs that impact the central nervous system mimic our own natural body chemistry. It was an honor and a privilege to have the opportunity to contribute to the Free Clinics' video on the effects of cocaine. I would be remiss to not mention Dr. David Smith, founder of the Haight-Ashbury Free Clinics. It was his vision and steadfast commitment that health care is a right and not a privilege. Two-thirds of a century later, we're just getting around to accepting that belief.

We bring our personal issues with us that are passed on from generation to generation. What appears to be an addiction to illicit substances can also be perceived as a genetic abnormality, which is why illicit substances are taken for medicinal purposes. Although users know what they're doing is illegal, they cannot figure out that something else is driving their behavior. There is only fear and thoughts of moral weakness.

People who seek high-sensation experiences are more vulnerable to substance abuse. Sensation-seekers tend to perceive more benefits

> *Who I was and how I identified myself*
> *at the time were tethered to football.*

and fewer risks in, for example, drinking than do low-sensation seekers. Would it be fair to say that football players are high-sensation seekers?

After the Cowboys game in November 1978, I couldn't wait to have dinner with my mother and take her back to her apartment. Afterward, I wanted to try and reproduce that feeling while celebrating. We had one day, maybe two, to enjoy the fruits of a victory, but a lost or bad game was never forgotten. Unaware at the time, I could later trace it back to high school. No matter how you categorize it, letting off steam, partying, or celebrating felt like an earned reward for the hard work we had put in, to be in that moment. I would also seek external relief for internal conflicts that stemmed from fears of failure—and fears of success. When the game ends, the industry steps in, and ruthlessness takes over. We all knew that our pro careers were going to end someday—it was inevitable, no matter how it ended. Then it was like having a broken heart. The differences was that you could never get away from the cause of it. My heart for the game was still there, but I was told to move on.

I was left trying to reconcile what had happened. At the time, the thought of fear never crossed my mind. But after leaving professional football, I began to gain insight into some of the issues I was dealing with and realized that fear was a part of it all. And fear has different manifestations, depending upon whether you are in fight or flight mode.

I didn't know or understand the impact of these forces until later in my life, but they were influencing the development of my personality. What came with success was visibility, which meant that to some extent you couldn't be yourself. You have to get in character, and then you become addicted to being that character, because being yourself is not emotionally safe.

The only thing that separated humanity was color. Whites could see a clear road ahead, and the decision was only whether to follow it or not. The road for blacks might seem easy at first, but at each crossroads the decision led to dead ends or long detours, which created repressed frustration. When I was younger, I didn't know that my habits reflected such frustration, that I was angry or fearful or had hidden issues, because I didn't have the information. One choice would have been to give in to hopelessness, something that I tried to ignore every day.

For black athletes, pro football is a devil's bargain. By the time we leave football—or football industry moves on—we have become more broken in body and spirit than before, emptier than when we first stepped onto the field, searching for answers to life's most indispensable questions: Who am I? What am I supposed to do?

One thing of which I was certain was that I could use my own story to help others.

The national reaction to the death of George Floyd in the spring of 2020 awakened many white Americans to a long-simmering issue that those of us in the black community have always known, racism and racist violence not only in law enforcement but also in communities at large.

Even most American attorneys are oblivious to the impact of race on the practice of law. In the trenches fighting for benefits the past four decades now, I have concluded that the majority of the attorneys who are white and work with people of color, particularly African Americans, prefer not to talk about race unless it arises in the context of claims of discrimination. Furthermore, if a person in the legal profession does harm and causes damage to another, my personal experience tells me that they will protect themselves and block justice for the victim by impeding their right to due process. If a judge denies a petition for joinder, for example, can the attorney still file it?

If you were the only black, female, transgender, or gay person involved, and things were happening without your knowledge or consent, would you call it discrimination or paranoia? When no attorney will take your case, I believe it is discrimination. After football, my life's work has been trying to help athletes make the transition from football. And because we have been lied to, taken advantage of, and violated, we have trust issues. I can attest from personal experience that this is true.

In 1998 I filed a suit for retroactive benefits against the NFL Retirement Board (NFLRB). The standard under the previous plan for entitlement to benefits required that the player be prevented from or unable to engage in any occupation or employment for remuneration or profit, according to the Bert Bell NFL Player Retirement Plan, Section 5.2.

I can say with great pride and joy that my disability payments have allowed me to live a better quality of life than if I didn't have the benefits. But how can someone work and hold on to a job after having twenty-four surgeries from professional football and leave the job without medical insurance and not need some assistance in some way?

The people who decide on qualification for benefits don't share the pain and agony with which many of us of former NFL players live. Somehow, we have to work out a happy medium among disability, workers' compensation, Social Security, and Medicare so that every former player is taken care of. A good place to start is to not break the law. Start giving the players notice about their rights to workers' compensation benefits. Above all, those who are responsible for assisting you should not be screwing you. This is why we need an association to ensure that the rights of athletes are enforced.

I was ultimately charged almost $9,000 in court costs and $75,000 in attorney's fees for the NFL Retirement Board (NFLRB). On top of this was the more than $1,200,000 they paid their lawyers to not pay me $162,000 in retroactive benefits (appendix G). The NFLRB was supposed to be my human resource department, but what was my union's position? "It was a modest fee," they said. Where the decision placed me and how much I was paid was irrelevant and had nothing to do with it, but no one said a damned thing. This is one of many events like those that Professor Ong refers to that happen over time and get repressed. It seems to me that there should be a whistle-blower program in the legal profession, but no one asked about those things. How do you get justice and due process?

Privilege comes in all colors, shapes, and sizes. Within my culture and family, I am privileged. There's nothing necessarily wrong with being privileged, because I've worked my ass off and sat through things that most

---

The NFL and the NFL Players Association should examine their cultural awareness.

---

would not have. In some ways, it's a blessing; however, I am unapologetic about it, because I've earned a privileged position in society and, though I may have outworked others, I don't think I'm better than anyone else. As far as I'm concerned, that is the black eye of privileged people—they think they are better than others! To me, privilege means a roof over my head, food in my mouth, clothes on my body, and some of the finer things in life: no more, no less. None of that makes me better than anyone else.

It is not the same NFL today as it was in the early years, long before my career. Most players in the NFL are of African American descent, and the subliminal message is that the league knows how to deal with it. However, when you take a closer look, most of the people who work with the athletes are white and probably have never discussed or understood the cultural differences involved. No wonder disputes or arguments arise. I say this having experienced insensitivity around cultural differences in dealing with my legal issues.

Learning from History

In the pursuit of my personal information from my attorneys and because of it being withheld from me, I felt the need to remind my attorney of some history and what has happened to African Americans when valuable information and the truth have been withheld from them. Too often, when an answer to a question of mine was not forthcoming and I persisted, the implied question to me in turn was "What is wrong with you?"

I am pleased that monuments that representing racism are being pulled down. For too long, unquestioned assumptions about certain historical figures have contributed to beliefs about their contributions to our history that don't match reality. Sometimes, this involves subtle acquiescence to a white supremacy.

Though people sometimes talk about reparations, what is needed at the highest level in this country is an apology to African Americans for slavery. We have apologized for the internment of the loyal Japanese Americans, but we have not thoroughly apologized to African Americans for slavery, which left a cloud of inferiority hanging over the heads of many and provided the fuel for bigotry. Even if such an apology were issued, it would take at least a generation to judge its sincerity. All that's really needed to enforce equal rights or nurture them going forward is to follow the Constitution. And this includes professional football.

I had a fair opportunity in high school, but my undiagnosed learning disabilities tied my hands—though I had no idea of this at the time. I began to question a lot of things but not my desire. When I think about life in Kashmere Gardens and the Fifth Ward's Kelly Courts, I realize that my ability to leave was a defining moment. And after I left for college, I thought I had put the negative experiences behind me.

I left the projects of Houston's Fifth Ward thinking I was crossing the tracks into a new adventure: one that would render me a better chance in life. Surviving my freshman year debacle and getting a degree was a game-changer. Graduating from the University of Kansas was a giant step in the right direction. As long as the outcome depended on me, I wasn't worried, because I was going to do the work. I was prepared to do whatever I had to do. All I asked for in return was a fair chance.

Going to the San Francisco 49ers was a dream come true, I thought. I was a pro football player. I had crossed the Rubicon, but I would come to understand that I came to this game with my eyes shut. When I realized that I would have to play running back in an NFL game two months later with a broken wrist, my eyes were wide open. I was expected to make good on an agreement that may have been an opportunity but was also a job with the San Francisco 49ers, a member of the NFL's consortium, an industry of professional football teams—a business.

I eventually would learn that the way I was brought up and what I experienced was grounding. Working hard didn't scare me. I would be all right, but trust abandoned me again. This time it was trust in my profession that was lost, because I was put in a vulnerable position.

The support personnel that professional athletes must choose from, surround themselves with, and put in their lives are there in some part because athletes are seen as being easy prey. Football players are not supposed to be smart, just strong and fast, purely physical.

Filling the Gaps

Lawyers, managers, agents, and others were not around before we turned professional. These are the people who fill the gaps between athlete and industry, seemingly at times without concern for boundaries when it comes to the players' needs.

In 1979 the movie *North Dallas Forty* was out when I was negotiating a new contract. At that time, I had set the Dolphins single-season rushing record while playing with a torn bicep muscle, broken ribs, and a bad knee and neck. After two surgeries in the offseason, I ran one of the fastest forty-yard times in training camp. I had been traded to the Dolphins the year before for two players and two draft picks after having done everything that was asked of me. In 1979 I went three weeks into the season unsigned, with the possibility of getting injured hanging over my head, upset and angry.

My attorney seemed to lack a sense of urgency. He told me, "Delvin, it's business." My response? "Bullshit, it's personal." That was the core of our differences.

At dinner with a friend who was a successful businessman, I shared with him why I thought athletes were at a disadvantage when it comes to business. I explained to him the difference between business for him and business for players, and why some leave professional football and have problems. His response: "That's what happens in businesses—you go for the throat and get what's best for you," or words to that effect. I told him that he had just identified the problem, but he couldn't see it as a problem. That is the conspiracy of silence: no one will tell you anything different. Business and football are both competitive. For businesspeople, however, the bottom line is money.

The owners had a lifelong love affair with business. The players' love affair is with the game.

Football players are not trained to make money. They are trained to play the game, to use their bodies, to physically impose their will on their competitors. Athletes play football for competition, to test themselves, and to evolve based on winning one-on-one challenges. They also compete for the love of it and for the basic need that we all have to belong, to be a part of something bigger than ourselves. In a nutshell, this disparity in motivation between businesspeople and athletes is a big reason why 85 percent of football players are divorced or bankrupt within three years of leaving the NFL. With no remaining purpose, their lives too often become empty of all meaning.

When football was industrialized, it put owners in a win-win situation. They had taken the game out of football. That doesn't make owners bad people or even wrong. However, if they are reaping all of the benefits of a business, then they should provide what all businesses provide for their employees: compensation for their injuries. But, as I will explain, they raise every barrier they can to provide players this basic benefit. At least this was so in my experience.

Who monitors the owners of pro football teams? Are they monitored at all? What are the standards? Aren't they supposed to run their businesses the way others run theirs and be held to the same expectations? I have heard so much in recent years about the rule of law. Is it for some and not for others, and, if so, who determines that?

I have more understanding now as I look back. All these questions began to change my perspective about professional football. However, what could I do about it, and how would I benefit from it? In my case, I was too late and too deep into the game to turn things around. An acceptance of my place with the organizations I played for was staring me in the face. I remember thinking, "How I could go through this without knowing what is happening?" Coaches, managers, and attorneys all told me to trust them, so I trusted those in charge that things would be fine.

But I was to find out differently. In my long battle for justice, the one person I could trust consistently was me.

I surprised even myself by learning the study skills and self-discipline required to earn a college degree in four years. I was also able to comprehend and implement some of the most complex playbooks in the NFL during the time I played. Nothing, however, prepared me for the maze I entered when I began learning about and fighting for workers' compensation and benefits for retired players, including myself.

Workers' compensation is the only remedy we have for dealing with job-related health issues: when a player leaves the game, their rights and responsibilities under both state law and NFL policy should be explained. Yet the NFL and NFLPA has ignored this simple requirement without repercussion, at least for the four decades I spent fighting for benefits. We leave the game not knowing what if anything is wrong with us.

As it turned out, many of the attorneys and human resource professionals I met along the way apparently also didn't understand the regulations. In fact, I have come to believe that my homework made me better educated on certain particulars of the law.

I have spent far too much time, money, and energy fighting not only for my own rights but also for those of every player who stepped onto a

Whose task is it to defend the defenseless
when the defenders of the rule of law
have broken the law to protect themselves?

field. The fight has been hard and at times nasty. But it has been worth it. It all started because I simply wanted to know why, and that began an odyssey that lasted far longer than my playing career.

First Contact

I suppose I should have had an early warning from my experiences with the NFL and the legal system, starting not long after my retirement from the league. I won a settlement for disability benefits in 1995, after the NFL Retirement Board (NFLRB) had initially denied my claim in 1983. But in 1993, a new collective bargaining agreement had been put in place that included a new plan for disability benefits. In 1998 I filed a suit for retroactive benefits.

The standard under the prior plan for entitlement to benefits required that the player be prevented from or unable to engage in any occupation or employment for remuneration or profit (Bert Bell NFL Player Retirement Plan, Section 5.2). The standard under the new plan, effective on July 1, 1993, only required that the player be "substantially prevented from or substantially unable to engage in any occupation or employment for remuneration or profit." Nowhere in the plan does it state that if a player was working at the time of approval, he would not be eligible for retroactive payment. It was a catch-22. You don't get help, so you have to work, but then they tell you that if you are able to work, you are not disabled. Six of us were involved in similar suits, and we were led to believe that, if approved, payment would be retroactive. However, we knew we could not work going forward, once we received the benefit.

A court initially ruled in my favor, but I lost in the Ninth Circuit Court of Appeal. In its brief, the defense cited the US Census Report's 1966 Statistical Abstract of the United States, based on income and race and stated: "These figures placed Williams in the top one-third of US household income during these years." The report showed that for all US households in 1994, average income was $32,264. The average for Asian Pacific Islanders was $40,482, for white households it was $34,028, for Hispanics $23,421, and for Blacks $21,027. I think the defense attorney made his point, which was, essentially, "To hell with the law, Delvin Williams should be satisfied with what he's getting."

As much as I did not want to believe it, I felt the sting of discrimination. It was there in the narrative and without shame. The sad part about it is that no one acknowledged it but me. Out of the seven of us, me, my two attorneys, and their four, I was the only African American. What else could I say? Three years before, in 1995, the NFLRB had approved my permanent disability. The only question remaining was whether I was injured, and the answer was yes. Where that award placed me in the income rankings and how much I made should have been irrelevant.

Fighting for Clarity

I remember when, in court one day, the defense attorney asked me a question. When I asked for clarification, he said, "I am not trying to trick you." When pursuing justice as the only African American in the court room, I thought many times that it would be helpful if this attorney and his legal colleagues—including my own counsel—were aware that I have a heightened sensitivity about accessing justice. Not realizing that you hear things like, "I have always told you and the other players I represent that I much prefer you have a little disability than become wealthy basket cases." Using the circumstance to justify that you're not hurt that bad. If I or any African-American said the opposite, it would be interpreted as playing a victim or using the race card. Framing such vernacular as support to some may be perceived differently to others.

Too many American attorneys are oblivious to the impact of race on practicing law. In the trenches fighting for benefits the past forty years, I have concluded that the majority of the attorneys who are white and work with people of color, particularly African American athletes, prefer to not talk about race unless it arises in the context of claims of discrimination. Such attorneys are unlikely to perceive the relevance of race to lawyering, as I can attest from personal experience. Again, lawyers approach client interactions with unexamined, often unconscious assumptions that their clients share the attorney's view (or should). If not, most will not discuss it with you. If you disagree with them, they may hear you, but too often they do nothing about it.

It's my belief that attorneys seldom pause to think about what their own racial and cultural assumptions are, let alone whether they are generally shared. To a point, we are all unaware of the cultural assumptions with which we function. Only when we are transported out of that culture by travel, experience, or education, do we begin to feel—if not know—that something is different.

Despite the best of intentions and all of their professional training and experience, some attorneys are oblivious to the scope and depth of the sensitivities generated by a client's racial experience. They don't know what it's like for a black man to be represented by white men and to be caught up in a process in which all of the white participants possess power over your fate. They cannot fathom how it feels to sense that your efforts to get correct information are being denied, that you are being told that up is down. A failure to recognize my cultural history makes it obvious that my attorney doesn't understand what it means to me. He can't know what it is to be a strong, intelligent, astute African American man yet experience powerlessness. By not understanding that, he has missed the big picture and is likely to proceed more toward his own benefit and less toward mine.

African Americans have a natural distrust of professionals they don't know, and, believe me, this often becomes a red flag. In my experience, it is the rare lawyer who would have spent time subjecting himself to the discomfort of analyzing my point of view and sense of what might go wrong. Most lawyers—at least most white lawyers—rarely have honest conversations with their clients about what it feels like to be represented by someone of

> *Because we don't know what we don't know, we're set up to be victimized.*

a different race, a different social and economic class, a different culture. When you don't feel understood as a client, trust and clarity are hard to come by. There was no timely denial of benefits on behalf of the Miami Dolphins. They were a month and a half beyond the statute of limitations deadline. Unless Miami produced a timely denial to avoid the statute of limitations, they were responsible to pay the benefit. They did not, and nothing was said. It happened on several occasions.

Legal scholars and professionals have devoted substantial energy, time, and thought to litigating, adjudicating, and writing about racism, but not so much about access to justice in sports. A growing body of literature exists on the experiences of minorities in law school, but not so much in sports. Numerous bias studies of court systems around the country have identified disparate treatment of minorities throughout the justice system, yet here I am, another "case study." Many have written and talked about the players as we enter life after football, but much less has been written about bias and its effects on access to justice at a time when justice is needed the most.

We have always looked to "the adult in the room" for guidance, but now that we are adults, there is with no guidance. What are the criteria for picking an attorney? How do you choose an accountant to manage your books? Do we know how to set a budget? Has anyone shown us how to create a life plan? No! Professional football players work six days a week at a job that is physically demanding to the utmost. And they work as part of the business world, alongside businessmen and business-women in large cities, where money flows and schemes are created.

I was told along the way and between practices, games, traveling, and surgeries, to ask questions if there was something I did not under-stand. I would often ask myself later, "Why ask questions if no one is there to answer?" But even worse is to be given inaccurate answers by those you thought were trustworthy.

Simply put, football players are not prepared by anything in their prior experience or training to answer questions or make decisions on the levels required in my experience. However, that does not mean we should not have access to accurate information or documentation we need. Given the time we have and what we do for a living as athletes, we are not trained to learn business and know the right thing to do. But if you tell us true and accurate information, we will understand, because that is what we do—we learn! Adding to my challenges, institutional rac-ism would sometimes rear its head in a setting where I would not have thought I would be confronted with it.

The Process Begins

Pro football players, like everyone else, wonder what will happen to us in retirement and how we'll deal with the transitions, let alone the injuries. I began learning about all this firsthand when, in August 1981, the Miami Dolphins released me and I became a free agent. The team did not provide an exit physical. Three weeks, later, the Green Bay Packers also released me, and my NFL career was over. Before leaving the practice facilities, I was given a physical that took about five minutes before being sent on my way. I had no way of knowing then the extent of the injuries I had sustained while employed by my two previous NFL teams.

I never knew (nor did most players) that we were covered by workers' compensation insurance. I should have received notice from the team alerting me to my rights and potential benefits and the time limits in which I had to exercise them. All businesses in the United States are required by law to have a workers' compensation benefit plan and insurance policy. Furthermore, the information should be posted in plain sight for all employees to see. But this was not my experience with my employers in the NFL.

My former teams provided no information regarding workers' compensation benefits.

In 1983, more than two years after being released by the NFL, I signed with the Oakland Invaders, a member of the now-defunct United States Football League. I was on their roster for two weeks before injuring my neck. I immediately retired from professional football, and I did not work again until I received my first paycheck from Pros for Kids in 1986.

Many years later, in 2010, I attended a conference in Las Vegas for the Retired Players Congress. I became aware—almost three decades after leaving professional football—that I was eligible for workers' compensation benefits for injuries prior to my retirement. In fact, all players are entitled to the same benefit, but teams and the players' union did not tell us. When I returned home, I found an attorney and began the process of filing for cumulative trauma injury compensation. There would be a number of hurdles to overcome.

The first thing I learned was that the California workers' compensation labor code had language for the situation I found myself in. First was "statute of limitations." In California, if you do not receive a notice from your employer about your rights to workers' compensation benefits, then the clock on the statute of limitations is not running. The second dealt with the type of injuries that I was living with and when they had occurred. The language in the California workers' compensation code states that you can have multiple dates of injury, namely for a specific injury but also for cumulative trauma, "called also cumulative trauma disorder, repetitive stress injury, repetitive stress syndrome, any of various musculoskeletal disorders as carpal tunnel syndrome or tendinitis that causes pain, weakness, and loss of feeling from repetitive movements, and damage to muscles, tendons, ligaments, nerves, or joints," according to the code. Having more than one date of cumulative trauma would be very important to my case because of how NFL players are moved around from one team to another but retain the same kind of working conditions. I could have cumulative trauma that began and ended with one team, and then have another case later when I was under contract with a different team. The California code also provides guidance about what counts as disability and what type of disability a worker can claim. Temporary disability exists if you temporarily can't perform your regular job. Permanent disability is determined if you do not recover 100 percent, and, in this case, you're entitled to a specific amount as a permanent disability award. Permanent disability awards are over and above any temporary disability payments and medical care costs. You may receive a disability payment even if you are working again. If you qualify for permanent disability, payments are due even if you "return to work, doing work you had previously been employed, and did not suffer any wage loss" (again, quoting from the code). Another important point was jurisdiction. The California labor code applies in California, but, while one of my employers, the Miami Dolphins organization, was outside of California, the code still applied because the Dolphins assumed the contract I was under with the 49ers.

So, in 2010, I hired an attorney, and we filed a claim for my workers' compensation benefit from the San Francisco 49ers and Miami Dolphins. He filed an application on August 11, 2010. He assured me that if I had not received a notice from my employers explaining my rights to worker's compensation, I was in good shape to prevail. But what I didn't know was what "prevailing" would mean. What would the payouts be? Would they be equal to what I suffered, what I had already paid for countless surgeries, and what I was legally owed? I expected that they would be, but ultimately I got caught up in the system instead. My experience was one of feeling talked over, cheated, and left out. I felt confusion and betrayal, and ultimately it came down to people who had power making decisions without me, without consulting me, without my best interests in mind. It was other people talking for me and not giving me what I was legally owed. Finally, it was about the teams, my former employers, protecting their interests at my expense. And ultimately it was about being a black man in the legal system.

The Medical Examination

To receive benefits, a doctor must determine the level of disability and the "permanent and stationary" date for you to receive workers' compensation. On March 21, 2011, Dr. Steven Feinberg, in his qualified medical examiner's (QME) report on my condition stated: "He is permanent and stationary. He became so within one year of his last football work engagement but would have a one-year period of temporary disability after each subsequent surgery (1983)." I've had more than seventeen post-football surgeries, but, as far as I can tell, I was only reimbursed for twelve.

The Value of the Claim

I would have two attorneys before all was said and done. In August 2011, when my original attorney began calculating what the claim would be and how much his fees would add to that amount, he sent me a letter laying out the case value of my workers' compensation claim. To the best of my knowledge, he was correct and on point as far as the labor code instructions. According to the pertinent section of the California code, section LC 5412, he estimated what my settlement would be if we were not past the statute of limitations for the claim. If we could show that I first learned of my legal right to workers' compensation in 2010, I had a claim to thirty-two years of weekly payments with a cost-of-living increase every year, raising that weekly rate. He explained that his fee was based on the entire settlement value of the case, which meant raising the settlement amount to include his attorney fee. But while I accepted those numbers, his calculations didn't necessarily cover all of the areas I expected to have covered. After he framed the issues, he was silent on matters including my permanent disability indemnity, temporary disability, and medical expenses, and, unless I brought it up, we did not discuss it. As a result, his calculations included the workers' comp claim for income lost due to injuries, medical fees resulting from workplace injuries, and his fees, but he left out the statutory disability indemnity payments for the cumulative trauma years.

But even those numbers proved to be wrong. When the case was still going in 2018, those 2011 calculations fell short of what the State of California said that I was due as someone whose first payments would be made in 2018.

Section 4661.5 of a legal case applicable in my situation—*Hofmeister v. W.C.A.B.* (1984) 49 Cal. Comp. Cases 438, the Court of Appeal, Second District—states that if an employer fails to provide temporary disability indemnity for two years or more after an injury, the temporary disability benefit rate must be the statutory rate prevailing *at the time the delayed payment is made*, which in my case meant whenever the case was settled, which would be 2018. Because by 2010 I had gone more than thirty years without being paid, I should have been paid at the statutory rate for the date of payment: at the 2018 rate.

But all of my attorney's numbers were from 2011. So I would get paid based on weekly rates that were already thirty years old. This was never resolved to my satisfaction.

The First Ruling

The judge who would be presiding over my case during the whole, long process was Joan Succa, an administrative law judge. She gave her first ruling on my case in 2014. This ruling was about statute of limitations. The defense was trying to have the case thrown out by proving that I knew that I had only a limited time to file a worker's comp claim. What was confusing to me is that they did not prove that they had given me a notice, which they couldn't—because they did not. Yet they would spend a total of nine years trying to prove that I should have known about something that they didn't tell me.

Judge Succa ultimately ruled in my favor on this matter. Her ruling also settled the 2010 cumulative trauma claim against the Dolphins and 49ers, indicating that the Dolphins and 49ers would be responsible for my injuries over a specific period of time. She found that there were two cumulative trauma events: the first one ended February 1, 1979, after my first season in 1978 with the Dolphins, after which the assigned contract from the 49ers expired; and the second trauma, which ended on my last day with the Oakland Invaders in 1983.

I would learn that at this time Judge Succa also refused the Dolphins and 49ers their request for joinder with the Oakland Invaders. Because it was to their advantage to have the Invaders pay some part of any settlement that I won, the Dolphins and 49ers were seeking to have the Invaders joined to the case as a codefendant. Judge Succa denied that request. But I would not be informed of this or have it explained at all until much later, when the request was made again and, for some reason, granted.

The Settlement

In March 16, 2018, I finally settled. For me, it had been thirty-two years. Judge Succa presided over the case for four years before reaching a decision. Our arguments were solid, and we felt good about where we stood on the issues of jurisdiction and the statute of limitations. But it was in the judge's hands for four long years. The defense's case, to my mind, was full of holes. Still, as anyone who has ever been involved in a lawsuit knows, you can't relax until the final ruling is made.

My settlement compensated me in part for the twenty-four surgeries over the preceding thirty-eight years, seventeen of which were post-employment. (I was actually paid for twelve.) At the suggestion of my attorney, it did not include payment for self-procured medical expenses of $161,000 or the $4,300 I paid to a vocational education professional. Most importantly, the settlement did not include any statutory disability indemnity payments that were due for the previous years.

In other words, my settlement paid for surgeries subsequent to my retirement from football, but the Dolphins and 49ers did not fulfill their workers' compensation obligation. I had not received the benefits of permanent and temporary disability to which I was entitled. Meanwhile, my former employers were still trying to band together to deny or limit my claims, something they had been working on since 2011.

The Joinder—Again

On or about June 1, 2018, three months after settling my claim against the Dolphins and the 49ers, I received a letter from ArrowPoint Capital, dated May 17, 2018. The letter was to inform me that they were denying my worker's comp claim with the Invaders. The dates of injury were the same period—January 1, 1974, to January 1, 1981—as determined in my claim against the Miami Dolphins and the San Francisco 49ers. But I had not filed a claim with ArrowPoint Capital, and it took another year for me to figure out how ArrowPoint was even involved. I would learn that they owned the insurance company that provided workers' compensation coverage for the now-defunct Oakland Invaders.

What had not been explained to me was that the Dolphins and 49ers had the legal right to attempt to include the Invaders by joinder into the settlement that they were obligated to pay. In 2011, and again in 2014, the defense had filed for joinder. This is something that the courts didn't seem to want to allow to happen. The courts denied the joinder in 2011, 2014, 2015, and 2016. If the joinder had been approved, the Invaders would have been responsible for a share of the payment, but the settlement amount would not change. I would get the same amount of settlement for a longer time period and from three employers instead of two. This was only going to benefit the Dolphins and 49ers as joint defendants; it would have no benefit for me, the injured party. While the labor code gave me the right "to proceed against any one or more employers," this right was taken away from me when the joinder was belatedly approved to add the Invaders to my existing case after my settlement had been approved. And even though this was all based on my original claim, I was never told that this was happening, nor did my counsel give me the opportunity to file a joinder. If it were not for the ArrowPoint denial letter, I would not have known anything about the joinder having been refiled, much less approved.

Combining the Invaders with the Dolphins and 49ers as defendants would change the judgment on my case. While the judge had ruled that there were two cumulative traumas extending through 1983, the Dolphins' attorney had argued that it was all one cumulative trauma extending through 1983, which would have added the Oakland Invaders to the claim. (The Dolphins and the 49ers were already jointly responsible due to the Dolphins having assumed my 49er contract for my 1978 season in Miami.) But the judge had never agreed with the Dolphins' rationale. Based on statements from Dr. Stephen Feinberg, Judge Succa concluded that my cumulative trauma, which had already existed as of 1979–80, did not extend continuously through to my 1983 Invaders injury.

Nevertheless, the joinder finally happened, even after Judge Succa ruled in my favor. It came during a transition in my legal counsel, and after the Dolphins and 49ers had been denied a joinder many times.

I was in Hawaii on vacation from May 29 to June 10, 2017. While I was gone, my attorney, whom I would subsequently replace, wrote in a letter dated June 6, 2017, that the defense attorney for the Dolphins was filing a joinder.

Remember, Judge Succa had denied this exact thing, as I learned in 2014. As part of her original decision on the joinder, she had stated that "[the Dolphins believe that] any cumulative trauma claim should be one continuous period ending with his last day of employment with the Oakland Invaders. However, Mr. Williams retired from the NFL in 1981. He did not go to work for the Oakland Invaders until 1983, creating a sufficient break during which Mr. Williams recovered sufficiently from his NFL days to play for the arena football team. Therefore, it is legally possible for Mr. Williams to maintain a separate cumulative trauma claim against the NFL teams who are subject to jurisdiction here in California."

Again in 2017, Judge Succa denied the Dolphins attorney's petition for joinder with the Invaders:

> The facts in this case clearly support the application of relation back doctrine as set forth in Labor Code §5500.5(a), as the reason there are no viable defendants from 2/1/79 until Mr. Williams stopped playing for the NFL in 1981 is lack of jurisdiction. Therefore, it is reasonable to relate back to the last carrier that is subject to California jurisdiction, which is the Miami Dolphins during the period of time Mr. Williams' S.F. 49ers' assigned contract was in effect. Mr. Buch's argument does not persuade me to change my decision.

Given all that, it still baffles me how and why that joinder kept coming up. I received multiple notices that a joinder had been ordered and served, and, although I had asked, my attorney did not provide documentation, and no one told me how and why it was filed. The notice from my lawyer said that "the Dolphins had requested joinder some years ago and that was denied. That request was now renewed, and in fact by order June 2, 2017, they have been joined." If it required approval, my counsel must have given it. I did not agree to a joinder, and I'm still not sure that it was authentic or legal.

Notwithstanding all that, my first notice that the joinder had been filed and approved was when I received a letter from ArrowPoint, denying me workers' compensation benefits for my injury when I was with the Oakland Invaders.

Keep in mind that with proper notice and consideration, I could have taken action regarding the joinder that would have changed the outcome to something much more favorable for me. The Invaders would have been responsible for their share of the settlement. However, with me out of the equation, the Dolphins and 49ers would simply collect the benefit of sharing the settlement with the Invaders, and I would receive nothing.

So I did not file the claim. Instead, the Dolphins did. They even used my name, because the filing was based on my original claim. All of this was done with my attorney's apparent approval; he knew all this was taking place but chose not to inform me. I couldn't do anything about it; the subject never came up.

When finally explaining Arrow Point's position to me, my attorney sounded like he was arguing for the defense. He told me that "the Defendant Dolphins continue to have a right to pursue contribution from the Oakland Invaders. Regardless of whether considered a contribution or a lien, the fact is that the Miami Dolphins have a right to seek some of their money back from the Oakland Invaders." He did not say what rights I had.

A Hard Choice

Prior to all this, in a letter dated March 8, 2017, my attorney had stated: "My advice is to not ask joinder at this point for a separate cumulative trauma involving the Invaders, but rather to wait until approximately 10 months after the Lewis report, which means to re-look [at] the situation in November 2017." This was the attorney I would be replace during that same year, long before November. He further stated, "The Invaders

CHAPTER 24

have nothing to do with this," adding, "You are going to have to make a decision as to whether you want to simply go on developing records and likely lose some permanent disability or file a new application against the Invaders and stretch your case out another couple of years. It is a hard choice."

In the end, even that choice was taken away from me.

A Black Athlete in the Legal System

While doing everything in my power—asking questions, sending letters, and even changing legal representation—to procure my benefits, I was still working with a disadvantage. I didn't have the extensive legal knowledge I needed, but those I hired did. To my disappointment, they proved to not have my best interests in mind. My core issues remain unresolved. The applicable law says, "Courts are required to construe the workers' compensation laws with the objective of securing for an injured worker the maximum benefit which he or she can lawfully be awarded." This is the law in California and most states, but that is not what happened in my case.

As professional football players, we were not told of our rights, which is against the law. Professional football is a business, and certain obligations come with owning a business. Workers' compensation is one of them, and it's the law. Everett L. Glenn, a contract advisor to professional athletes, has stated: "There is power in unity, and only by coming together can sport or society tackle the issues that challenge both."

A conspiracy of silence exists when members of a group, either explicitly or in an unspoken way, agree to stay quiet about an occurrence, situation, or subject in order to promote or protect their interests. This can also include keeping secret certain information which, if exposed, could be damaging to the group, its interests, or its associates.

A customary explanation for the traditional lack of legal malpractice filings had to do with such a conspiracy of silence that encouraged lawyers to refuse to assist the client if it meant legally attacking a professional colleague. The notion that lawyers consciously conspire in this way seems far-fetched. To me it seems more likely that lawyers' avoidance of suing each other and even just giving expert testimony in a case is a result of assumptions and understandings embedded in the common legal culture.

Charles W. Wolfram opined in a 2006 *Hofstra Law Review* article: "Aggrieved clients no longer lack lawyer champions. . . . A lawyer's filing suit against another lawyer on behalf of a legal-malpractice claimant is hardly stigmatized today or even significantly noticed, at least in most legal communities." On the basis of my experience, I beg to differ with Mr. Wolfram. As a client, I don't believe I had a legal champion in my corner. Further, I believe that there is a conspiracy of silence among the pro football team management and attorneys, driven by the long-term financial outcomes. I experienced discrimination at each level of my journey. Certain groups can and do thrive on the athletes' lack of knowledge and experience about what is in their best interest. Keeping us uninformed and misdirected in these networks controlled by like-minded individuals has life-altering effects for football players.

During my own search for legal assistance, it was obvious to me that my efforts were being repressed. After unsuccessfully reaching out to several attorneys over the years, I found that they all were quick to decline. I don't need to be hit over the head with a sledgehammer to realize this was not random. After they read the information I presented, it seemed to me that they had detected nefarious activity and wanted to steer clear. It is odd to think that the attorneys could tell me what had been done right but would not discuss my reasoning for making the complaint. If you kill someone you can get an attorney, possibly pro bono. However, if you are defending yourself and fighting for your rights, you cannot find an attorney.

Under the current system, the client loses any structured role in the process; the "rules" do not assign the client any specific opportunities to speak before the court other than if the client chooses to testify. Likewise, the "rules" do not require the client's signature on most documents submitted to the court and do not even require the litigant's presence in pretrial conferences, which are meant to enhance the management of the dispute and possibly facilitate its settlement. The client has no knowledge or information of what was said in these meetings other than what one's attorney divulges.

How could I fall through the cracks and not receive benefits? How could that happen to someone with my medical issues after being in court for ten years and even enduring seven surgeries during the trial? One way it could happen is through a sustained effort of highly placed individuals, some of whom could have included my representatives. Not being allowed to be in the courtroom denies the client's access to justice. In my case, being shut out had a major impact on the accuracy of the information presented and especially on my understanding and ability to provide input into my own case. The depth of misinformation is pervasive. We need substantive changes in how these cases are reviewed to drill deeper into what needs fixing, to find out why the system isn't working.

Since Then

At the time of this writing, I am still attempting to win from the NFL what I believe I am entitled to: benefits for temporary and permanent disability and full medical reimbursement due to injuries sustained during my playing career. My legal difficulties have redefined my friendships with people I've known for years who happened to be attorneys. The belief that my personal information was privileged proved to be a myth. The only privileged information, it seems, is exchanged between the attorneys, and they decide what you should know. Getting misguided information and sending originals of important documents to my attorneys never to get them back are examples of how I believe my case was mishandled. Missed filing dates of which I was not informed, followed by the excuse that nothing was going to happen, and release of personal information that I asked my attorney to retain in privacy: these circumstances undermined my confidence that I was receiving fair representation. Such actions give the impression that counsel is acting not in my best interest but in theirs.

While multiculturalism may now be a central component of basic education in the schools training educators and counselors, it is still all too foreign to those in management of professional football and in pro sports in general. While it is true that players are paid far better today than those of us who played thirty or forty years ago, players still need help with the larger questions of life after football. Meanwhile, the fans think players don't need help. After all: "Look at how much money they're making."

It's obvious we see the world differently, but we don't acknowledge it. The wrong of discrimination perpetrated on athletes is unconscionable.

I have fought to stand up when I felt discrimination. But it hurts to have someone disrespect you and attempt to punish you for questioning their actions.

Building bridges across the void—finding out what binds two individuals and helps them communicate openly and effectively across cultural and racial divides—is hard work. We all strive for financial equity, but professional football are in it for more than the money. But when we are retire or are released, equity becomes no more than a fleeting thought. The majority of football players in the NCAA and NFL are African American, and we don't talk about the differences in experience that create the basis for misunderstanding and injustice. After George Floyd was murdered in Minneapolis in May 2020, frantic conversations happened, though the powers that be failed to make many necessary changes. When former 49ers quarterback Colin Kaepernick peacefully protested systemic inequities, he was vilified. Such outcomes leave me, as a black man, feeling emotionally abused and isolated, though I'm told to "get over it." It is critically important that we acknowledge our own attitudes, beliefs, and feelings before we knock someone else's.

In my case, the failure to effectively navigate these divides was coupled with neglect of a client's interests and effective legal representation. When representing people of color, what matters to a given attorney may not matter to a person of a different ethnicity; the differences are nuanced. As clients, we come to attorneys and put our trust in their hands. If violated, that trust becomes a burden. Understanding subconscious racism and the dynamics of privilege, learning how to recognize that in ourselves and others, is an important step in bridging the divide.

The Room for Improvement Is Huge

Athletes mirror society, and so does management. The discipline, drama, hard work, pain rituals, sacrifice, and strategies for winning in sport are also tools for success in life. On the other hand, the same exploitation, greed, and racism that exists in society can also be found in sport. Institutional racism runs deep in the fabric of our society, and sports are no different. One example is the stand taken by University of Missouri football players in 2015 that resulted in the resignation of the school's chancellor. The players charged that the university and its administration had done too little to combat racism on campus. It was another instance where sport mirrors life.

In 2020 the NFL made history by fielding an all-black officiating crew. Bear in mind: this was 2020, when the league was one hundred years old. My point is that the NFL and its attorneys should examine their cultural awareness, but they may not care. Most of the players in the NFL are of African American descent, so the subliminal message is that the NFL knows how to deal with the cultural differences. However, when you take a look, the people around the athletes are mostly white. Do they ever discuss or understand the cultural differences among themselves? Having experienced insensitivity toward cultural differences while dealing with my legal struggle, I believe much of the problem is caused by the huge gap in understanding and awareness.

Starting from no black players in the early NFL to the current majority of Black players on its teams today, the NFL took eighty years to create a diversity plan for African American coaches, scouts, and front-office ranks. I have spent forty years navigating the benefits system, thinking the problem was me. The NCAA's economic model is based on the revenue sports of basketball and football, which are dominated by Blacks, financing the non-revenue sports dominated by white athletes. According to NCAA president Mark Emmert, "Black athletes generate more scholarship funding ($2 billion) than any other source except the federal government." Does any of this matter to the people who are making the decisions at the highest levels? My experience tells me that it does not.

In 2007 I traveled to Washington, DC, along with other former players and interested parties, to meet with a Senate committee that was investigating the NFL's retirement system. As part of his testimony before that committee, Daryl Johnston, former running back for the Cowboys, said,

> Delvin Williams, who played eight years as a running back in the NFL, experienced this [difficulty with receiving benefits] firsthand. After eight years, six surgeries, two concussions, broken ribs, a dislocated thumb, knee and spinal injuries, as well as numerous other joint and vertebrae injuries, his professional football career ended in 1981, when the Green Bay Packers released him. He was one of approximately 285 out of 7,000

retired NFL Players who received degenerative disability benefits. However, it did not come without a fight and persistence. He started the process in 1983 and was awarded a football degenerative disability benefit in July 1995—twelve years later! In twelve years, he was turned down twice and lost at arbitration before being awarded the disability pension benefit.

The NFL mirrors the discrimination we see in society. To not pay players the benefits we are legally entitled to, particularly workers' compensation, is de facto discrimination against the players, and has racist outcomes for a person of color. It mimics the inequity we are seeing in society today. The long-range impact of the inequities at this level may be invisible to the naked eye. The NFL players today should be better off than the generations that came before them. Their access to 401K plans, severance pay, education plans, and similar benefits are all for the good. There are long-term care and "88 plans" (named for the great John Mackey, who proudly wore No. 88 for the Baltimore Colts) that benefit some, not all. Things are getting better, and I envy the guys who benefit from those programs.

However, anytime I see a retired player limping or having a physical problem—like John Mackey himself, who died too young at sixty-nine and spent the last years of his life needing constant nursing care, unable to manage for himself because of dementia accelerated by head injuries during his playing career—I think about how it could have been eased. A huge part of the answer would have been as simple as making sure we had thorough exit physicals and were given notice of our right to workers' compensation.

Meanwhile, the conspiracy of silence and discrimination are still happening. It is a disgrace to a great game and the great players who built it into the favorite sport of millions of Americans.

Lessons from the Fifth Ward

Growing up in my neighborhood, if you asked a question, you expected an answer. A man of principle would give you an answer. As I have mentioned, I reminded my attorney of what has happened when important information and the truth is kept from African Americans. In my old neighborhood, withheld information was especially critical if it was about your business or money. Not getting a truthful answer could lead to a physical confrontation. That is not an alternative for me today. But how do you get your information after you ask and they refuse to answer or, worse, ignore you? My cultural upbringing and understanding would have no influence on my decisions, because the rules I was under as an adult were different. We're living a double life, and, as Deon Cole says, "We can't be black all day!"

When information is withheld, it's easy to believe something is going on, usually nothing good. Yes, withholding specific information may be intended to avoid giving false information about changed circumstances, but each individual, regardless of ethnicity or cultural beliefs, should be treated with respect and dignity and told what they need to know. If not, you might as well take whatever you want from people. If you are not going to give me my information because when I ask for it, I can become the problem.

Inasmuch as I didn't know the impact my cultural environment growing up would have on me as an adult, I would eventually live the way I was brought up. What I experienced as a youth was grounding. Working hard didn't scare me, and so I thought I would be all right in the world. But, over time, my trust in this assumption abandoned me. I questioned and doubted what I saw and felt to be true, because I didn't want to believe the NFL and NFLPA would abandon me, along with every other retired player. All the players' association members at that time experienced the same things. This was my profession, but I was put in a position to be victimized by it.

Becoming a victim is one thing I vehemently rejected, and the guys I knew who played professional football did not embrace the concept either. Furthermore, they worked like hell not to be victims. For anyone who suited up and stepped across that white line and onto the field to have career success, chances are that they are not victims in any area of life. For that reason, fighting the emotion of being put in the category of victim is hard. The emotions come up as if I somehow allowed it to happen. I may have been victimized, but I'm not ready to be a victim. As a group of players, we didn't know then that workers' compensation was a remedy for our injuries, because we didn't get the notice we were covered.

However, when college football players are elevated to the professional level, they have a target on their back that says "vulnerable." Contrary to what we believe, regardless of good intentions and the ability to work hard, you just don't know what you don't know. The remedy to vulnerability is knowledge and honesty. If you don't have the knowledge, you can only be guided by the proverb "to thine own self be true" and act in accordance with what you know.

As I've noted, the support personnel we have to choose from and surround ourselves with in our lives are there because we are professional athletes and therefore easy prey for the unscrupulous and manipulative. When discussing athletic prowess, some assume we're not intelligent. And certainly, as in all disciplines, there are some who are not the sharpest knives in the drawer. But the skills of professional football players are often less transferable to other professions.

The lessons and information I took from my youth in Houston's Fifth Ward were reminders and guideposts throughout my journey. I used them to measure success or setbacks, winning or losing, compromise or no compromise. The memories of sight and sounds of my old neighborhood, community, and cultural experiences are poignant. All of life's circumstances in childhood there shaped and motivated me. Throughout my years I would meet challenges at every level with a sophistication relevant to my age and experience, but it was always grounded in those earliest experiences. I cannot emphasize it enough: the impact they had on me—subliminally, as a reservoir of hope and the will to succeed—has played a huge part in whatever success I've achieved, including my tangled journey through the NFL pension and benefits system.

Sportswriters, fans, and others who endlessly second-guess decisions made by players and coaches are known as Monday morning quarterbacks. It's much easier to criticize after the fact that than to make split-second decisions in the heat of battle with a three-hundred-pound lineman chasing you.

The choices I made in my life range from the bad to the good to the indifferent. However, I refuse to be a victim. I take full responsibility for the way I have lived, and I believe I have exceeded the low expectations that were set for me way back in the Fifth Ward. Most of all, I have exceeded my own limited expectations for what I could be and do.

Retirement from professional football was both less and more than I had expected it to be. I went from the lows of trying to find myself and reconnect with my daughter to the highs of Pros for Kids and a state dinner at the White House. I learned that you may retire from sports or even business, but you never retire from life.

The last thing I want to do is come across as a bitter former player. Football created opportunities for an education, provided a good living,

Professional football is a business that rewards you handsomely for a few years but can take a physical and emotional toll that lasts a lifetime.

and introduced me to people and took me to places that a kid from Fifth Ward of Houston never could have imagined. But football also affected much of my body and part of my soul. I simply want to set the record straight and do the right thing, first for my generation and then for the players who have followed.

As a young kid, I saw grown men being paid to play the game of football and thought, "What a great job that would be." However, you couldn't have convinced me that I or any player would have the physical and mental problems we're seeing in football players today. Once again, it's what you don't know that can hurt you. Today's pro game has changed dramatically from the game it was. We knew little about the business and entertainment side of it. We looked past the medical issues, because they blocked our path to manhood. After all, men don't complain.

As a player, it was hard for me to reconcile the pain and punishment I put myself through just to see it as a business or even entertainment, for that matter. That's where the franchise owners wanted us to be. It was still a game for us, but we were vulnerable to the professional football indus-try. Furthermore, there were no tax breaks, depreciation, nontaxable expenses or write-offs for the punishment. Playing with pain was part of the price of admission to the NFL. The sacrifice was suffering through the pain for the team, but the team moved on and left players behind, discarded. Then the pain was not just for a day, a week, or the next game. I didn't know that I would be left alone to deal with the damage for the rest of my life.

During those early days of retirement, I sat and thought about the trajectory of my life. It became clear that I was not the man I thought I was. I grew up around the hustlers and confidence men on the streets of Houston. At some point, it dawned on me that understanding these con-fidence men reveals a great deal about how the NFL treats its former players.

There were signs I refused to see be-cause of a blind pursuit of ambition for what my dreams held for me. That drive, the pursuit of something better in life, was a disguise for the innocence and vulnera-bility that we brought to the game. We had to be physical. Those who lasted have the

We needed football more than the game needed us.

CHAPTER 25

scars, bruises, aches, and pain to prove it. Those who did not, struggled with the self-imposed perception of failure.

Every day and every year, teams confirm my observations by discarding wounded warriors for newer, younger, and more enthusiastic players in pursuit of the dream. The old horses, now damaged goods, are put out to pasture.

If I learned anything from those early years of observing my culture and developing an enormous level of street cred, it was that street smarts are developed on the backs of gullible people with their misguided hopes as they watch their dreams go down the drain. Those people knew nothing about the confidence game, how con men use trust to scam them. They are sold ideas of a brighter future and buy into these concepts that hold no value. Visions of more money and a better life are only a dream, although there is a short-lived positive experience of that idea. Just as in the confidence game, they are tricked and defrauded after having gained confidence in the system.

After my first professional football game, I was made aware of what it would take to succeed on this level, which was playing with broken body parts, disfigurement, and pain. I was willing to do what it took, because we were a team and family. We were supposed to take care of one another, and our leaders told us it would be okay. By being in the NFL, I thought I had made it to the other side, to a life free from the struggles that came with living in the hood.

I had observed, participated in, and now was evaluating my physical experiences without the value-added immediate gratification. It was replaced with my reaction to the pain, involuntary nerve twitching, and discomfort.

"Fans don't know," former New England Patriot Ronnie Lippett said. "They have no clue. And you think the NFL is going to tell them? I'm just so happy that the senators and congressmen and congresswomen took notice of how they have been cheating us. And that's the only reason (players are) getting the help that we're getting now. And it's only been in the last two years that anything has started to change."

Kudos to those who have transformed their playing days into a career after football. But many others delayed their disengagement and went back to a different reality. I assumed that disability plans were designed to assist players who were having physical and mental problems. I thought my union would make sure that my human resource department would guide me through the process to make sure there were no problems. I thought the system would work for us—but I was wrong.

Fanning the Flames

After years of repressing the anger and frustration of one's truth about that experience "for the good of the team," one's insides burn. If you don't figure that out until you are out of the game, it's too late. The team makes promises, making you think you're part of a big, happy family, but, like a thief in the night, they're gone.

When that anger and frustration manifests and affects me, I search my soul for the reason why I believed in the promise of fairness. Had I been delusional? Had there really been a promise that we were family, or was it about my own familial needs? There's a lie that's built into the promise. The promise became my problem, and they stopped listening. I experienced the feeling that came with holding in the lies I was told and accepting the blame to be a part of the team. As soon as I thought it was safe to put my bullshit detector away, I was surprised that the anger and resentment returned. Once again, I felt the remnants of the perpetual paradox of pain.

Pride evaporates in midair when you hear the words "The coach wants to see you, and bring your playbook," when you're told you're not wanted anymore, to "sign here" with not even a thank-you. Most egregious is knowing that you had a remedy for your injuries but never were told. You find out how little you really mean to the team for which you worked.

Some say people play games because they want to escape reality. We know the human ability to compete is very powerful. Psychological needs are largely satisfied when we play games. Autonomy is met, because we have control in games and we play voluntarily. The reason we are so attracted to games and get spellbound and even obsessed is that a few of our basic needs are met.

Key components of games include goals, rules, challenges, and interaction. Games generally involve mental or physical stimulation or psychological roles. The need for relationship is fulfilled, because we are able to interact and compete with others in a way and world that is different from real life. Those all contribute to continued play.

Many games help develop practical skills, serve as a form of exercise, or perform educational simulation. Abraham Maslow in his hierarchy of basic needs model identifies components available to us in sports such as football that are important to our human development.

But if you play football long enough, you will get injured. In my fifty years of being involved in or around the sport of football, I do not know one person who played for any period of time and did not get injured. Concussions and other types of repetitive, play-related head blows in American football have been shown to be the cause of chronic traumatic encephalopathy (CTE), which has led to debilitating symptoms after retirement—including memory loss, depression, anxiety, headache, and sleep disturbances—and to early deaths.

Wally Hilgenberg played sixteen years as an All-Pro center for the Minnesota Vikings. He was a starter on all four of their Super Bowl teams. He died on September 23, 2008, of amyotrophic lateral sclerosis —or Lou Gehrig's disease—which many medical authorities felt was exacerbated by his football career. When his widow, Mary, found out that she was ineligible for financial; support, she told Sylvia Mackey: "All those years he played. All he gave to that game. And now they just spit on his grave."

Football for all of these reasons is a young man's sport. I hope that athletes of the future will learn that football on all levels is still a game. My generation of pro football players lost our innocence and idealism regarding the game, what it meant, and how it changed us. I got caught up in the marketing and public relations of the industrial business model and saw a means to an end. I wanted to get paid to play a game. Given my view of the world as a starry-eyed kid, what else would I think?

Part of the beauty of the game is that there are rules and regulations, boundaries and guidelines, and you either win or lose. Football players, especially professionals, are used to rules and regulations and assume that they will be followed and enforced for the integrity of the game. However, the health of the player is important. As a business, football should have all of the normal protections for individuals. The young live in the glory of a string of hundred-yard moments. But in this glorious and often brutal business, the dues often get paid later.

Bottom-Line Mind-Set

The industrialist mind-set does not look at the individual as much as it does profit and loss. There's a gap where the pro football industry and player care do not meet. When I wake up aching most of my mornings or see a retired player at post-career functions, I am reminded of the neglect and indifference the football industry has shown regarding the plight of its retirees' health and the current players' lack of concern about the treatment of retired players. In the industrialized thinking, the human being is an entity, a commodity, a brand.

Everyone who knows me understands that I am an optimist. I have had a tough but wonderful life, thanks in large part to family, friends, teachers, and coaches who believed in me, even at times when I may not have believed in myself.

My peers are my team now, and they may not have the ability or resources to advocate for themselves. All too many men who played in the NFL during my time are no longer with us, and those still alive are living in pain and struggling to make ends meet. Saddest of all, many of are left without tools to compete off

When will institutions step up and raise awareness of players' physical and mental health?

the field while they wait for the unspoken promise to be fulfilled. To put it simply, all I have ever wanted since leaving football is for the NFL to take the lead in doing the right thing.

As a boy, I saw an opportunity for me to have the life that I dreamed of having. I simply am opposed to the way that we have been treated as former players. I think it's imperative to make it a requirement of having a thorough psychological and physical examination. To make individual therapy part of any examinations. The player has a better chance of knowing if it is just depression from exiting the game or neurological damage. I hope that the settlement and new collective bargaining agreements will bring healing and let us move forward. The NFL needs to be fair to its community of retired players, not just its current ones. Retired players are their sons who would like to be welcomed home.

Now and Then

I recently met a wonderful woman, got married, and bought a house in the Sierra Nevada foothills of California. As I sit here today watching the NFC championship game between the San Francisco 49ers and the Green Bay Packers, I'm having a bit of nostalgia. Although I did not play a game with the Packers, they were the team that released me. I am watching the game without any reservations or ill will toward either of the teams.

However, I am reminded of historic times with the 49ers. Seeing the way the 49ers run the football, I am nostalgic for 1976. That was Monte Clark's only year with the 49ers, and the game was fun. He moved Wilbur Jackson and me into the same backfield instead of competing against one another. We would end up having our best season together and individually, rushing for just five yards short of two thousand yards combined. I had 1,203 yards, and Wilbur had 792 yards.

Late in the season we played the Minnesota Vikings, who had won their division championship and were in the playoffs. We were struggling to right ourselves from four straight losses. The Vikings had one of the best defenses in the league with a front line of Carl Eller, Jim Marshall, Alan Page, and Gary Sutherland. Jim Plunkett, our quarterback, had been hurt, and we had to start rookie Scott Bull. That Monday night, for only the third time in the history of the NFL, two teammates each rushed for more than 150 yards in a game. Wilbur had 156 yards, and I had 153. The other tandems to have done that were Jim Brown and Bobby Mitchell, and Emerson Boozer and Jayhawk John Riggins. I would go over one thousand yards for the season on that night.

I am taken back to the day I was asked by 49ers co-chairman John York to be the honorary captain for a game against my other former team, the Miami Dolphins. Until that day, I had never been honored by any of the teams I played for. Dr. York made that day feel special. I hadn't realized it until the game was over, but that was the first post-football honor that I received. That made it even more special, because it brought closure to my time with the 49ers and the Dolphins. As I went out on the field for the coin toss, highlights of my career were played on the scoreboard screen. It brought a sense of closure to me.

The 49ers and Packers NFC championship game that sent the 49ers to Super Bowl LIV was poetic enough to bring final closure to it all.

Thank you for reading my story. I hope something I said challenges, motivates, or inspires you. I am happy to say that after a lifelong search for my identity, with many twists and turns, I am at peace with who I am and where I am today.

Life is all about what you don't know. Although I still don't have all of the answers, I have learned to ask the right questions and demand answers. Although I am at peace with my life, I will never stop fighting for those who shared the same experiences—especially those who no longer are able to speak for themselves.

British prime minister Winston Churchill once gave a commencement speech at Harrow School, his alma mater. The audience must have anticipated a stem-winder, but it was brief, not much more than seven hundred words. The gist of it would be remembered: "Never give in," Churchill said. "Never, never, never, never." Many people—teammates, coaches, opposing players, media, and fans—have shared their opinions about Delvin Williams. No one could ever say that I gave up fighting for what I believe to be right.

As long as we have breath, the final chapter has not yet been written for any of us. Peace be with you.

AFTERWORD

TIM ANDERSON,
SAN FRANCISCO 49ERS,
1975

I hope you have enjoyed reading the amazing story of Delvin Williams. More importantly, I hope you have been inspired.

I knew Delvin was a special player from the first time I saw him on the football field. He had blazing speed, could change directions on a dime, and could shoot through a hole in an instant. Delvin was what football players call "deceptively fast."

I also knew from the moment we met that he was an even more special person. Delvin and I have been best friends since the day we met and roomed together on the road. After football, we worked together to start Pros for Kids, and we remain close all these years later.

One lesson I have learned is that what life hands us is not always going to be good, but it is going to teach us a lesson. Delvin may have been dealt a worse hand than most, but he has played it well. He's one of those people you just can't count out. It was unbelievable how one guy could go through so much yet come out successfully on the other side. Delvin also is one of the hardest-working people you will ever see. He really is special.

The best thing I can say about Delvin is that if he tells you he is going to do something, he is going to do it. That's the biggest no-brainer—you have to show up, and Delvin shows up. Delvin is a very good guy to have as a friend, teammate, and business partner.

Whatever life has in store for you and me, I hope we can face it with the same grace, determination, and positive attitude. Thank you, my friend.

High School Football Accomplishments

Kashmere High School, Houston

- All-City first team
- All-District first team
- All-Regional first team
- All-Southerner
- *Parade* magazine All-American
- 1,806 rushing yards (school and city record)
- 20 touchdowns (school and city record)

College Football Statistics

University of Kansas (Big Eight Conference)

RUSHING

YEAR	GAMES	ATTEMPTS	YARDS	AVERAGE	TOUCHDOWNS
1971	11	102	509	5.0	2
1972	11	67	352	5.3	2
1973	12	208	788	3.8	9
TOTAL	34	377	1,649	4.4	13

RECEIVING

YEAR	GAMES	RECEPTIONS	YARDS	AVERAGE	TOUCHDOWNS
1971	11	9	67	7.4	1
1972	11	5	28	5.6	0
1973	12	37	303	8.2	1
TOTAL	34	51	398	7.8	2

NFL Statistics

RUSHING

YEAR	TEAM	GAMES	ATTEMPTS	YARDS	AVERAGE	TOUCHDOWNS
1974	SF	13	36	201	5.6	3
1975	SF	14	117	631	5.4	3
1976	SF	12	248	1,203	4.9	7
1977	SF	14	268	931	3.5	7
1978	MIA	16	272	1,258	4.6	8
1979	MIA	14	184	703	3.8	3
1980	MIA	15	187	671	3.6	2
1981	GB	1	0	0	0	0
TOTAL		99	1,312	5,598	4.3	33

RECEIVING

YEAR	TEAM	GAMES	RECEPTIONS	YARDS	AVERAGE	TOUCHDOWNS
1974	SF	13	1	9	9.0	0
1975	SF	14	34	370	10.9	1
1976	SF	12	27	283	10.5	2
1977	SF	14	20	179	9.0	2
1978	MIA	16	18	192	10.7	0
1979	MIA	14	21	207	8.3	1
1980	MIA	15	31	671	6.7	
1981	GB	1	0	0	0	0
TOTAL		99	152	1,415	9.3	6

Awards and Recognition

HIGH SCHOOL

- First team All-City
- First team All-District
- First team All-State
- First team Alp Regional
- First team All-Southerner
- Bill McMurray's All-Greater Houston Team
- *Parade Magazine* All-American

UNIVERSITY OF KANSAS

- Gale Sayers scholarship award
- Leading rusher two out of three years
- Second-leading rusher in Big Eight Conference
- Second team All–Big Eight
- Second-round draft pick of San Francisco 49ers
- Graduated with a BS in education despite being academically ineligible as a freshman
- Moved mother out of the projects and into a new home

SAN FRANCISCO 49ERS

- In 1976, set 49ers team records for single-season rushing with 1,203 yards; single-game rushing with 194 yards; and single-game carries with 34
- Selected All-Pro following 1976 season
- Led team in rushing in three out of four seasons
- NFLPA 1,000 Yards Club Award

MIAMI DOLPHINS

- In 1978, set team single-season rushing record with 1,258 yards
- Led team in rushing in two out of three seasons
- Selected All-Pro following 1978 season

- First running back in history to rush for 1,000 yards in both NFC and AFC conferences
- First running back in history to be named All-Pro in both NFC and AFC

PROS FOR KIDS

- Founded National Sports Career Management, the first substance abuse prevention program in professional sport
- Pros for Kids was first organization to design a curriculum with athletes as instructors
- Awarded first contract for a substance abuse program employing athletes as positive role models
- First athletic organization to have First Lady Nancy Reagan as guest speaker
- First nonprofit to run summer camps for kids focusing on academics and athletics
- First official guest of First Lady Nancy Reagan after leaving the White House

RECOGNITION

- President Reagan's Private Sector Initiative Commendation, 1988
- Better Health and Living Award for Americans Who Have Made a Difference, Sports Category, 1987
- California Partnership Award presented by California Private-Public Partnership Commission, 1986
- Stanford Mid-Peninsula Urban Coalition's 1986 Founders Award
- Recognition from Rep. George Miller, Sen. Pete Wilson, Gov. George Deukmejian, Mayor Art Agnos, the FBI, the DEA, the U.S. Attorney General's Office, and Northern California Olympians

COMMUNITY SERVICES

- Christmas in April, Advisory Committee, 1995
- San Francisco School Volunteers Eye on the Prize Committee, 1994
- Human Rights Commission, Committee on African-American Parity, 1994
- San Francisco Mayor's Job Corps Task Force, 1994

- Economic Opportunity Council of San Francisco, Board of Directors, 1993–1994
- Haight Ashbury Free Clinics, Board of Directors, 1987–1991
- San Mateo County Parks and Recreation Commission, 1988–1991
- San Francisco Special Olympics, Board of Directors, 1986–1987
- California State Department of Education, Physical Education Model Curriculum

COMMITTEES

- San Francisco Mayor's Narcotics Task Force, 1986–1987
- San Mateo County Juvenile Justice and Delinquency Planning Commission, 1985–1987
- San Mateo County Drug Abuse Prevention Task Force, 1984–1985
- NFL Alumni, San Francisco Chapter, 2002

NOMINATIONS AND INDUCTIONS

- Nominated (not elected) Pro Football Hall of Fame's Class of 2001
- African American Ethnic Sports Hall of Fame, 2008
- Prairie View Interscholastic League Coaches Association, 2011

Football-Related Surgeries

YEAR	INJURY
1970	Left ankle
1972	Upper right arm
1975	Right wrist bone graft
1977	Left thumb and right toe
1979	Upper left arm and left knee
2001	Total left hip replacement
2002	Right wrist (carpal tunnel) Right radialectomy
2005	Arthroscopic debridement of right wrist Left shoulder arthroscopy Sub-acromial decompression Distal clavicle excision Arthroscopic synovectomy Arthroscopic excision of ganglion cyst
2006	Arthroscopy of right wrist and debridement of triangular fibrocartilage
2008	Bunionectomy on right big toe
2009	Removal of bone spur on left ankle
2012	Subacromial decompression Rotator cuff debridement L-5 synovial cyst excision
2014	Total right hip replacement Bone graft and reconstruction of left hip
2015	Bone spur excision on right hand
2017	Left wrist (carpal tunnel) Right rotator cuff

Medical and Legal Resources

FAIR (FAIRNESS FOR ATHLETES IN RETIREMENT)

www.pensionparity.com

FAIR is a 501[c](3) nonprofit organized to represent the voices of NFL players who played before 1993 to help them obtain pension parity in the negotiation for the 2021 collective bargaining agreement. FAIR is committed to working with the NFLPA and the NFL to find a solution that allows for these great players and their loved ones to live with dignity.

GRIDIRON GREATS ASSISTANCE FUND

www.gridirongreats.org

The Gridiron Greats Assistance Fund's mission is to assist retired NFL players who were pioneers of the game and who have greatly contributed to professional football's status as the most popular sport in America. The Gridiron Greats Assistance Fund provides hands-on assistance to help retired players and their families deal with hardships they face after football. The services include medical assistance, transportation costs for medical evaluations and surgeries, housing assistance, financial assistance for utilities, medication, and coordination of services for food, automotive payments, and childcare.

NFL PLAYER CARE FOUNDATION

www.nflplayercare.com

The NFL Player Care Foundation (PCF) is an independent organization dedicated to helping retired players improve their quality of life. The PCF addresses all aspects of life by providing programs and assistance with medical, emotional, financial, social, and community issues.

Motion Protesting Attorney's Fees Requested by NFL Players Association

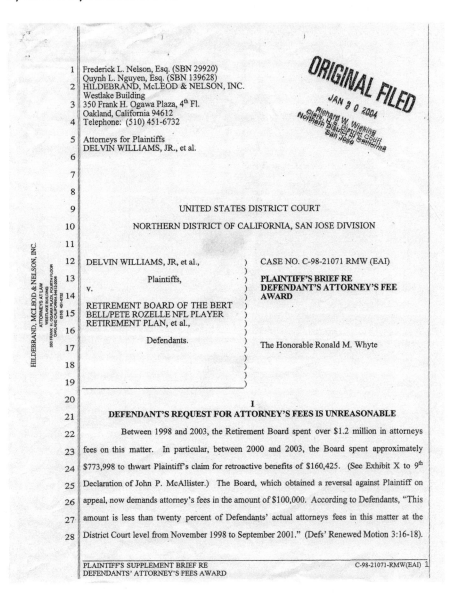

1 Frederick L. Nelson, Esq. (SBN 29920)
   Quynh L. Nguyen, Esq. (SBN 139628)
2 HILDEBRAND, McLEOD & NELSON, INC.
   Westlake Building
3 350 Frank H. Ogawa Plaza, 4th Fl.
   Oakland, California 94612
4 Telephone: (510) 451-6732

5 Attorneys for Plaintiffs
   DELVIN WILLIAMS, JR., et al.
6

7

8

9   UNITED STATES DISTRICT COURT

10   NORTHERN DISTRICT OF CALIFORNIA, SAN JOSE DIVISION

11

12 DELVIN WILLIAMS, JR, et al.,   )   CASE NO. C-98-21071 RMW (EAI)
)
13   Plaintiffs,   )   **PLAINTIFF'S BRIEF RE**
)   **DEFENDANT'S ATTORNEY'S FEE**
14   v.   )   **AWARD**
)
15 RETIREMENT BOARD OF THE BERT   )
    BELL/PETE ROZELLE NFL PLAYER   )
16 RETIREMENT PLAN, et al.,   )
)
17   Defendants.   )   The Honorable Ronald M. Whyte
)
18   )
)
19   )

20   I
21 **DEFENDANT'S REQUEST FOR ATTORNEY'S FEES IS UNREASONABLE**

22   Between 1998 and 2003, the Retirement Board spent over $1.2 million in attorneys

23 fees on this matter. In particular, between 2000 and 2003, the Board spent approximately

24 $773,998 to thwart Plaintiff's claim for retroactive benefits of $160,425. (See Exhibit X to 9th

25 Declaration of John P. McAllister.) The Board, which obtained a reversal against Plaintiff on

26 appeal, now demands attorney's fees in the amount of $100,000. According to Defendants, "This

27 amount is less than twenty percent of Defendants' actual attorneys fees in this matter at the

28 District Court level from November 1998 to September 2001." (Defs' Renewed Motion 3:16-18).

PLAINTIFF'S SUPPLEMENT BRIEF RE   C-98-21071-RMW(EAI) 1
DEFENDANTS' ATTORNEY'S FEES AWARD

HILDEBRAND, MCLEOD & NELSON, INC.
ATTORNEYS AT LAW
WESTLAKE BUILDING
350 FRANK H. OGAWA PLAZA, FOURTH FLOOR
OAKLAND CALIFORNIA 94612-2006
(510) 451-6732

1 By their statement, Defendants' motion for attorney's fees appears to be less for remuneration

2 than for the purpose of serving as an exemplary penalty. Regardless of whether or not the

3 $100,000 represents a fraction of defendant's actual attorney's fees, it is nevertheless an

4 unreasonable and excessive amount to require someone, who is dependent on welfare and

5 disability checks, to pay. The substantial fees claimed by Defendants should be drastically

6 reduced to an award appropriate to Plaintiff's financial situation.

7 　　　Plaintiff Delvin Williams' sole sources of income are welfare benefits from the NFL

8 Retirement Plan and disability benefits from the Social Security Administration. These benefits

9 are taxed. The welfare benefits from the Retirement Plan are not guaranteed for life; at the

10 Board's discretion and not more than every six months, Mr. Williams must repeatedly submit to

11 qualifying physical examinations conducted by Board-assigned physicians, (despite the

12 permanent nature of his disabilities). Mr. Williams' discretionary income, net long-term expenses,

13 is around $17,406 per year. In December he assumed custody of his grandson, Je'Marcus

14 Williams, who is 13 years old. Mr. Williams will be responsible for raising his grandson until he

15 reaches the legal age. He will also provide financial assistance to his daughter and Je'Marcus'

16 mother, Dositheia Williams, when she is released from jail in June 2004. Dositheia has substance

17 abuse problems. Mr. Williams intends to support her until she gets back on her feet. Under these

18 circumstances, Mr. Williams will suffer an extreme financial hardship should he have to pay a

19 substantial attorney's fees award to the Retirement Board, which has net assets of over $600

20 million. (See Exhibit 19 to Declaration of Delvin Williams.)

21 　　　Although this Court initially awarded Delvin Williams his benefits claim, the award

22 was unfortunately reversed on appeal. The appeals process concluded, Defendants renewed their

23 motion for attorney's fees and asked to be awarded a substantial sum. Thereafter, this Court

24 awarded Defendants "a portion of their attorney's fees in an amount to be determined."

25 (December 29, 2003 Order 6:9-16) The Court also ordered Defendants to meet and confer with

26 Plaintiff's counsel pursuant to Civil L.R. 54-5(b)(1). Id.

27

28

PLAINTIFF'S SUPPLEMENT BRIEF RE
DEFENDANTS' ATTORNEY'S FEES AWARD   C-98-21071-RMW(EAI) 2

1   At the suggestion of defense counsel John McAllister, Plaintiff faxed to the Board a

2   settlement proposal for the Board to consider at its January 15, 2004 meeting. In his proposal,

3   Mr. Williams stated that, as of December 2003, he assumed custody of his 13-year grandson,

4   because his daughter is a crack addict and currently in jail. Moreover, his daughter will need his

5   help and support when she is released. Given the financial burdens he had undertaken and further

6   expects to undertake, Mr. Williams proposed a settlement of $10,897 to be paid in two years.

7   The proposed settlement is 10% of the $100,000 that Defendant requested for attorney's fees and

8   10% of the $8,897 that Defendants submitted for costs. (See attached proposal as Exhibit 18 to

9   Declaration of Delvin Williams.)

10   On January 19, 2003, Mr. McAllister informed Mr. Nelson that the Board had rejected

11   Mr. Williams' proposal. The Board, without budging from its original figure, made a counter-

12   proposal which was that Mr. Williams pay $100,000 over ten years without interest; this meant

13   the Board would deduct $833.00 per month from Mr. Williams' monthly welfare benefits.

14   Plaintiff rejected this counter-proposal. (See Declarations of Frederick L. Nelson and Delvin

15   Williams.)

16   The Board's demand for $108,897 in attorney's fees and costs is unreasonable in light

17   of its net assets of over $600 million and the fact that Plaintiff only receives welfare plan and

18   social security benefits. Mr. Williams' proposed award of $10,897 for both fees and costs should

19   be granted.

20

II

21   **PLAINTIFF WILL SUFFER UNDUE FINANCIAL HARDSHIP SHOULD
A SUBSTANTIAL AMOUNT IN ATTORNEY'S FEE BE AWARDED**

22   In general, courts should express a "bias" against demanding attorney's fees of

23   Plaintiffs in ERISA cases. Jaffe, supra, 2003 WL 22697729, *2, citing Salovaara v. Eckert, 222

24   F.3d 19, 28 (2nd Cir.2000) and Foley v. Bethlehem Steel Corp., 30 F.Supp.2d 366

25   (W.D.N.Y.1998); West v. Greyhound Corp., 813 F.2d 951, 956 (9th Cir.1987). The "culpability"

26   of a losing Plaintiff "significantly differs" from that of a losing Defendant: "A losing Defendant

27   must have violated ERISA, thereby depriving Plaintiffs of rights under a pension plan and

28

PLAINTIFF'S SUPPLEMENT BRIEF RE   C-98-21071-RMW(EAI) 3
DEFENDANTS' ATTORNEY'S FEES AWARD

1 violating a Congressional mandate. A losing Plaintiff, on the other hand, will not necessarily be

2 found 'culpable,' but may be only in error or unable to prove his case." <u>Marquardt v. North Am.</u>

3 <u>Car Corp.</u>, 652 F.2d 715, 720 (7th Cir.1981). Thus, the refusal to award attorneys' fees and costs

4 to ERISA Defendants, even "prevailing" Defendants, would rarely constitute an abuse of

5 discretion. <u>Id</u>. at 719. However, should attorney's fees be awarded to a plan Defendant, the

6 award should be reduced to reflect the individual Plaintiff's limited ability to pay. <u>Childers v.</u>

7 <u>Medstar Health</u>, 289 F.Supp.2d 714, 719 (D.MD.2003) (**requested lodestar of $21,574 reduced**

8 **by 75% to $5,393.50**; court noted that party required to pay had dependent children; <u>Jaffe v.</u>

9 <u>Intern'l Brotherhood of Teamsters Local 282 Welfare Pension & Annuity Trust Funds</u>, 2003 WL

10 22697729, *2 (E.D.N.Y.2003) (**$99,522 fee award reduced to $20,000**; court noted the

11 plaintiff's age, his impaired health and unemployed status).

12   In this case, Mr. Williams would suffer undue financial hardship should he be required

13 to pay any substantial amount of attorney's fees beyond his proposal of $10,897 in two years.

14 In December 2003, Mr. Williams assumed legal custody of his 13-year old grandson Je'Marcus

15 Williams and will have custody of him until he is of legal age. Mr. Williams' daughter and

16 Je'Marcus' mother, Dositheia Ross, is 34 years old and a crack addict, with a history of

17 recidivism. She can no longer care for her son. In December 2003, Dositheia granted Mr. Williams

18 the power of attorney over Je'Marcus. Dositheia was arrested for two counts of possession of

19 drugs, i.e., cocaine, on December 23, 2003, and was sentenced to one year in the Harris County

20 Jail in Houston, Texas. When Dositheia is released from jail on June 22, 2004, (assuming she

21 serves her sentence without incident), Mr. Williams will financially assist her until she gets back

22 on her feet. Mr. Williams expects to pay and/or contribute between $500 - $1,000 per month

23 towards her rent, utilities, groceries, etc. Mr. Williams anticipates that Dositheia will need his

24 financial assistance for a year to a year and a half, perhaps longer if she suffers a relapse. (See

25 Declaration of Delvin Williams.) Having never assumed the care of a child before, Plaintiff does

26 not know the cost of raising a teenager from age 13 to 18, and through college; however, he

27

28

1 believes the cost of raising his grandson and supporting him through college will be significant.

2 (See Declaration of Delvin Williams.)

3 Mr. Williams will be 53 years old in April 2004, and he is totally and permanently

4 disabled. Mr. Williams relies on approximately $110,000 per year from the NFL Retirement Plan

5 and about $15,000 from the Social Security Administration for his income. Defendants' demand

6 of $100,000 for attorney's fees is almost an entire year of income for Plaintiff. In light of Mr.

7 Williams' financial situation, Defendant's demand is unreasonable and should be denied or

8 drastically reduced.

9 Furthermore, the Plan is well funded, thereby rendering a $100,000 attorney's fees

10 award as excessive and unrelated to remuneration. The NFL Retirement Board's "Summary

11 Annual Report," dated March 15, 2003, provided that the value of plan assets after subtracting

12 the liabilities was $691,110,650 as of March 31, 2002. The Plan experienced an increase in its net

13 assets of $16,664,662 and had total income of $62,518,973. Taking into consideration changes in

14 market conditions from 2002 to 2004, the Fund's net assets have likely increased significantly.

15 From March 17, 2003 to January 27, 2004, the Standard & Poor 500 has increased 32.5% (March

16 17, 2003 / 862.79 and January 27, 2004 / 1144.05). By contrast, $100,000 represents about 80%

17 of Plaintiff's annual income (from welfare plan and social security benefits) before taxes. Fee

18 awards under ERISA should not be intended to be excessively punitive. Ursic v. Bethlehem

19 Mines, 719 F.2d 670, 677 (3rd Cir.1983) An attorney's fee award of $100,000 would be an

20 exemplary sanction in Plaintiff's situation.

21 **II**

22 **DEFENDANTS' ACCOUNT AND SUMMARY OF**
THEIR ATTORNEY'S FEES IS UNREASONABLE

23 Defendants maintain they have spent over $1.2 million in attorney's fees between

24 1998 and 2003—about 70% was spent against plaintiff's retroactive benefits claim of $160,425.

25 By contrast, Plaintiff's two previous attorneys and current attorneys previously claimed a

26 combined attorney's fee award of $311,363.50. The following comparison of yearly totals shows

27 the disparity in costs, which indicates unreasonable fees:

28

PLAINTIFF'S SUPPLEMENT BRIEF RE   C-98-21071-RMW(EAI) 5
DEFENDANTS' ATTORNEY'S FEES AWARD

HILDEBRAND, MCLEOD & NELSON, INC.
ATTORNEYS AT LAW
WESTLAKE BUILDING
350 FRANK H. OGAWA PLAZA, FOURTH FLOOR
OAKLAND CALIFORNIA 94612-2006
(510) 451-6732

1 **Defense Counsel**

2 | Dates | Hours | Fees |
   |-------|-------|------|

3 | Nov.-Dec. 1998 | 155.75 | $ 28,657.50 |

4 | 1999 | 1,812.15 | $413,781.25 |

5 | 2000 | 827 | $226,328.75 |

6 | 2001 | 362 | $109,850 |

7 | 2002 | 669.75 | $221,097.50 |

8 | 2003 | 578 | $21,722.50 |

9 | Total | **4,404.65** | **$1,214,576.25** |

10 (Refer to Exhibit X of Ninth Declaration of John P. McAllister.)

11 **Plaintiff's counsel**

12 | Dates | Hours | Fees |
    |-------|-------|------|

13 | Previous counsel | | |
14 | Aug. '98 – Dec. '99 | 227.10 | $56,775 |
    | Chuck Teixeira | | |

15 | Aug. '98 – Dec. '99 | 695.33 | $152,663.50 |
16 | Clapp, Maroney | | |

17 | Present Counsel | | |
    | Dec. '99 – Oct. '01 | 405.75 | $101,925 |
18 | Hildebrand, McLeod & | | |
    | Total | **1,328.18** | **$311,363.50** |

19
20 (Figures derived from Court Order, filed April 29, 2002, pp. 5-8, and attached as **Exhibit 2** to

21 Declaration of Frederick L. Nelson.) As can be seen by a comparison of the hours, defense

22 attorney's fees are approximately $903,212.75 more than Plaintiff's previously requested fees.

23 The amount of Defendant's attorney's fees is unreasonable and excessive in light of

24 defense counsel's expertise, skill, familiarity and extensive experience defending similar ERISA

25 cases in which disability/welfare benefits were denied under the same NFL Retirement Plan.

26 Defense counsel was already familiar with the applicable terms of the Retirement Plan and ERISA

27 law, even before this action began from previously litigated cases such as Courson v. Bert Bell

28 NFL Player Retirement Plan, 214 F.3d 136, (3rd Cir.2000), Dial v. NFL Player Supplemental

---

PLAINTIFF'S SUPPLEMENT BRIEF RE
DEFENDANTS' ATTORNEY'S FEES AWARD
C-98-21071-RMW(EAI) 6

HILDEBRAND, MCLEOD & NELSON, INC.
ATTORNEYS AT LAW
WESTLAKE BUILDING
350 FRANK H. OGAWA PLAZA, FOURTH FLOOR
OAKLAND CALIFORNIA 94612-2006
(510) 451-6732

1 Disability Plan, 174 F.3d 606, (5th Cir.1999), and <u>Sweeney v. Bert Bell NFL Player Retirement</u>

2 <u>Plan</u>, 961 F.Supp. 1381 (S.D.Cal. 1997) affirmed in part, reversed in part and remanded by

3 <u>Sweeney v. Bert Bell NFL Player Reitirement Plan</u>, 156 F.3d 1238 (9th Cir. 1998). This list does

4 not include unpublished and/or nonappealed cases.

5   Both, the Hildebrand firm and the Groom Law Group, filed virtually the same number

6 of briefs, dispositive motions and counter-motions in 2000 and 2001. Yet, while attorneys at the

7 Hildebrand firm reported approximately 405.75 hours in their previous fee request, defense

8 counsel claimed approximately 1,098 hours. Defense counsel's claimed hours are unreasonable as

9 the litigation of this case was limited to the pre-existing Administrative record compiled by its

10 client the Retirement Board, written discovery and depositions were not required, and a jury or

11 bench trial never occurred. Further, portions of Defendants' briefs (e.g., describing Plan terms)

12 were boilerplate and rote. The ERISA standard of denying benefits in this case was the same as in

13 other cases revolving around the denial of Plan benefits: the abuse of discretion standard. Only

14 one Plan applied, with the same plan terms. Simply put, defense counsel was not faced with

15 novel issues of fact or law.

16   Additionally, defense counsel could rely on the Retirement Board, their own client and

17 the Plan Administrator, to assist them in becoming familiar with Mr. Williams' file and

18 application process. Prior to this action, Plaintiff's counsel at the Hildebrand firm were not

19 familiar with the NFL Retirement Plan or ERISA law. They were required to spend time

20 familiarizing themselves with the Plan terms, the application process, and Mr. William's file.

21 Nevertheless, plaintiff's counsel only reported 405.75 hours, while defense counsel claimed over

22 two times more the number of hours. The Supreme Court provides that the trial court may reduce

23 the hours submitted for attorney's fees "if the case was overstaffed and hours are duplicated, or if

24 the hours expended are deemed excessive or otherwise unnecessary." <u>Hensley v. Eckerhart</u>, 461

25 U.S. 424, 432-434 (1983); <u>Mogck v. Unum Life Ins. Co. of America</u>, 289 F.Supp.2d 1181, 1191,

26 1195 (N.D.CA 2003) Defendant's time records indicate that there were at least three attorney's

27

28

1   working on this case at all times, and more so at other times, repeatedly reviewing each other's

2   work.

3   In 2001, defense counsel Douglas W. Ell was billed at $420/hr., John P. McAllister at

4    $340/hr., William F. Hanrahan at $345/hr., and Alvaro I. Anillo at $275/hr. In the ERISA context,

5   the Third Circuit pithily notes that, "A fee applicant cannot demand a high hourly rate—which is

6   based on his or her experience, reputation, and a presumed familiarity with the applicable

7   law—and then run up an inordinate amount of time researching that same law. Double dipping, in

8   any form, cannot be condoned. Our cases supply no authority for rewarding non-stop meter

9   running in law offices. See Prandini I, 557 F.2d at 1020. ¶[T]here must be a correlation between

10   the 'hours worked' and 'the total recovery. . . . The trial court must consider the relationship

11   between the fee award and the amount of recovery." Ursic, supra, 719 F.2d at 677. Virtually all

12   the work defense counsel did after January 2000 revolved around the denial of plaintiff's

13   retroactive benefits claim for $160,425. Even assuming $100,000 is only 20% of Defendants'

14   actual fees as they claim, it is excessive in light of the relatively miniscule amount of benefits

15   Defendants prevented from being distributed (cf. Plan assets of over $600 million), and in light of

16   their attorneys' expertise, skill, familiarity with ERISA law and extensive experience defending

17   against similar benefits claims.

18   Additionally, a substantial attorney's fees award against Mr. Williams will have a

19   chilling effect on other Plan participants who may want to file meritorious claims but who be

20   inhibited by a large fee award against a fellow Plan member receiving only welfare benefits. If

21   word is spread in the community of disabled NFL ex-football players that the Board obtained a

22   substantial amount of fees against Mr. Williams, other participants who are wrongfully denied

23   benefits will be discouraged from asserting their rights under the Plan and ERISA.

24   ///

25   ///

26   ///

27

28

PLAINTIFF'S SUPPLEMENT BRIEF RE
DEFENDANTS' ATTORNEY'S FEES AWARD
             C-98-21071-RMW(EAI) 8

1

III
CONCLUSION

2

3   For the foregoing reason, plaintiff respectfully requests that, If any fees are to be

4   awarded, that the Court award attorney's fees and costs in the amount of $10,897 in light of Mr.

5   Williams' financial situation.

6

7

IV
REQUEST FOR PROTECTIVE ORDER

8   Pursuant to the Court's Order, filed December 29, 2003, Plaintiff files the Declaration

9   of Delvin Williams under seal. Plaintiff also requests the Court for an order directing that

10 Plaintiff's papers concerning his ability to pay not be disclosed or used outside the litigation of

11 this matter for any reason whatsoever. FRCP 26(c)(2) The basis for Plaintiff's request is that the

12 information filed under seal is extremely confidential and personal as it concerns Plaintiff's entire

13 financial status and contains private information about Plaintiff's daughter.

14 Dated: January _30_, 2004

15   HILDEBRAND, McLEOD & NELSON, INC.

16

17 By: _Frederick L. Nelson_

18   FREDERICK L. NELSON, ESQ.
                                            Attorney for Plaintiff
                                            DELVIN WILLIAMS, JR.

19

20

21

22

23

24

25

26

27

28

PLAINTIFF'S SUPPLEMENT BRIEF RE
DEFENDANTS' ATTORNEY'S FEES AWARD   C-98-21071-RMW(EAI) 9

Frederick L. Nelson, Esq. (SBN 29920)
Quynh L. Nguyen, Esq. (SBN 139628)
HILDEBRAND, McLEOD & NELSON, INC.
Westlake Building
350 Frank H. Ogawa Plaza, 4th Fl.
Oakland, California 94612
Telephone: (510) 451-6732

Attorneys for Plaintiffs
DELVIN WILLIAMS, JR.

UNITED STATES DISTRICT COURT

NORTHERN DISTRICT OF CALIFORNIA, SAN JOSE DIVISION

DELVIN WILLIAMS, JR.	)	CASE NO. C-98-21071 RMW
Plaintiffs,	)	**DECLARATION OF DELVIN WILLIAMS PURSUANT TO COURT ORDER OF DECEMBER 29, 2003,**
v.	)	
RETIREMENT BOARD OF THE BERT BELL/PETE ROZELLE NFL PLAYER RETIREMENT PLAN, et al.,	)	
Defendants	)	The Honorable Ronald M. Whyte

I, Delvin Williams, declare as follows:

1.   I am the Plaintiff in the above-entitled action and I have personal knowledge of the matters set forth herein. If called as a witness, I could and would competently testify under oath to the contents thereof.

2.   The Retirement Board's demand for any substantial amount in attorney's fees would cause an extreme financial hardship for me. My gross income is comprised of $110,000 in welfare benefits I receive from the NFL Retirement Board, and $15,100 in Social Security benefits. These benefits are taxed. I have no other sources of income. In 2003, my anticipated total income tax expense will be approximately $24,995. In 2003, my home related

1 expenses (for a condominium) were $42,207; my auto related expenses (for two cars) were

2 $9,714; my medical and health-related expenses were $11,502; miscellaneous expenses

3 concerning a credit card, legal/professional fees and investment deposits amounted to $20,276.

4 (These figures are set forth in a spread sheet attached as **Exhibit 1** and supported by

5 documents attached as Exhibits 2 through 17, inclusively, below.) In 2003, my total income

6 less total expenses left me with $17,406 of discretionary income. This figure does not include

7 non-necessary or non-material expenses, such as entertainment expenses, gift expenses, or

8 nominal daily living expenses.

9

10   3.   I do not expect my income to increase, nor do I expect my expenses to

11 decrease. I do, however, expect my recurring expenses to increase significantly because I now

12 have custody and responsibility for my grandson, Je'Marcus Williams, and I will need to

13 provide financial assistance to my daughter when she is released from jail. I also expect my

14 expenses to increase significantly in the near future due to the previous award of court costs

15 against me in this action. I will be 53 years old on April 17, 2004.

16   4.   Attached as **Exhibit 1** hereto is a true and accurate copy of an Excel

17 spreadsheet printout indicating my income and expenses for 2003. This sheet was constructed

18 with figures from the following exhibits and does not include non-necessary or non-material

19 expenses, such as entertainment expenses, gift expenses, or nominal daily living expenses.

20 Monthly expense figures have been multiplied by twelve months to get yearly figures

21 comparable with my yearly income. All figures have been rounded to the nearest dollar. The

22 majority of these expenses can be found in **Exhibit 4**, my end-of-the-year, 2003 Quicken

23 Personal Finance Spending statement, and in **Exhibit 5**, my December 31, 2003 US Bank

24 Statement. This printout represents with accurate detail my true and actual income and

25 expenses for 2003.

Motion Protesting Attorney's Fees   295

HILDEBRAND, MCLEOD & NELSON, INC.
ATTORNEYS AT LAW
44 THIRTEENTH STREET
OAKLAND, CALIFORNIA 94612-2809
(510) 451-6732

5.   Although not listed in **Exhibit 1**, I will need to adjust the above-described expenses to accommodate the costs that I will incur in caring for my grandson and helping my daughter on a long-term basis. In December 2003 I assumed legal custody of my 13-year old grandson Je'Marcus Williams. Je'Marcus' mother and my daughter, Dositheia Ross, is 34 years old and a crack addict. She can no longer care for her son. In December, Dositheia granted me the power of attorney over Je'Marcus. On December 23, 2003, Dositheia was picked up for two counts of possession of drugs, i.e., cocaine. She violated her probation and was required to serve a one-year sentence in the Harris County Jail, at 1200 Baker Street, Houston, Texas 77002-1260, Case No. 09721520940945. She is expected to be released on June 22, 2004, if she serves her sentence without incident. When Dositheia is released from jail, I will financially assist her until she gets back on her feet. Although I do not know the extent of the financial assistance she will need from me , I expect to pay and/or contribute between $500 - $1,000 per month towards her rent, utilities, groceries, etc. Dositheia will likely need my financial assistance for a year to a year and a half, perhaps longer if she suffers a relapse. My grandson will remain with me. I will have complete financial and physical custody of my grandson through his high school years. Having never assumed the care of a child before, I do not know the cost of raising a boy from age 13 to 18, and through college; however, I believe the cost of raising my grandson and supporting him through college will be significant. Dositheia also has an eleven-year old daughter whose father is currently in the process of obtaining custody for her.

6.   I have about $26,000 of equity in my condominium, $10,532 in savings and $45,122 in a Charles Schwab investment account. My total assets amount to approximately $81,654. I opened a Charles Schwab investment account for my two grandchildren's college educations. I am the only one in my family from my generation and my daughter's generation

296

APPENDIX G

HILDEBRAND, MCLEOD & NELSON, INC.
ATTORNEYS AT LAW
414 THIRTEENTH STREET
OAKLAND CALIFORNIA 94612-2603
(510) 451-6732

1   to finish college. I do not consider the Schwab account a liquid asset as I only intend to use

2   my investments for my grandchildren's educations. The money in my savings account is set

3   aside for taxes and personal emergencies.

4

5   7.   Attached as **Exhibit 2** hereto is a true and accurate copy of my 2002 Form

6   1040 U.S. Individual Income Tax Return.

7   8.   Attached as **Exhibit 3** hereto is a true and accurate copy of my 2002 Form

8   540 California Resident Income Tax Return.

9   9.   Attached as **Exhibit 4** hereto is a true and accurate copy of my end-of-the-

10   year, 2003 Quicken Personal Finance Spending statement. This statement is a true and

11   accurate reflection of my actual spending for 2003. Most of the spending information in this

12   statement is directly and electronically tied to my US Bank transaction records. All other

13

14   transactions were entered into Quicken in a timely manner based on actual transaction receipts.

15   The margin of error between this record and actual spending receipts for 2003 is nominal.

16   10.   Attached as **Exhibit 5** hereto is a true and accurate copy of my December

17   31, 2003 US Bank Statement. This statement reflects the month of December and presents a

18   full and accurate reflection of my regular monthly spending requirements. Multiplying these

19

20   figures by twelve months gives accurate results to compare with my yearly income. Because

21   many of my bills are automatically paid electronically every month, I do not receive monthly

22   statements to present to the court. Examples of these payments include my Blue Cross of

23   California payment, my Capital One credit maintenance payment, my Charles Shwab

24   automatic deposit, and my Village Sierra condominium dues. This statement also shows

25

26   checks for uninsured medical and dental expenses, charity donations, and utility payments.

27   11.   Attached as **Exhibit 6** hereto is a true and accurate copy of my December

28   31, 2003 Charles Schwab account statement. This statement reflects my entire personal

Motion Protesting Attorney's Fees   297

HILDEBRAND, MCLEOD & NELSON, INC.
ATTORNEYS AT LAW
414 THIRTEENTH STREET
OAKLAND, CALIFORNIA 94612-2603
(510) 451-6732

1 investment savings and equity ownership. One thousand dollars a month is drawn directly

2 from my US Bank account into this Schwab account.

3   12.   Attached as **Exhibit 7** hereto is a true and accurate copy of my August 12,

4 2003 Citimortgage Home Mortgage statement. This statement shows my monthly payment

5

6 and the total principal balance owed on my condominium.

7   13.   Attached as **Exhibit 8** hereto is a true and accurate copy of my January 1,

8 2003 Santa Clara County Assessors valuation report of my condominium.

9   14.   Attached as **Exhibit 9** hereto is a true and accurate copy of my 2003

10 Property Tax Bill.

11   15.   Attached as **Exhibit 10** hereto is a true and accurate copy of my 2003

12

13 Farmers Homeowners Insurance statement.

14   16.   Attached as **Exhibit 11** hereto is a true and accurate copy of my City of

15 Mountain View, CA, Utility Bill.

16   17.   Attached as **Exhibit 12** hereto is a true and accurate copy of my December

17 18, 2003 Gas and Electric Bill.

18   18.   Attached as **Exhibit 13** hereto is a true and accurate copy of my November

19 23, 2003 SBC Phone and Internet statement.

20

21   19.   Attached as **Exhibit 14** hereto is a true and accurate copy of my January 7,

22 2004 Audi Financing statement for my 2001 Volkswagen automobile.

23   20.   Attached as **Exhibit 15** hereto is a true and accurate copy of my May 18,

24 2003 State Farm Automobile Insurance statement for my 2001 Volkswagen and 1979

25 Mercedes.

26

27   21.   Attached as **Exhibit 16** hereto is a true and accurate copy of the Power of

28 Attorney and custody granted to me for my grandson, Je'Marcus Williams, from my daughter

Dositheia Ross.

       22.   Attached as **Exhibit 17** hereto is a true and accurate copy of the birth certificate for my 13-year-old grandson, Je'Marcus Williams.

       23.   Attached as **Exhibit 18** hereto is a true and accurate copy of my proposal to the Retirement Board, dated January 12, 2004. In the proposal, I disclosed to the Board that in December 2003, I assumed custody of my 13-year grandson, because my daughter, Dositheia, is a crack addict and currently in jail, and that she will need my help and support when she is released. Given the financial burdens I have undertaken and further expect to undertake, I proposed a settlement of $10,897 to be paid in two years. The proposed settlement is 10% of the $100,000 that Defendant requested for attorney's fees and 10% of the $8,897 that Defendants submitted for costs. Defendants rejected by proposal and did not budge from their original demand of $100,000. It would be a financial hardship for me to have to pay more than the amount I proposed.

       24.   Attached as **Exhibit 19** hereto is a true and accurate copy of the NFL Retirement Board's "Summary Annual Report," dated March 15, 2003. As can be seen by the summary, the value of plan assets after subtracting the liabilities was $691,110,650 as of March 31, 2002. The Plan experienced an increase in its net assets of $16,664,662 and had total income of $62,518,973. Taking into consideration changes in market conditions from 2002 to 2004, the Fund's net assets have likely increased significantly.

       I declare under penalty of perjury under the laws of the United States that the foregoing is true and correct and can competently testify thereto if called before a court of law.

       Executed this ____29____ day of January 2004 at _Oakland_, California.

                       DELVIN WILLIAMS

HILDEBRAND, MCLEOD & NELSON, INC.
ATTORNEYS AT LAW
464 THIRTEENTH STREET
OAKLAND CALIFORNIA 94612-0603
(510) 451-6732

INDEX